PRIMITIVE ART

PRIMITIVE

ART

ITS TRADITIONS AND STYLES

PAUL S. WINGERT

NEW YORK · OXFORD UNIVERSITY PRESS · 1962

PREFACE

As an introduction to primitive art, this book endeavors first to isolate the concept of the term and then to examine the various attitudes and approaches that have prevailed or presently do prevail toward this art. A method of approach is therefore proposed that involves: 1) the investigation of the physical, psychological, and sociological backgrounds so that the reader can envisage the full cultural context in which a work was produced; and 2) the analysis of the objects created in the three major areas, that is, in Negro Africa, Oceania, and North America so as to discover the formal art properties and aesthetic qualities that characterize the numerous styles within the traditions of these regions. Such a methodology is necessary in order to comprehend the significance of the art forms, since by this procedure the objects are not isolated from the positions they occupied, culturally and aesthetically, in the lives of these peoples.

For the sake of clarity I have limited the number of areas for discussion, and merely refer in very general terms to such areas as Indonesia, Micronesia, Australia, South America, and Eskimo North America. Other areas have, unfortunately, had to be omitted entirely, including Madagascar, Nicobar, and certain Southeast Asian and Malayan regions. Moreover, within the major areas selected for a more comprehensive consideration, further restrictions had to be imposed, since it was impossible to treat all of the styles in every area. These omissions do not reflect on the importance or quality of the styles not included. The choice of styles and examples treated here was dictated by the desire to consider selective, representative styles and works that would exemplify the traditional arts of these major regions in the primitive world.

The use of the term "traditional" perhaps needs some explanation. It is used here to mean the art that existed as a part of the cultural complex of the various peoples at or before the time of prolonged or continuous European contacts. That is, "traditional" forms refers to the art produced by peoples with the same motivations as had existed long before the disruptive influences of European civilization were brought in: such art still performed the same functions and had the same meanings for the people who created it as it had had in past generations. Some may take issue with this interpretation and insist that traditional art still persists in a great many regions of the primitive world, and that it was not, by any means, "killed" by European contact. This criticism is only partially justified. The one area where art flourished after contact was on the northwest coast of North America; there the riches acquired in the dealings with fur traders during the first half of the nineteenth century led to a climax in the development of the elaborate art forms. In a few other areas, Western influences are still marginal, especially in certain areas of the western Pacific. But in the majority of African and Polynesian areas where any semblance of traditional art survives, it has lost its verve and its quality because of the total modification of its motivations, functions, and meanings. It is somewhat comparable to being able to find creations made in sixteenth-century western Europe which are executed in terms of pure Gothic traditions. Progress and/or change in a way of life must inevitably lead to modifications and alterations in methods of artistic expression. By the traditional arts of primitive peoples, therefore, I mean that which was produced as an outgrowth of their cultures as they had developed by the time of continuous European contact.

The significance of primitive art against the background of world art is an important topic in its own right. Therefore it is sufficient at this time to say that the one is incomplete without the other. As mentioned hereafter, primitive art, with certain important exceptions, must be dated from the nineteenth and early twentieth centuries. For the art historian and for the serious art connoisseur or collector, this art has certain very important advantages over the study of other traditions. For one thing, there is not the vast bulk of historical and analytical literature, so that it is possible for the individual to exercise his own powers of perception and analysis without any fixed attitude to direct or curtail his observations. In other words, when dealing with primitive art, the scholar and the art connoisseur can with all freedom express their own aesthetic interpretations and judgments.

Paul S. Wingert

New Year's Day 1962
Auckland, New Zealand

ACKNOWLEDGMENTS

Appreciation and gratitude are herewith extended to the personnel of the many museums in Europe, America, and the South Pacific who throughout the years have made available for study their entire collections and have facilitated this study in so many different ways. Without their invaluable assistance this book could not have been written. To single out individuals from the numerous museums would be unjustified—hence this expression of thanks is intended to be all inclusive. The travel necessary to examine the widely scattered collections of primitive art was made possible by a grant in 1952 from the Wenner-Gren Foundation for Anthropological Research and by a 1955 Guggenheim Foundation Fellowship. Gratitude is here expressed for this assistance.

Particular and deep-felt gratitude is due Mr. Arthur A. Cohen of New York City for his constant encouragement and faith in the value of this work and for his sincere encouragement that withstood the pressure and tribulations of a moderate time span. Thanks are also extended to Mr. Sheldon Meyer and Mr. John Begg of Oxford University Press in New York City for their considerable interest in the manuscript, their editorial criticisms, and for easing the publication and production pains. Comparable thanks also go to Mr. Aaron Asher, Director of Meridian Books, for his editorial contributions. I am indebted also to Mrs. Sheila Crowell and Miss Florence Warshawsky for diligently copy-editing and proofreading the text.

Special appreciation for aid in securing illustrative material is here given to Mr. Cory L. Reynolds of the Museum of Primitive Art in New York City, to Mr. Harry A. Franklin of the Franklin Gallery in Beverly Hills, California, to Dr. Frederick F. Dockstader, Director of the Museum of the American Indian in New York City, and to Dr. Roland Force, Director, Bernice P. Bishop Museum, Honolulu. To Mr. Edwin C. Vogel, Mrs. Siegfried Peierls, and to Mr. and Mrs. Edgar Peierls go my deep thanks for their encouragement and for their belief in the significance of this work. And last, but most important of all, the greatest appreciation is herewith accorded my wife for her stimulating enthusiasm for this work, for her invaluable aid in editorial suggestions, and for the arduous task of typing and preparing the text for publication. Her aid contributed greatly to the completion of this work.

Of the illustrations, the following photographs were taken by the author: Figs. 3, 8, 16, 17, 18, 19, 20, 21, 22, 23, 24, 27, 29, 30, 31, 32, 33, 34, 35, 36, 37, 39, 40, 41, 42, 43. 44, 45, 48, 49, 50, 52, 53, 55, 56, 61, 62, 63, 64, 65, 66, 67, 68, 69, 70, 71, 72, 73, 74, 75, 76, 77, 78, 79, 81, 83, 85, 86, 87, 88, 89, 90, 91, 92, 93, 95, 96, 97, 98, 99, 101, 102, 103, 104, 105, 106, 107, 108, and 109. Credit is here given for the following: Figs. 7, 9, 12, 14, and 28 to Mr. Charles Uht, New York City; Figs. 84 and 110 to Mr. Reuben Goldberg, Philadelphia; and Figs. 1, 10, 51, and 54 to Mr. Peter Furst, Los Angeles. In all other instances, the illustrations were provided by the museums or collections in which the subject belongs. Credit for permission to publish all of the figures was given by the various museums and collections, and thanks are herewith accorded for that permission.

CONTENTS

LIST OF ILLUSTRATIONS

AFRICA

xiii

xiv

PRIMITIVE ART

INTRODUCTION

At the beginning of the fifteenth century, when the Great Age of Discovery began, the whole of the Western Hemisphere and the vast area of the Pacific Ocean, as well as the extent and continental status of Africa, were unknown. Within three hundred years, however, the world as it is now known was largely discovered. Since then, extensive explorations and scientific expeditions, which are still continuing, have further revealed the true character of these previously unknown parts of the globe and the ways of life of the numerous peoples who inhabit them.

These expeditions and explorations led the Darwin-inspired evolutionists of the late nineteenth century to designate these peoples as "primitive," since it was considered that their life patterns represented an earlier cultural phase through which the great civilizations of the world had progressed. The numerous and diverse art forms found among the Negroes of Africa, the peoples of the Pacific Ocean area, and the American Indians were therefore logically known as "primitive art." But shortly after the beginning of the present century, scientific investigations began to discredit many of the premises of the evolutionists. It became evident that the cultures of these peoples, which had only just recently become known, did not represent an earlier phase of our civilization. On the contrary, it was recognized that these cultures were neither in an early formative nor a late stagnant stage of development; rather that they had achieved a maturity within the contexts of their own

beliefs, institutions, and technologies which was basically different from that of the highly evolved civilizations
of the world.

With these differences in mind, scholars sought a term
by which this art could be classified or categorized, the
most frequent choice being "Primitive Art." In recent
years, an unwarranted reaction to this term has led to
lengthy disputes and to searches for a new title. What is
more acutely needed, however, is a definition of terms.
As in any field of art history, nomenclature often needs
explanation or even justification. Although there was a
historical reason for describing the arts of peoples
outside the direct influence of the great centers of
civilization as primitive, the term, already proved invalid,
has continued to be used, often in an ill-defined and
confusing manner. Fundamental to this confusion are
the several meanings given to this word within totally
different contexts, particularly by art historians and connoisseurs. For example, early phases within the historical
development of painting in the various European countries have been considered primitive, such as Flemish
or French primitive painting. By this it is meant that the
painting dates from an early period in the historical
development of the art of these particular countries.
While these works frequently appear to be anonymous,
they can often be accurately dated, or even authenticated as painted by a specific artist. Used in this way,
primitive means both chronologically early and technologically formative or immature since it refers to the
beginning of an art development.

For entirely different reasons, certain recent artists
such as Henri Rousseau and Grandma Moses have been
considered "primitives." Here the term characterizes
artists who have not received professional training and
who paint with a personal, naïve quality in their mode
of representation and interpretation of subject matter.
Moreover, their manner of painting is not akin to the
traditional, academic, or avant-garde styles of their day.
It is, in fact, a unique and highly personalized, untutored
art expression. This is not an early phase within a histor-

4

ical development, but is a "sport," in the biological sense of the word, that is, a spontaneous deviation from the norm. Used in this connection, primitive means the untrained, the naïve, and the nonconformist art. This has nothing to do, as does the first example of this term, with an early chronological period. Instead, the term "primitive" has in this context acquired a totally different meaning.

Not all the variations and usages of this term are the result of legitimate confusions relating to contextual matters of periods of time. Among many art historians, connoisseurs, and even dilettantes, the word "primitive" has also been, and is often still, commonly used in a variety of derogatory ways. If a work is inept or technologically crude, if it is puerile expressively, it is said by these people to be "primitive." This terminology means that to those who are evaluating it the work is of inferior quality. In this usage, "primitive" becomes a comparative term, and denotes a lack of quality in every respect. Hence, a work of the Middle Ages, the Renaissance, or even an earlier period may be considered "primitive" in just the same way as any contemporary art form that lacks refinement or fails to produce aesthetic pleasure.

It is evident from these discrepancies that the word "primitive" is one of many which have a considerable elasticity of meaning. Thus when such words are used, a definition of meaning and intended usage should be given. Unfortunately, this is seldom done, and the lack of a clear definition contributes strongly to the confusion surrounding the meaning of the word "primitive." This is especially true of the many instances when anthropologists and archaeologists apply the term to cultures outside the spheres of influence of the so-called great civilizations. It is necessary, as a consequence, to distinguish between these great civilizations or high cultures and the cultures of primitive peoples.

Any comparison between the so-called high and primitive cultures discloses that a number of features and institutions that have led to the development of the great civilizations are conspicuously missing in primitive societies, and that this absence is in good measure responsible for their "low" cultural status. Important among the features that they lack is a written language. Ideas and events cannot be recorded, transmitted, or disseminated, and it is impossible to share knowledge, a fact that seriously interferes with any concrete, scientific developments. Even more important is the absence of any concept of political organization, which is necessary before manpower can be trained and utilized for the construction of roads, aqueducts, or monumental architecture; in fact, such loosely organized peoples cannot maintain a standing army. The development of religious institutions into a theocratic state which can achieve comparable ends is also missing among primitive peoples.

The distinctions noted above are all too often either completely ignored or insufficiently recognized, largely because no clearly evolved concept of primitive cultures as distinct from high cultures has been developed. Because of this lack of thought or perception, the high cultures of the Inca area of the Andes and those of Central America and Mexico have often been considered "primitive." The misuse of the term has even been applied to the ancient Paleolithic and Neolithic cultures, and to the prehistoric beginnings of the high cultures. This confusion has been made almost complete by including with, or relating to, primitive art the various folk arts, the art of children, and even the work of the mentally deranged.

To some extent it is for these reasons that various attempts have been made to find some other appellation by which these most recently discovered peoples might be designated. Such terms as "native" and "aboriginal" are inappropriate, since all persons are native to particular areas, while aboriginal peoples are the prehistoric populations of the world. "Nonliterate" and "tribal" are other terms frequently used, but these, too, are unsatisfactory. "Nonliterate" was coined especially to replace primitive and can only mean peoples who are not literate —that is, who have not learned to read; this designation

6

is applicable to all of the illiterate peoples of many countries and hence has a restricted usage. The word "tribal" is little more satisfactory as a replacement, since a good number of primitive peoples are not organized in a tribal pattern, and it is erroneous to consider them in this way; at the same time, numerous tribes, such as those of the Islamic peoples, have high cultures.

What word, then, is suitable to define these peoples, called by their discoverers "primitive"? Since the last war, they have been categorized as the peoples of "underdeveloped" areas. This cannot mean, however, underdeveloped with respect to the history of their own cultures, but only by comparison with the technological standards of the high cultures of the world. It is apparent that the term "primitive" was not used because of its derogatory implications, and to discredit them as being so is only out of a false respect for the sensitive feelings of these peoples who have so recently become "our brothers." Perhaps even a sense of guilt, a remembrance of past exploitations and intentional disruptions of their ways of life, is somewhat responsible for the concept of these peoples as "underdeveloped." It would seem that by far the word most applicable to these societies is the one given to them historically, namely "primitive." But this is not because they represent the fumbling, early beginnings of civilization; rather, it is because these cultures show developments more closely allied to the fundamental, basic, and essential drives of life that have not been buried under a multitude of parasitical, non-essential desires. These are not, in so many of their aspects, simpler cultures; and certainly within their own tenets, they have had a long and evolved development. That the rate of change has been slow is a consequence of their conservatism, a concomitant of their close adherence to tradition, that is, to those ideas and practices which, through time, have been established as valid. It seems highly desirable to accept "primitive" as a reasonable term, and to make clear that its use in designating these cultures must be thoroughly understood.

Used in this way, "primitive" refers largely to the Negro peoples south of the Sahara in Africa; to the Eskimo and the American Indian, excluding the high cultures of the Andean region, Central America, and Mexico; and to the peoples who inhabited the islands of the Pacific Ocean, Australia, and certain areas of the islands off the coast of Southeast Asia at the time of their discovery. In relation to these cultures, "primitive" is a meaningful word of historical status, which refers to the cultures existent largely in those parts of the world brought to light during the Age of Discovery and subsequent explorations. When used in this context, it has no derogatory connotations, and to give it such shows a lack of knowledge or a personal bias.

"Primitive art," as a term denoting the art of primitive peoples, defines the art and in no way refers to kind or quality. And the fact that primitive art is the art of primitive peoples is in no way a characterization of the forms. It would seem obvious that some specific ideas or concepts must be formulated to give the term "primitive," with respect to art, some special significance. In other words, the concept of primitive art must be localized or defined before any study of it can be attempted. Only when this is done can the various misconceptions and misuses associated with this art and the term by which it is designated be successfully alleviated.

Primitive art refers to the artistic output of literally thousands of often small, areal cultures, each of which developed and nurtured its own art tradition. In every instance, their art was inextricably associated with such major cultural facets as religion, society, economy, and politics. The beliefs, ideas, aspirations, and fears which implemented these cultural forces served as motivations for the art expressions of these people. While it is apparent that the art styles of neighboring peoples over a small, or sometimes even a sizable, area show some analogy or even affinity of one for another, they do not resemble each other so closely as to deny any unique development or interpretation by each cultural group. It is this very uniqueness that makes it possible to recognize or distinguish between styles, and this in turn indicates a sufficiently long period of germination and development for the eventual crystallization of these elements of style to have taken place. Once this is recognized, it becomes evident that the art expressions of primitive peoples have attained a thorough maturity and that they have a definite meaning within the contexts of their numerous evolved and developed cultures. Thus it can be seen that an understanding of primitive cultures is surely a prerequisite to a more complete appreciation of their art. Even a brief familiarity with the institutions and beliefs of primitive peoples is sufficient to reveal their remarkable dissimilarity with those of the high cultures, particularly in the Western world.

It is fundamental to any valid concept of primitive art that these important differences in beliefs and practices be fully recognized. Through this recognition and insight comes the realization that to compare the meaning of the forms of primitive art with those of high cultures or of the prehistoric age, of children or of the insane, is completely illogical. The very appearance of primitive forms differs, especially in their resemblance to life forms. It is essential to recognize these highly unusual shapes for what they are: the expressions of deeply rooted art traditions which dictated to a great extent the basic designs that the professionally trained primitive artists were required to follow. In other words, it was specified that an art form, commissioned for a specific practice, agree in general with the forms traditionally used. Primitive art is, therefore, not a free, uncontrolled, and untutored creation.

Technical proficiency was, as it has been among all artists, the heritage of the primitive artist. The belief still prevails, however, that a crude and fumbling technique, which at best can only partially realize the desire of the artist, is a characteristic of primitive art. Nothing could be further from the truth. There certainly can be found mediocre or even inept examples of this, as is the case of any other art in whatever time or place, but the instances of them are in proportion, too. Involved in the

9

misconceptions surrounding primitive art is the additional, mistaken belief that smooth, polished surfaces and refinement of detail stamp a work of sculpture as superior to one in which a vigorous and dynamic realization of form is achieved by an equally strong and direct technique which lacks polish and refinement. If, however, rougher style were given an elegance of finish, and smoother style received an abrupt and dynamic treatment, the results would be unsuccessful or even incongruous. Technique and style go hand in hand, one being developed for the realization of the other.

The technique and training of the primitive artist were combined to form essential works of art, fundamental to the particular art and the particular society which spawned them. It is often difficult for outsiders to realize fully the aesthetic qualities of these objects because of an unfamiliarity with their subject matter and with the needs for which they were created. In fact, many of those whose interests in art are restricted to one or more art eras of the high cultures, particularly those of western Europe, maintain the idea that primitive art is not quite an art: it has a barbarous ("unfamiliar" or "unknown") subject matter and an inaccurate or gross misrepresentation of the human form. As indicated, a lack of knowledge is responsible for the first of these views, and a prima facie refusal to look at the work sufficiently to realize that basic art principles are as much involved in a primitive work as in any other art form compounds the error. This is not so much the harboring of false concepts as it is a protective evasion from having any concepts at all with regard to these objects. In other words, no effort is made to understand the work, and the art is given no chance to vindicate itself since it is not even carefully observed or studied.

Another equally erroneous concept of the art maintains that direct contacts with high cultures supplied the form and design elements which were then diffused throughout the far-flung primitive world, and which in the process were often debased and misunderstood. Although it cannot be denied that between contiguous groups there was a certain amount of diffusion, via borrowings of forms and design elements, this was naturally contained within a relatively small area due to geographical limitations as well as cultural affinity and hostility patterns. To apply such "borrowings" to the artistic production of the entire primitive world is to believe in the impossible as well as the improbable. For example, according to the theories of total diffusionism, the art elements of the Marquesas Islands in the eastern Pacific derived directly from early Chinese bronzes, while the bronzes and terra cottas of Ife and Benin in southern Nigeria owe their technique and characteristics to influences from Egypt and the Mediterranean world. Supporters of this opinion believe that primitive art is in general merely a backwash from that of the high cultures. The more avid of them agree with many of the obsolete theories of the early diffusionists, who maintained that in art, basic style elements were discovered but once, and then radiated outward from the single center of their discovery. This means that the creative invention of these elements occurred but once in all the history of mankind. To prove or to substantiate these ideas, the adherents of diffusionism compare specific art elements taken from within the context of one style to those with a superficially analogous appearance found within the context of a totally different style and milieu, often separated by thousands of years as well as miles. In their evaluation of primitive art, the diffusionists often "find" in the occurrence of these questionable analogies an indication of origins for the art. Without any genuine evidence of contacts between one given culture and another, these dubious analogies are frequently "discovered" without the presence of any other basic, cultural analogies. Such proof cannot even be credited as a theory, but only mentioned as an unsupported idea which in reality has no bearing on the understanding or appreciation of the art styles or the people who created them.

PART I

ART IN THE LIFE OF PRIMITIVE PEOPLES

The art of primitive peoples includes sculpture, painting, and architecture, as well as the utilitarian crafts of textiles, ceramics, and basketry. Sculpture, however, has been by far the most widespread mode of artistic expression. Carving, either in the round or in relief, in such materials as wood (the most preferred material), stone, ivory, bone, and shell was the chief sculptural technique. Modeling, however, was also an extensively developed sculptural medium. In some areas, figures were modeled in clay and fired as terra cottas, while in others they were merely sun-dried. In still other cases, as for example in various regions of Africa, figures and reliefs were modeled in beeswax and cast in brass, bronze, gold, or silver. Engraving and low-relief carving appeared throughout the primitive world on animal horns, gourds, bamboo, shell, bark, and hide.

Compared to the significance of sculpture, painting and architecture were of decidedly minor importance. Painting was most commonly used to further define the sculptured forms, although in many cases it was an adjunct to them and gave them an increased meaning.

In some areas, however, painting was a highly significant and totally independent art. Geometric, descriptive, or narrative forms were painted on wooden panels and house facades, sheets of bark, and treated surfaces of animal skins. Vegetable and mineral pigments were frequently used as simple and transient water colors, although some peoples mixed them with oil, thereby giving the paints a more permanent character. Another use of painting was that of ceremonially decorating the body and/or the face with prescribed designs and colors. The importance of this custom, as it pertains to the painting of figures and masks, must be taken into account.

The development of architecture also is of some significance for the understanding of primitive art. While in many instances buildings were of a purely utilitarian character, interesting techniques were frequently used that gave to the structures a certain artistic appearance; and in some areas of the South Seas and the Americas, decorated buildings of a superior character and importance were constructed which were motivated by ceremonial and aesthetic ends. Carved and painted, or merely painted, forms were frequently attached to these buildings to contribute to their functional and artistic purposes. A variety of materials was used in these structures including wood, stone, clay, grass, leaves, bark, hides, and mats. The structural members were held together, sometimes by mortising and grooving of parts, but more usually by lashings of vegetables or animal fibers.

The utilitarian crafts, such as textiles, ceramics, basketry, and, in some areas, stone work and metallurgy often attained a high level of proficiency. Decorative designs compatible with, and often growing out of, the technique were frequently applied to purely utilitarian objects for no other reason than to give them a more pleasing and attractive appearance. There is little doubt that most of these designs were the result of the aesthetic impulses of the artist and that they gave pleasure, as the objects were used, because of rather than in spite of the totally unnnecessary, decorative adjunct.

1

THE ARTIST: His Patron and Public

In primitive societies the artist was, in almost every instance, a professional who worked on commission. His client or patron was usually an elder, a leader, or a spokesman for some particular group that needed the artist's services. In many areas the artist was trained by serving a long apprenticeship on the basis of his interests and his talents, although among some groups the right to become an artist was inherited within a family line of chiefly or near-chiefly rank. In some regions, however, there were no trained artists as such, since every man at some time in his life, according to his attainment of various social ranks, had to carve and paint various required ceremonial objects. But it was the professional artist who was held in high esteem, particularly in Africa, where, in some areas, he also had religious and political status. It is important to keep this in mind, since it so completely refutes the all too commonly held belief that the primitive artist was completely "free" from all restraints.

The exercising of these restraints and controls on the artist by his society in general, and by his patrons in particular, meant that the traditional art styles in every area of the vast primitive world were perpetuated and held fast by the conservatism of the group that maintained the apprenticeship tradition. This was in its character as academic as the most academic traditions against which the "discoverers" of primitive art were in revolt during the early years of the present century. Every area and, in fact, often each small region had its own traditional art style, which was maintained by the apprenticeship tradition. The basic premise of this system was that the apprentice be trained to follow the age-old ideals of representation and expression common to his village or tribe; thus the proportions and shapes within a design, and the manner in which they were arranged and stressed, were taught him by his patrons as "right," that is, as traditionally correct. For centuries and centuries, these areas, no matter how large or small, had developed, through contacts with neighboring peoples and the creative interpretations of their own artists, their particular mode of representation, interpretation, and expression of the forms requisite for ceremonial and secular use. In no instance are these forms in an early or "primitive" stage of development; and there is no way of telling why certain patterns evolved and were crystallized rather than others. Perhaps in the future archaeological investigations may shed some light on the earlier forms from which the historical styles of primitive art, as they are known today, were derived. It is certain that the inherent conservatism so fundamental to primitive cultures perpetuated throughout long periods of time the basic essentials of their art styles.

It must not be construed, however, that the primitive artist was so completely restricted by the traditionalism of his training that he was a mere copyist and could, because of social restraints, be nothing more. It must be recognized that the fundamental shapes, forms, and patterns of his style were fixed by tradition; but it is just as evident that most of the pressures for the invention and development of new forms were self-induced, coming from an innate aesthetic desire rather than being demanded by the group. The master artist could, in primitive cultures just as in high cultures, endow the traditional forms with his own interpretation and insight, and these in turn sprang from his personal genius as a perceptive and creative artist. Thus, in primitive art, as in all art, there are examples of poor workmanship just as there are masterpieces and mediocrities. Because an artist was inept or crude does not mean that he has produced important works of primitive art. Due to the rigors of apprenticeship training, a high level of achievement prevailed in this art; but this must not be confused with the great accomplishments of the master artists of primitive societies.

The works created by the primitive artists were generally more than objects of aesthetic pleasure; they were requisite forms made for the economic, social, and/or political needs of the community, from materials thought to contain a vital force of their own. From existent knowledge, it is evident that the artist recognized his somewhat ambivalent role in his association with the forms he created. Various restrictions and even taboos surrounded the handling of his materials because of the belief in their inherent possession of spirits or powers of their own. His early apprenticeship had acquainted him with the necessary procedures to control and allay these forces, that is, there was a certain amount of magic involved in this aspect of the artist's endeavor. In this "controlled" material he created, following traditional patterns, his own renderings of the requisite forms. He thus had first to overcome the power latent in his materials before he could shape them to his will. The force within his materials was always, even when controlled, an active element that combined with the created entity of his forms to give them greater significance. It is no wonder that the artist was often completely exhausted after he completed his creative efforts.

The lengthy and exacting training period which enabled him to produce the objects and handle the materials also included teaching of the more prosaic requirements of his craft. As part of his apprenticeship, an artist had to make and give shape to his tools. From present-day knowledge, it would seem that he adopted the basic forms of these tools from those of his master, although it is clear from the evidence at hand that he frequently adapted them and, in fact, modified them to be a more efficient set of implements. All too often it is said that primitive peoples accomplished wondrous things with their tools. This was not the case. The primitive artist had, in fact, extremely efficient tools, which were sufficient to his needs and which he used with complete manual control to achieve the desired effects.

It is also important to keep in mind that the primitive artist was a participant in the social and ceremonial functions at which the objects of his creation were used. Thus he observed the physical and psychological significance of the objects as they functioned within the setting for which they had been commissioned. The result was that he could, and did, as numerous examples show, modify his interpretations of the traditional forms by emphasizing or minimizing various parts to give a work added force and meaning and to achieve more powerful aesthetic expression. His participation had particular significance since the forms of primitive art were substantially derived from human and animal forms; thus by his observation of his fellow men during moments of physical and emotional stress at ceremonial and ritual occasions, he was better able, due to his powers of perception and his great sensitivity, to endow the traditional art patterns peculiar to his culture with the creative force of his personality.

The demand for the artist's work depended upon the extent to which his work showed this creative force, that is, his success in fusing tradition with invention and innovation. The patronage of the primitive artist came from the elders, chiefs, priests, or leaders who directed or controlled the fundamental aspects of life—religion, social relationships, economic practices, and political and judicial controls. In many groups, some form of art was required to implement all of these basic activities; in other areas, figures, masks, or other ritual objects might only be used in certain religious ceremonies. But there were no primitive peoples, however meager their cultural attainments, who offered no patronage to the artist.

Although knowledge of the roles of the patron is considerably limited, it seems that he sought out and commissioned the artist to produce a specific kind of traditional object for a particular use. Only in relatively few areas, particularly in western Melanesia, did the patron dictate to the artist the design elements a work had to include. Most often he exerted no control whatsoever on the artist, although he would not accept his work if it deviated too far from the traditional standards. In other words, the artist had to be "right" in his basic interpretations of traditional design elements. The patron also functioned, in some known instances, as connoisseur and appraised the aesthetic content and quality of the objects. This practice may have been more widespread than is now known and may have been an important factor in maintaining the high level of artistic achievement that prevailed in so many areas of the primitive world. It is known that in various regions individual artists attained a renown far beyond the limits of their village, and that competition sometimes prevailed among the artists. Under such circumstances, the patron was of decisive importance. He was not, however, the only critic of the artist and his work: the public had a strong voice and was highly interested in the artist's achievements. The clear integration of art with all of the major facets of primitive cultures made it so much a part of life's experiences that all members of a group were familiar with it and acted as the "public" for whom the art was essentially made. In the case of secret societies or special groups, the art forms were, as a rule, only seen or used by that group. Nevertheless, it would appear that the people were familiar with the art forms used by most societies, although they did not know the complete meaning of the objects any more thoroughly than the people of the Middle Ages comprehended the full meaning of the sculptures on a Gothic cathedral. In both cases, a complete knowledge of the art forms was enjoyed by a relatively small group—by the theologians in the Middle Ages and by the elders, chiefs, or priests in primitive societies. There is no denying, however, that art played a greater part in the lives of primitive peoples than in the lives of men in Western civilization during recent centuries. That primitive peoples had an exceptionally acute aesthetic response to their art because of their constant contacts with it seems an unwarranted assumption. The range of individual aesthetic sensibility was probably no different among them than among any other group of peoples. They were, however, undeniably more aware of their art because of its constant association with the most vital experiences of their lives.

2

THE NEED FOR ART

A widespread need for art was in many instances due to the great diversity of religious beliefs and practices. One of the most common of these was the concept of the importance of ancestors for the welfare of the living. In many areas it was believed that after death the spirit of the deceased would proceed to another world where he would be in contact with the spirits and forces that controlled and determined all the activities and happenings of the living. The spirit of the ancestor was in a position to aid or to harm his descendants. Particularly in Africa, but in certain regions of Indonesia and Melanesia as well, these beliefs gave rise to various forms of ancestor worship in consequence of which ceremonies were performed to petition the beneficence and to avoid the wrath of the ancestors. In some areas it was believed that at least a certain portion of the innate spiritual power and energy released from the body at death could be ritually persuaded to take up its abode in a carving provided for that purpose. Thus, during ceremonies the actual power of the ancestor could be invoked by directing the rites to the figure. In other areas, it was thought that by ritual petition the spirit power of the ancestors could be persuaded to inhabit temporarily—that is, for the duration of a specific ceremony—a particular figure, mask, or other carving created for just that purpose, making this power accessible for direct ceremonial approach. Such permanent or temporary containers of ancestral spirit power were believed by these people to denote, tangibly, the actual presence of the ancestor.

Among other peoples, numerous carved, painted, or fabricated objects of prescribed and traditional design were symbols peculiar to the ancestor and, when used ritually, served as evidence that the rites were being symbolically directed to the ancestral being. These symbols might be given human or animal form or they might be purely abstract, geometric designs. In only a few instances were the forms used in this type of worship a realistic representation of the physical appearance of an ancestor. More often these forms were given a particular appearance which had been traditionally used for the designation of ancestors. Possible exceptions are the sensitively naturalized bronze and terra-cotta heads of Ife and the early, naturalistic bronze heads from Benin, two adjacent areas in West Africa. In other areas of Africa, as for example the Ivory Coast and the Western Congo, there are some indications that a very broad, generic portraiture may also have been intended.

In Africa and Melanesia, another consequence of ancestor belief gave rise to sculptures made especially to serve as memorials to house the deceased. Mortuary ceremonies were performed by some groups out of respect for the ancestors, at which time the sculptures were particularly revered. Afterwards, no rituals were conducted involving the carved forms, which merely existed as an evidence of esteem and respect for the dead. In some other areas of Africa, and especially among the American Indians, numerous objects, including pottery vessels, stone pipes, and small figures were frequently buried with the dead to serve at least partially as tokens of esteem. The belief that the dead had to be interred with prescribed paraphernalia and ritual was directed toward two ends: 1) to ensure a successful journey to, and abode in, the realm of the dead; and 2) to show sufficient respect for the dead so that his soul would not return to harm the living. These precautions were certainly associated with ancestor worship, as well.

Other religious concepts among primitive peoples often included beliefs in various spirits of a different nature. It was believed that some of these had at one time been humans who attained supernatural status because of the greatness of their achievements while alive, achievements that were believed to have been accomplished only as a consequence of power derived from great spirit alliances. However, numerous other supernatural spirits who were not of mortal origin had, according to myths and legends, specialized powers to control such natural phenomena as rain, lightning, and the fertility of crops, animals, and human beings. They were also entitled to preside over the majority of the activities of man, such as hunting, fishing, and craft pursuits, and to protect against and cure diseases. It was thought that, when properly petitioned or appeased, many of these spirits could be persuaded to act in benevolent fashion toward man, rather than to be malevolent, as would otherwise have been their nature and practice. Other kinds of supernatural spirits were less inclined toward malevolence and still others were benevolently disposed. But appropriate rites to insure maximum protection were directed to all supernatural spirits.

To implement the numerous rites associated with these spirits, sculptured figures, masks, and other ritual objects, together with the requisite costumes or attachments, were almost universally used. Although the specific provinces of their activities and the very nature of many of these spirits were often vague, the majority of those represented sculpturally were usually given stylized or fantastic shapes which were obviously derived from human form. Thus, a marked degree of anthropomorphism prevailed, even in the conceptualization of supernatural beings.

Still another religious concept found in numerous areas of the primitive world was the idea that a superior being or force prevailed over all others. Sometimes this being was associated with mythological ages; in other instances he was the primary force of the cosmological era from whom stemmed the origins of the universe, with all of its elements, and the very life power of plants, animals, and human beings. The concept of this being was often very vague or even nebulous, and practically no petitions or rituals were ever made to him. This was true even in regions where he was considered the superior deity in a specific pantheon of gods. In these pantheons, the gods were highly specialized, each with a limited and particular province of activity to which he had been assigned by the superior deity. These domains included the forces of nature, such as lightning, rain and storms, and all of the pursuits and vicissitudes of man, as hunting, fighting, disease, and death. Often each family, group, or village had its own tutelary or protective deity, while various other gods were also ceremonially honored or petitioned. In a few areas of the primitive world, priests officiated at shrines where the god was worshiped. Whatever the rites performed to placate, honor, or petition a deity, they always followed a traditionally prescribed pattern.

As in ancestor or spirit worship, primitive man preferred to have some tangible symbol or representation of the deity to which he could direct his ceremonies. This was due to the belief that at such times preliminary rites could endow the symbol or the representation with the actual presence of the god. Thus carved masks or figures in human form, or sometimes objects of abstract shapes, were commissioned from the sculptor. For the consummation of deity worship, art forms were, then, highly necessary, traditional elements. In all of the religious practices thus far considered, the principal actors or characters in many of the ceremonial dramas, that is the ancestors, supernatural spirits, or deities, received their sanction from, or had their prototypes in, the mythology or oral literature of a people, in itself another highly developed art form.

Two other areas of primitive man's beliefs, those of magic and divination, have strong religious implications. Magic, in brief, is the concept that certain desired ends may be achieved, or harm, disaster, or evil avoided, if a prescribed formula for contacting particular spirit powers or supernatural forces is followed. The carrying out of such formulas was often left to specialists or professionals who knew all of the intricacies involved in these procedures; but various forms of magic were frequently performed by an individual for his own protection or to achieve a desired end. Sculptured objects, including figures and masks, were often used in magical practices, together with a number of other, sometimes unpleasant materials, including grasses, blood, animal skins, and viscera. In some cases, carvings were given magical potency by the application of certain colors or painted designs; in other instances the shape of the sculptured forms was in itself sufficient.

Another important magical object was the so-called "fetish," an object that had an indwelling power capable, when properly invoked, of curing disease, causing destruction, or giving protection. In many "fetishes" this power was derived from magical substances that had been attached to or inserted into the object to activate it. When supplications or petitions were directed to a "fetish," following a traditionally prescribed pattern, it was believed that the power within the object would, through its supernatural spirit alliances, strive to achieve the desired results. The distinction between a "fetish" and an object used to achieve magical ends is that the spirit power is localized in a "fetish" and has merely to be ritually activated to become operative, whereas in the performances of the other magical rites, the spirit power first had to be localized before it could be invoked. Great numbers of figures, masks, animal forms, and abstract objects had to be furnished by the artist for use by his patrons in these countless, magic-working ceremonies.

Divination, like magic, was a common practice among primitive peoples. It was, in substance, an effort, through a prescribed use of certain objects, to foretell future events, to discover the propitiousness of a given time for a specific act, to reveal the guilt or innocence of an accused person, and to accomplish various other comparable purposes. In a few areas there existed both a god and a cult of divination, and in all areas it was an appeal to supernatural powers or beings for guidance. It is apparent, therefore, that there was some religious sanction for this custom. Here again, the artist was often called upon to carve and embellish the varied and diverse objects used in divination practices and rites.

For the purpose, then, of controlling or directing the unknown forces from which came death, sickness, and various other disasters, magic was employed; it involved the manipulation of either a dynamic, spirit-charged object, or of materials or substances which, in combination, became volatile, dynamic spirit agents. Divination, on the other hand, was concerned with foretelling future events and with discovering the reasons for the perpetration of various crimes such as thievery, murder, and death, through the prescribed use of inherently powerless elements. An example of this is the practice of throwing kola nuts which are supposed to fall in a patterned way because of the intervention or will of supernatural spirits. The diviner can then read the answers to his queries according to the patterns which he has been trained to interpret. In other words, in magic the spirits are involved directly, and in divination, indirectly.

Since they have a distinct bearing on art, important differences between ancestor, spirit, and deity beliefs and practices, and those involving magic or divination, should be carefully noted. The actual presence of the spirit or of a symbol standing for it was often believed necessary before the rites and ceremonies could be performed. As already noted, there were numerous instances in which various sculptures acted as repositories for, or were representatives or symbols of, the ancestors, supernatural beings, or deities. If these rites were enacted carefully and in a traditional manner, the people felt reasonably confident that all would go well. In magic, a different belief and attitude prevailed. It was believed, but without the same degree of assurance, that if certain traditional formulas consisting of actions, chant, and/or the use of potentially spirit-charged materials were correctly enacted, a dynamic, supernaturally charged spirit force would be released which had the capability of achieving the desired ends. However, uncertainty existed, since the performances of counter-magic or the presence of a stronger version could negate the original action. The rites of magic were, therefore, tense, dynamic, and frequently even dangerous since a slight mistake could bring disaster. Sculptures made for use in the performance of magic were usually more summary in shape and less carefully rendered or finished, since the surfaces and sometimes the entire form were hidden by the addition of other materials and substances.

The close integration of all aspects of life within primitive cultures makes it difficult if not impossible to single out rites with purely religious, magical, or divinatory significance as distinct from those with social, economic, or even political importance. Most ceremonies, although religiously inspired and sanctioned, usually involved several phases of the major, cultural aspects and were strong factors in the maintenance and continuance of cultural solidarity. Ancestor rites, for example, not only honored the ancestor and petitioned him for health and well-being, but also requested fertility of the crops and animals that formed the basis of each particular economy. Other religious ceremonies were directed toward the deities and supernatural spirits solely for the protection and fruitfulness of crops. All craftsmen and artisans, as well as hunters and fishermen, had their special forces, whether ancestor, spirit, or deity, to whom they directed their petitions for help and protection. In all cultures religion is a strong socializing force. But due to the extensive participation of primitive peoples in so many of what were often spectacular and dramatic ceremonies, religions had an almost incalculable social importance. Even political customs had, at times, the religious sanction of ancestors, supernatural spirits, or gods. Therefore, before the full significance of an art that is so completely a part of its cultural fabric can be perceived, it is necessary to examine insofar as possible the motivating forces that led to its creation, the manner in which it functioned within the cultural setting, and the meaning it had for those who used it.

3

MOTIVATIONS

In any culture and in any historical epoch, the motivations that lead to the necessity for creation of art forms stem from the methods developed to gain satisfaction and fulfillment of the basic, fundamental needs of man through the implementation of his traditional beliefs and aspirations. These needs are, and have always been, common to all mankind, but the implementation of their fulfillment is different in every culture. The desire for some form of security, and therefore an assurance of survival, is one of the essential drives, perhaps the most elemental drive, of all living matter. Plants, animals, and humans alike make every effort to adapt and defend or protect, so that they may sustain themselves and their descendants. In a nonscientific, primitive society, much depends upon an ability to cope with the unknown forces of nature since life itself is at stake. Beliefs arose about the causes and effects of certain natural phenomena, and out of these, certain ceremonies and rites were gradually developed to assure some security and survival in an uncertain, arduous, and frequently hostile world. The ancestors, supernatural beings, and deities were petitioned for rain, for the fertility of crops, and for the abundance of animals as staples essential to the maintenance of life, that mankind might survive; and often at the same time, these beings and powers of the universe were placated, that they would not withhold these needs and thus wreck adversity and destruction. Security, or protection against accident, disease, and death (where primitive belief did not associate cause with effect), was often sought through magic appeals to or through specialized spirits. Indeed, because of a lack of association of effect with cause, it was believed in many areas that without frequent ceremonies honoring and petitioning the various spirits and beings according to traditional patterns, a latent malevolency could come from any of these ostensible forces for good. The innumerable rites directed to these forces were, therefore, inevitable attempts to assure some security and survival against patent odds. It is obvious that for humanity as a whole these were a set of cardinal needs, and a great deal of primitive art was created to implement such imperative requirements.

Another almost comparable set of needs centered on the desire for continuity and stability. A paramount characteristic of primitive cultures is a rigorous adherence to tradition, which necessarily results in the growth of strong conservatism. The external evidence of the need for continuity and stability can be seen in the numerous societies, practices, and ceremonies centered around strong traditions, often of a distasteful or even injurious nature to nonparticipants, which were evolved as an outgrowth of those needs and were such an important aspect of life. Secret societies, for example, with the indoctrination of youth into adult society, were one of the powerful institutions in the achievement of this end: they not only gave a continuity to the culture by insuring recurrence of traditional practices, but also served as strong stabilizing elements in often small and loosely organized groups. Certain ceremonials, which are sometimes referred to as "plays," involved mythological characters as well as minor deities. These acquainted the spectators with their traditional "literature" and often their cosmology, thereby contributing a comparable cultural role. Ancestor beliefs also were a strong force in satisfying the need for continuity and stability, but, as previously noted, they also played an important part in assuring security and survival. The vast quantity of art objects used in numerous ceremonies aimed at the attainment of these primary desires indicates that these events served as one of the major motivations toward art.

Still another critical need in primitive life was the maintenance of equilibrium and balance. This involved, among other things, the sometimes precarious and uncertain relationships between the living and the dead, especially the newly dead. Many primitive peoples believed that until mortuary rites had been performed the spirit or soul of a person, liberated by death, was at large, and in that state was capable of taking revenge or otherwise seriously harming his descendants and other survivors in the community. Important ceremonies were necessary to change his status from that of a living member of his family and village to a possibly beneficent ancestor of the group, since the interval between these two roles was a dangerous one of imbalance when man was completely vulnerable because no controls existed for his protection. The rites enacted after death were, therefore, of the greatest importance: they assured the transformation of a dead person into an ancestor spirit by ritually conducting his soul or spirit-being to the other world where the ancestors dwelt; thus they restored the balance and the certainty of relationships, regenerating the state of equilibrium.

While essential whenever an individual died, these rites were of added significance upon the death of important persons such as headmen, chiefs, elders, or priests. Although not attended by comparable dangers, a similar situation of imbalance prevailed with every change of status wrought by the passage from childhood to adulthood, marriage, and childbirth. As a result societies, sometimes secret, existed in many parts of the primitive world, their major function being to induct the youth, at the age of puberty, into the state of manhood via special, traditional initiation ceremonies. This generally applied only to the boys, but there were instances of female initiation as well. The youngsters were instructed in their new roles as adult members of the group and, in certain instances, were taught the inviolable nature and importance of certain customs and traditional beliefs. This change in status was often marked by special scarifications of the face or body, by tattooing, or by the wearing of arm bands, belts, nose sticks, hair ornaments, or sculptured breast pendants such as small ivory masks. In many areas, marriage and birth, which likewise affected the balance within a culture, were also celebrated by important ceremonies and rituals. The majority of these rites needed to accomplish the critical changes of status, and aptly called by one scholar **"rites de passage,"**[1] required from the artists large quantities of carved and fabricated objects and must, therefore, be recognized as powerful cultural motivations for artistic development.

The need for a societal equilibrium and balance was in many respects an outgrowth from, or at least closely related to, the essential human desires for security and survival, continuity and stability. To satisfy these needs, primitive man developed an often intricate series of rites and ceremonies which, without scientific knowledge of the forces of nature and of disease, enabled him to gain peace of mind through exercising certain controls over the unknown, the dreaded elements by which he was surrounded. These basic needs, which can be equated with religious, economic, and social beliefs and practices, served as powerful motivations which ultimately led to the production of the largest proportion of primitive art.

Not all of the art of primitive peoples, however, was motivated by these basic needs. In mankind there is an innate desire to display one's achievements whether in social, economic, or other spheres of activity. This desire, depending upon circumstances, can be called vanity or an assertion of personal prestige. Evidences of vanity and prestige-seeking are very old, appearing in many of the most ancient archaeological records. They are known to have served as strong motivations for art objects in bygone Western and Eastern civilization, and clearly they occupied the same role among primitive peoples. For example, not all face and body painting, scarification, or tattooing was religiously or socially prescribed by tradition. It appears that a good deal of it was used as an expression of sheer vanity, while some of it denoted the rank or status of an individual within his group, and thus had prestige value. The sculptor enhanced his figures and masks with designs culled from those he observed on the faces and bodies of his associates; thus the motivation that led to the expression of a personal vanity served indirectly to inspire details on art objects. But art was also directly involved in the need to express personal vanity and prestige, as is clearly evident in such objects as richly carved hair combs, lime containers and spatulas, tobacco pipes, drinking cups, neckrests, and stools; in the wide variety of ornaments worn on the arms, legs, breast, nose, and ears; and in the shaping and decoration of pottery and wooden bowls, jars, and cups. Many of these objects were of personal prestige value, clearly indicating that the economic status of an individual was such that he could afford these luxuries or display items, or that his rank was high enough that he was eligible to possess them.

In all the needs that motivated art objects, there is an accompanying desire common to all mankind from the earliest Paleolithic times onward — the apparent need for aesthetic expression and creation of form. Rarely was the mask or figure for a given ceremony or rite required to contain any artistic quality for the successful fulfillment of its purpose; yet artists were commissioned to shape these objects, and in very few cases did they fail to give the forms an objective or external aesthetic expression and appearance beyond the demands of their subjective or internal content. Even the stone tools and a wide variety of weapons and purely utilitarian objects used by primitive man had an aesthetically satisfying shape and finish that did not purport to increase the efficiency of the implements. No matter how meager the development of a culture may be, there is invariably some evidence of the fulfillment of this universal need for aesthetic expression — the shape given to a utensil was often not for the sake of greater usefulness, but solely for the pleasure that the form could give to those who used it, as well as to its maker. As an important need, which in most cases led to direct or indirect motivations for the creation of art forms among primitive peoples— no less than it did among others—the desire for aesthetic expression must be kept in mind for a fuller comprehension of the art, or for any meaningful evaluation of it.

4

FUNCTIONS

In discussing primitive art the term "function" has a specialized meaning, since the general use of the word — i.e., the purpose or use for which an object was made to serve — is inadequate. It refers only to the practical aspect of a work (e.g., the wearing of a mask) and does not include the particular significance of the work in question while it is in use, which is the primary function. The term may therefore be defined as: the overt and tangible implementation of the means by which a fulfillment of the basic needs or drives underlying the fundamental motivations is attained. During the performance of some ancestor rituals, for example, a carved figure may have served as a container for the ancestral spirit, in which case its primary function was to provide for the requisite presence of that spirit at the ceremony. Other figures often served as symbols of the ancestor's presence or were generic representations of him to which the rites were directed. Every figure and mask and, for that matter, all ceremonial objects had their own particular function without which the desires responsible for motivating art forms could not have been satisfied. It is, therefore, highly essential to consider the specialized functioning of each object or type of object within its own cultural context.

An example of what is meant by "function" can be seen by examining the events which once took place in South New Guinea, along the beaches of the Papuan Gulf east of the Purari Delta. If crops had been meager, or an unusual number of persons had died over a span of time, the elders of a clan, realizing that the security and survival of their group were threatened, would decide that a ceremony honoring beneficent, traditional, supernatural beings must be held in order to avert total disaster. Each clan had as its special benefactors a certain number of these supernatural spirits and possessed the right to represent them by constructing and painting tall, oval-shaped masks (Fig. 60). Since it was essential that these spirits be present at such a ceremony, a large house was erected with a prescribed amount of wood for the heavy log framework and a heavy thatch covering for the roof. In this house, each clan would make its own masks, keeping them out of sight of the women and children. Every mask was a unique representational form just as every supernatural being was a distinct individual; but all were made in the same way and were decorated with a shared vocabulary of geometric symbols. Each mask consisted of a light, palmwood armature, the front and back covered with a natural-colored, light gray-tan bark cloth on which designs were affixed by sewing strips of cane onto the surface. The designs were then painted in delicate pastel colors, and grotesque facial features were delineated in cane stitched to the front surface of the lower part of the mask, which fitted over the head of the wearer. For the mouth, a large, carved, wooden, crocodilelike snout fitted with sharp wooden slivers for teeth was lashed into place. The making of the masks was a co-operative clan endeavor under the direction of an elder who dictated the designs from memory. Because of the many interdicts and restraints associated with the mask-making, plus the necessity to grow and accumulate the quantities of food required for the feasts

60

which accompanied the ceremony, preparations frequently lasted as long as five years.

When everything was finally ready, the masks were ritually indoctrinated; and on the following day, at sunup, the ceremony began. From the great, high door of the special house where they had been secretely made, each mask, worn by a clan member, emerged individually to take its proper place in the ritual proceedings. For several days, the clan members walked around the villages and along the shore, grouped around one or another of their own masks, singing and rejoicing in their presence. It was a time of pleasure and of almost hysterically charged excitement and exuberance. During these few days other ceremonies were held for the initiation of the youth into adult society, at which time still other spirits, represented by conical masks of similar construction, were in attendance. At the end of the ceremonial period, all of the great masks re-entered the special house for the last time and continued through to a sacred court behind it, where they were ritually thanked for their presence and were then destroyed by fire.[2]

This ceremony was motivated by the need to alleviate disease and for some assurance of survival, which depended upon improvement of crops; the supernatural beings were honored and entertained since it was believed that they had the power to rectify both disorders. To appraise these beings successfully of the continuing respect and esteem in which they were held, some direct contact was necessary, and this was provided by their representation in the masks. The functioning of these forms in this instance was, by their depiction of the spirits, to act as proxies for them; and so they called the attention of the supernaturals to the many honors being accorded them, that the needs that brought the ceremony into being might be allayed.

Initiation rites were held at this time because of its sacred and propitious nature, since it was believed in this region that only then would there be sufficient, direct spirit contact to achieve the drastic adjustment involved in this critical alteration of status. But there was still another fundamental need satisfied by the performance of these rites — the desire for continuity and stability in the way of life of the people. In this ceremony, the presence of the spirits contributed a strong religious aspect, the control and direction of the elders being vested in the religious and political leaders. In addition, the need for great quantities of food served as an economic stimulus; and the identification of clan members with their own supernatural spirits, when combined with the feasting and dancing, provided a marked, integrating, social force which led to a decided stability and cohesion for the group.

The big Papuan Gulf ceremonies and their accompanying initiation rites were motivated by several of the essential needs of primitive man; and in them, the art forms served a vital function. Every important aspect of culture was an element of concern in this important ceremony; and all of the essential motivations that spring from the needs of a people, and require implementation through art forms, were involved both directly and indirectly in this communal ceremony. This may be considered, then, a classic example of how completely integrated a role was played by art in all phases of primitive culture.

The forms themselves had far greater significance of function than their mere appearance as objects worn in the ceremony. Although the forms and the symbolic designs on them were only partially understood by the community at large, there was sufficient comprehension on a generalized level to evoke an Aristotelian, cathartic type of response. On that basis alone, the success of the ceremony was assured, while because of it the art became so charged with spirit power that the major masks or dramatis personae had to be destroyed for the general safety, since contact with them might be fatal because of their recent association with spirit powers.

The full significance of the designs on the art forms was known only to a select group, the clan elders. This was in spite of the common clan knowledge of their own traditional designs which they recognized by appearance and of which they had limited knowledge. The emotional response came from the recognition of these clan-owned symbols by which their supernatural spirits were represented in terms of the designs within the context of the forms. This was the real function of these spectacular Papuan Gulf art forms.

In many ways analogous in purpose to the art forms from the Papuan Gulf — though completely dissimilar in appearance — were the art forms found among certain of the American Indians. The False Face Society, which existed among the Iroquois tribes of New York State, used in their rituals a wooden mask with a somewhat more restricted function and motivation than the first examples (Fig. 117). The need to be protected against destruction by disease, the causes of which were unknown, and so to survive, inspired the ritual wearing of carved wooden face masks by members of the False Face Society. In this instance, however, observers of the rites had full knowledge of the mythological inspiration of the form.

117

It is explained in Iroquois myths that these masks were originally given to man in the distant past by the great supernatural beings with whom they had come in contact. The supernaturals offered them protection against disease if they followed a prescribed pattern of ritualistic activities and wore a wooden mask carved and painted in a specific way. This mask represented the appearance of these beings and had to be accompanied by appropriate gestures and by the carrying of a turtle-shell rattle during ceremonial use. At times of serious illness, a few members of the Society, wearing their masks and shaking their rattles, would ritually exorcise the evil spirit of disease from an individual; and every spring, members of the False Face Society would visit each house and cleanse it of any disease that might have been lurking there and banish impurities that had accumulated during the year. The benefits of the curative powers of the Society could thus be individually acquired in cases of emergency, or could be dispensed in a communal, therapeutic manner throughout the tribe.

Iroquois False Face masks, together with all the para-phernalia and ritual of the Society, were derived from a deeply religious experience: the initial contact with the supernatural beings when the knowledge of and right to wear the masks were obtained. When they were carved, religious offerings of tobacco were made at all stages of their creation. In order to retain the power that was be-lieved to be inherent in all growing things, a power at one with that of the supernatural beings, the mask was cut within the living tree (usually an ash tree). When it was cut free, the great gash was treated so that the tree would not die. The identity of the mask was clearly estab-lished by the time it was removed from the matrix — that is, it was blocked out and given its shape and final sur-face design while still attached to the living trunk — but its full character was only acquired when the details of physiognomy and the requisite color—either red or black, or a combination of the two — was given to the surface.

These masks were the particular property of the False Face Society, and they had, in general, a certain sense of sanctity which related to their religious motivation and to the traditional rites associated with their use. The primary function of the Society was, through the use of the masks and their accompanying ritual, to bring the force and power of the supernatural beings to bear upon such problems as curing disease and ridding a com-munity of incipient illnesses and/or lurking, malevolent spirits. Each carved mask represented the actual pres-ence of a supernatural being, and the wearer, for the duration of the ceremony, lost his own identity. He acted, instead, through the mask to achieve the desired ends. Since rituals involved only members of the False Face Society, they were socially unimportant as a cultural factor, and they did not have economic or political over-tones. Compared to the great Papuan Gulf masks, these American Indian forms were not as integrated with the varied aspects of the life of a people. However, they did serve as important aids for the maintenance of continuity and stability in the traditional relationships between the tribes and their beneficent supernatural beings, relationships that contributed strongly to the much needed feelings of security and survival.

A still different function of masks was found among the Ibibio peoples of Nigeria in West Africa, where the Ekpo Secret Society played an important cultural role. The rituals of this Society were performed in the strictest secrecy and any nonmembers found encroaching on the area where the meetings were held were surreptitiously killed. The Ekpo served a dual purpose: to honor the ancestors and, through terroristic methods, to maintain a social and political status quo. Certain religious sanctions were involved by their calling upon the power and prestige of the ancestors for support, although certainly at the time of European knowledge of the Society, its rites and, in fact, its **raison d'être** were oriented toward social and political ends. The numerous masks (Fig. 20) used by the Ekpo members were varied in design and dynamic in form, some of them clearly derived from human facial types, others a fantastic combination of human and weird animal forms. These masks were said to represent spirits from the underworld whose character and actions were wayward and unpredictable, as exemplified by their destruction of property as well as of human life — thus they were frequently known as "destroyers" or "avengers."

20

It would seem likely that the Society originally sought to achieve security by appealing to the ancestors for their protection and general beneficence, the rites probably being conducted and participated in only by the important elders of the group. Over the years, however, probably through the self-interests of these "big" men, the original religious character was gradually modified and the Ekpo became a strictly secret society of socially repressive nature which acted as a controlling factor in the political life of the community. It also played a judicial role, since persons adjudged by the Society as guilty of ambitions for powers and position, as well as disrespect for authority, often had their property destroyed and/or were severely beaten as a deterrent to others who might wish to overstep the bounds of tradition. The basic motivation, therefore, became an outgrowth of an almost pathological need for continuity and stability on a status quo basis.

The primary function of the masks also seems to have undergone a drastic change over the years. Originally they were either the symbols or representations of ancestors whose presence was requisite when honors were paid or petitions directed to them, while later, although the ancestors were still present as minor motivating forces, the masks had ceased to function as their representations. Instead, they now depicted the underworld spirits who carried out the decisions and dictates of the Ekpo and were consequently held responsible for the resulting death and destruction. These were demoniac spirits who were under the control of the Society and from whom its members derived their power; and in this capacity the masks functioned as oppressive agents for the maintenance of stability for the desired social and political order. Since it was apparently felt necessary for at least some of these masks to have the fantastic if not terrifying appearance of the wayward spirits, one of their functions was to produce this effect. On the basis of the variety of their designs and forms, it appears that the artist was given a good deal of freedom to interpret his representation of the spirits. The more naturalistic representations found in some Ekpo masks were, on the other hand, probably a typological continuation of the forms that had previously represented the ancestors.

57

In some respects, the spectacular masks used by the Sulka peoples of the northern area of New Britain in Melanesia had a motivation and function comparable to those of the Ekpo (Fig. 57). These helmet-type masks, which fitted entirely over the heads of the wearers, were constructed of a light cane armature covered with narrow strips of pith from a species of reed, and had a few attached wooden details. The entire surface was painted crimson and sharp, acid green in striking juxtapositions, with some of the details left in the light neutral tan of the wood and pith. In appearance, these are among the most striking of primitive masks. They were worn by members of a secret society whose primary function was the initiation of adolescent boys into adult society. Closely associated with this purpose was that of maintaining—by terroristic methods—the traditional division of the sexes, setting the women and children apart from the adult males. The crucial change in a boy's status was dramatized by surrounding the period of transition with an aura of secrecy, mystery, and suspense. Here, too, the preservation of the status quo was a vital, subjective factor, while objectively the masks were said to represent dangerous supernatural spirits from the jungle, capable of destroying a boy who showed signs of fear or timidity during the initiation proceedings, a period of exacting ordeal. The boy was told at this time that the masks were disguises worn by mortal men who were merely impersonators of the supernatural spirits.

These Sulka masks were motivated by two interrelated needs: to achieve at this period of crisis occasioned by the change in a boy's status the maintenance of an equilibrium and balance in the social, economic, and political life of a community; and, through the traditionally prescribed initiation rites, to contribute to a continuity and stability of group beliefs and practices. The only suggestion of any religious motivation appears in the ostensible role of the supernatural spirits, although the actual purpose of the masked figures seems to have been—by the time of European contact with and knowledge of the Sulka—to terrify the women and children who believed that the masks were the actual spirits. Through their actions and appearances, the initiation period was given an intense quality of melodrama and mystery. Like the Ekpo masks, these weird forms may also have had at one time a religious character, representing the supernatural beings whose power was invoked by the elders for the protection and well-being of those undergoing initiation. By European days this concept was somewhat removed, for the women and children sincerely believed that the spirits could surely destroy the boys whom they dragged away from their homes in the opening act of the initiation melodrama. If the boys did not survive the rigors of the initiation ordeal, death was credited to the super-natural beings, just as death and destruction had been ascribed to underworld spirits by the Ekpo members.

Certain masks, therefore, had among both the Sulka of New Britain and the Ibibio of West Africa an ostensible and a hidden function: they were generally believed to represent a particular class of spirits characterized by their dangerous and potentially destructive temper-ament, in which case the mask functioned to create terror or apprehension; the same objects were known by members of the secret societies to be disguises behind which certain individuals could assume the cloak of anonymity and perpetrate acts of violence to enforce the traditional organization of a community. Conse-quently, the mask functioned both as a means of con-cealing the identity of the wearers and as an agent through which their will might be enforced on the group. Although the basic motivation behind the Sulka masks seemed to have undergone a drastic expansion by the time of European intervention in New Britain, the masks still satisfied, by their use in initiation rites, the primary need for continuity and stability through ritual, as well as ensuring a cultural equilibrium and balance in the face of the vital change in status that resulted from the inclusion of the initiates into their new group. By instilling in the youth—by means of the dreadful experiences of indoctri-nation—a proper respect for authority and position, they could prevent the growth of anarchy and the eventual dissolution of the community which might have resulted from the entry into adult society of successive groups of self-assertive adolescents. This problem was handled by various other peoples throughout the primitive world in ways comparable to those of the Sulka, masks, figures, and a variety of other art forms often being used with a very similar function.

Quite different, however, from the terroristic function of the Sulka and Ekpo art forms were the figures of the Baoule peoples from the Ivory Coast of West Africa, which, as among many primitive peoples, were as impor-

tant as masks in ceremonial and ritual use (Figs. 1, 2).
While several influences lay behind the carving of the
human figure, which functioned in a variety of different
ways, only those associated with the ancestor cult will be
considered at this time, since they reveal additional
relationships between art and life. At the time of European contact with the Baoule, the carved human figure
was used extensively in ancestor rites in addition to the
mask which also played a significant role. When a person
died, a trained professional sculptor was commissioned
by the family of the deceased to carve a likeness of the
dead person, the likeness consisting largely of rendering such details as the style of hairdress and the unique
facial and body scarification patterns upon a generic
figure, common in style to the traditional mode of representation of the village or area. The figure was then
placed by the grave of the dead person for a sufficient
time for his spirit, or at least a sufficient portion of it, to
take up residence in the carving. Afterwards, the sculpture was placed in a special house in which all of the
sacred carvings—ancestral and otherwise—were stored
when not in ritual use. At certain prescribed and special
occasions, the figures were taken from the house and
special ceremonies to honor and propitiate the ancestors
were enacted.

1

The fundamental motivations of these carved figures
involved both the needs for security and for cultural continuity, since it was believed that at death some portion
of the soul or spirit of the deceased went on to the
superior world of the hereafter. There it was in constant
contact with the great deities of the fairly well-developed
Baoule pantheon and with a variety of somewhat volatile
supernatural spirits. It was believed that by performing
certain ritual practices, petitions and honors addressed to
the ancestors were conveyed by them to the great deities
and spirits, and that through this intervention the possi-
bility of successful responses was distinctly favorable.
Subsistence and protection against unknown forces thus
directed in the rites were surely of great importance;
but the possibilities suggested by the position held by

the ancestor as a link between the past, present, and future was of still greater significance. The continuance of life, as well as an assurance of life for future generations, were all involved in the ritual directed to these ancestor figures of the Baoule. The motivations, therefore, evolved from some of the most elementary of essential human needs.

In function, these carved, wooden ancestor figures made their ritual appearance as proxies of the actual person and, in substance, served as objects that contained the requisite portion of the soul or vital essence of the ancestor. They were the visible and tangible means by which the spiritual force or power of the ancestor was contacted. Since these were religious sculptures, the knowledge of what they represented and of the purposes they served heightened the aura of sacredness with which they were surrounded.

2

The elegance and refinement of shape, surface, line, and detail that the Baoule artists so consistently gave to these figure sculptures is a strong argument in support of the theory that these objects also served as forms of aesthetic quality and importance—that they gave pleasure as artistic expressions independent of their primary function. This aspect of primitive art—objects intentionally created with aesthetic quality—has all too often been ignored or even denied in favor of expositions of its more practical purposes; but on the basis of the rather meager information available about the recorded responses to ritual objects as artistic forms, it seems certain that the artist was striving for that result and that at least some of his "audience" responded to it. This observation must be applied to all examples of primitive art. Perhaps Baoule sculptures in particular functioned rather more heavily than in other areas as emotional stimuli for religious and aesthetic responses. In any case, the motivations seem clear-cut: to secure and continue the spiritual, physical, and economic welfare of the community.

Although ancestor beliefs were of the utmost significance among primitive peoples, those beliefs did not always give rise to such active, ritualistic relationships as are found among the Baoule. In the Central Congo, for example, among the Bushongo (Bakuba) peoples, royal portrait figures were carved in commemoration of their kings and functioned largely as memorials to them. According to information culled from somewhat conflicting data, an early king who reigned over this large confederation of tribes sometime before 1600 commissioned a portrait figure of himself to be carved as a memorial to which his people could turn for inspiration in time of stress or need; thenceforth, this practice became standard among successive rulers, each of whom left his own testimonial (Fig. 31). From a study of the relatively few surviving royal figures, it is quite evident that the portrait character was largely a generic representation with the personalized elements reserved for, and evident in, details only—such as a slightly greater portliness in one carving than in another—and in such unique features as the carving on the low pedestal in front of the figure, which refers to that contribution of the king to his people that either the elders or the sculptor (the choice is not known) considered significant and most worthy of representation. The figure was carefully kept within the royal compound and, so far as is known, was not used in any rituals.

31

These Bushongo royal portrait figures were largely motivated by an individual desire for that ultimate form of prestige which would continue beyond the grave—immortality. Also involved was a shameless, personal vanity. The belief that the spirit power of the ancestors was a force to which his descendants could appeal for help and protection was inherent in the function of these carvings as memorials that were turned to in times of dire trouble. More specifically, these portraits were remarkable symbolizations and pictorial expressions of the weightiness and omnipotence of African kings. They may, therefore, be considered as obliquely associated with ancestor-cult beliefs, but in a very specialized way. Further examples of ancestor memorial figures are to be found in other parts of Africa, among the American

44

Indians, and in the art of peoples of the Pacific Islands, although motivation and function differ from group to group.

44

32

33

22

39

Strong personal prestige or vanity motives for the Bushongo figures is in no way unique, for among primitive peoples generally this is an important motivation for some of their most finely realized and creative forms. Further examples of Bushongo vanity-inspired art forms are the carefully carved drinking cups (Figs. 32, 33) and the boxes of various sizes and shapes which were made for the wellborn and affluent peoples as objects of social status. Similar carved or fabricated forms, including neckrests (Fig. 44), stools (Figs. 22, 39), pipes, various kinds of containers, moccasins, hairdresses, and the facial and body scarification and tattooing patterns were all art forms of prestige-vanity value. Within this category, art was not as traditionally prescribed or restricted, and there was a greater latitude in the culturally accepted forms. In art of this nature there is often refined, artistic expression and rendering underlying these objects with a less important content since the surface patterns and often the shapes themselves had only a decorative significance and served only to enhance the object. Some of the designs, however, had a symbolic significance generally understood by either the clan or by the community as a whole; or the design elements might have had meaning only to the artist who gave them his own unique ideas as content. While the majority of art forms in this category functioned as societal prestige objects and/or as evidence of position or economic affluence, to achieve this function most satisfactorily a particular stress was laid on a high level of artistic quality; thus, a closely related function was to give aesthetic pleasure—that is, the cliché "art for art's sake" could be applied to these works. On the basis of the strong, secondary motivations and functions of the Bushongo royal portrait figures, these forms may be at least partially classified with this group.

Among the peoples of western New Ireland in Melanesia, an ancestor belief somewhat comparable to that of the Bushongo peoples led to spectacular ceremonies that were only somewhat differently motivated and to art forms that functioned in a mildly analogous way to the royal portrait figures. In New Ireland, at one time, mortuary rites were held every three or four years, ostensibly to honor those who had died during that period. Although differently motivated from those of the Papuan Gulf peoples, these ceremonies were again directed by the clan elders. Here, too, each clan "owned" a number of representational and design forms which they used in the carving and fabrication of the mortuary-ceremony sculptures. At these rites several categories of ancestors were honored: the great cosmic beings, that is, the sun and the moon, from whom all order and life in the universe began; the legendary ancestors, those demigods and culture heroes who had in the remote past been human beings affiliated with specific clans; and those individuals who had recently died in the community. The rites and all of the objects made for use in them were known as the Malagan. While this ceremony was a commemorative one held to honor all the ancestors, it was a gala occasion without somber mourning, a time of rejoicing in the presence of all the ancestral symbols.

The Malagan had a complex set of motivations. All of the primary or basic needs and desires that served as stimuli for art forms were involved in this ceremony, but several of them stand out as leading to the elaboration in performance of these rites at the time of European contact: 1) the desire for continuity and stability; 2) the need for equilibrium and balance; and 3) the need for prestige-vanity satisfaction as well as aesthetic pleasure. These varied inspirations led to the great profusion of art forms and, to an extent, to their highly developed style and quality.

When the elders of a clan began the exacting and costly preparations for staging a Malagan ceremony, they procured the services of the most accomplished artists available to carve and fabricate the necessary objects. These artists worked within an enclosure especially constructed for that purpose, under the direction of the elders, who guided their choice of clan-owned designs and symbols which had to be included in the objects.

The dynamics of this culture were such that, to uphold clan prestige, each Malagan had to be more spectacular, more original in creating something new within the pattern of existing art traditions. These "new" designs were actually merely elaborations of the traditional motifs and elements. This led to inventiveness and creativity as ends in themselves—a pattern that is found only rarely among primitive peoples, since traditional designs have to be complied with and the creativity has to take place within set patterns.

66

As a consequence of this freedom, the designs from New Ireland became extremely elaborate while maintaining the ancient, basic patterns. Malagan art, which included single-figure compositions, series of forms arranged either vertically or horizontally, and a number of masks of different designs (Fig. 66) was, therefore, a deliberate attempt to achieve novel and spectacular effects that would bring praise and prestige to the clan from whose designs they were composed. This cultural necessity to stage bigger and more spectacular Malagan rites led to an elaboration in the art that had achieved, by the time of European contact, an extraordinary richness of composition in which traditional design elements were combined with virtuosity in a fabulous fashion.

This ceremonial art of New Ireland served largely a symbolic purpose. The clan-owned design vocabulary consisted of a variety of naturalistic and geometric forms: numerous bird, fish, and snake representations; bird and fish heads used by themselves or in fantastic combinations to form weird human eyes, nose, or mouth elements. Attempts have been made to translate and record the meanings of this symbolic language, but it appears that the various forms and designs had not fixed meanings either singly or in combination. For example, a particular geometric pattern could refer to the sun or the moon, or it could be a detail within a form that referred to a culture hero. To understand fully the specific function of any Malagan carving, whether figure or mask, the clan elder who directed the shaping of forms and the painting of surface designs would have to act as interpreter for it. In view of the extraordinary complexity of this art, it seems unlikely that all the clan members understood the entire significance of the wide range of forms; rather, the art functioned for them as symbols honoring all the categories of ancestors.

Since these New Ireland forms were motivated by a desire for prestige, which could be attained only if the art produced was more spectacular than that of the previous Malagan staged by a rival clan, a drive toward virtuosity of designs led to the creation of new, aesthetic forms of expression. The response to this aspect of the art seems to have been unquestionable, since from it the clan as a whole was elevated, even if only temporarily, in social prestige, which lasted until a rival clan staged the next and still more spectacular ritual. The art functioned, therefore, as a culturally dynamic force, one that gave strength of continuity to the relationships of the present with the past and fostered a strong adherence to the traditions of the group.

On the large island of Malekula in the central New Hebrides group of Melanesian islands, far to the east of New Ireland, and on the neighboring island of Ambrym as well as various smaller ones nearby, art also functioned as an essential factor in a complex series of ceremonies associated with what was undoubtedly the most intensely dynamic culture of the southwestern Pacific. A single, basic concept led to rituals of ostensibly social and religious character: the one a communal ceremony, and the other strictly under the aegis of a secret society. In both instances, the central idea was that all during their lives men had to accumulate enough spiritual power through prescribed rites and ceremonies, that they would be able at death to attain the hereafter, there to assume a place sufficiently important that they could aid their descendants. These survivors, in turn, were striving, with the help of their ancestors, to achieve a comparable place in the hierarchy of society, first among the living, and then among the dead. At the time of European contact with these peoples, this power was observed to have been acquired, whether in public or private ceremonies, through a sacrificial animal, the boar, which had ritually gained power; this power could, by proper ceremonial procedures, be transferred to the person offering it. The symbols of this animal's power were its tusks, with the degree of their curvature indicating the greatness and extent of its spiritual force. For this reason, the upper incisors of the animal were removed when it was still quite young, and it was carefully tended so that the tusks would develop to the required shape.

The pressure on each individual to amass power throughout his lifetime resulted in the formation of a prescribed series of grades through which he would pass, beginning as a boy of six or seven years of age. Passage into each grade required certain traditional types of carvings to be used; in some areas these were figures, and in other areas or grades they were masks. Two other necessary parts of the transformation were the accumulation of a specified amount of foodstuffs for the accompanying feasts and, most important, the sacrifices of a number of tusked boars, each of which had to have the necessary accouterments significant of their power. When the requisite art forms had been prepared and the food had been accumulated, such cere-monies were performed either as public, communal affairs or as secret-society rites. They were a vital and continuous necessity throughout each man's lifetime, since only through them could the power so essential to the attainment of the hereafter be acquired. In a culture of this type, there could be no status quo; instead there was a constant, cyclical fluidity that was reflected in the ceremonial complex. Clearly, the desire for a continuity of relationships between the past, the present, and the future was of paramount importance to these people who concentrated all their efforts on passing success-fully through life, which was but one phase of the vast cycle of existence and was, therefore, like the grade societies, merely another level to be attained.

The motivations underlying this art included almost the whole gamut of desires leading to artistic expression. The drive for cultural continuity was the most strikingly evident, being, in fact, so strong as to be almost obses-sively dominant. But the grade societies were so much a part of New Hebridean life that it may rightly be said that all phases of life were associated with them. The fundamental need for assurance of security and survival was also an inherent motivation intensively involved in the development of these societies and their art forms. The forms required for use in the grade-society rites functioned as an implementation of the forces out of which they grew. The figures erected or, in other instances, the masks worn for these ceremonies had a symbolic, ancestor content: they referred to both an early and a recent ancestor who had achieved the grade to which their user aspired—thus a religious sanction and meaning was given to the carvings. This placed the rites, whether public or secret, under the aegis of the ances-tors, endowing these rites with at least some degree of religious basis.

Other recurrent symbols in grade-society art were the hawk and the solar disc. Each of these forms referred to the great culture hero who had brought the boar to the people as a sacrificial animal so that its power could be accumulated toward achievement of the ancestral world after death. In addition, this culture hero assisted the dead by being present at the moment when their spirits embarked on the way to the hereafter and by abetting their powers in the afterlife. This being—visualized but not represented in anthropomorphic form—had a religious significance. Thus it seems that the strongest influences on the grade-society rites were of a religious nature; but practically all the other major cultural facets were involved, at least to some degree, in these complex rituals. The social role of the grade societies was of extreme importance. Since the progression within a grade society was advantageous to everyone, these societies gave a remarkable cohesion to the otherwise loosely organized group by sharing matters of vital interest to the entire community as well as to each person as an individual. These rites also functioned as a societal catharsis, in which respect they were similar to the great ceremonial cycles of the Papuan Gulf. Through the feasting and group dancing, the tensions and conflicts of the community were resolved, thus making for a greater communal feeling within the group.[3]

The figures and masks, as indispensable parts of these ceremonies, had a threefold sociological function: 1) they were symbols of the higher social grade being gained by the individual who was staging the rites; 2) they displayed the symbols of his ancestors who had reached that social level; and 3) they were of symbolic importance to all of the participants since they, too, were benefiting in a communal sense from the advancement of one of their own group. However, because of the unique quality of symbolic representation contained in each of the art forms used for these purposes, they could serve only once.

While New Hebrides art objects have no overt economic or political significance, they stand in a secondary relationship to these cultural factors, for the dynamic aspect of the grade-society complex placed a premium on the economic endeavors essential to success of the rites; and the elders in whom political power was vested

77

were always of an advanced level in the grade societies. Some of the ceremonial objects used, however, were personal possessions, such as the adze-shaped clubs with which the sacrificial boars were either actually or ritually killed during the ceremonies (Figs. 77, 78-79). The ones only ritually killed were tapped on the head with one of these clubs, thus rendering them unavailable for any further rites. A number of these clubs were handsomely carved with one or more human face forms in relief. Such carvings can only be judged as having additional prestige value growing out of their artistic quality and the extent to which they gave aesthetic pleasure.

Another New Hebrides art form that served as a measure of rank or social status was the slit gong, the upper end of which was also carved with a human face in relief. There was considerable range in the size of these objects, which were used during the grade-society rites and at other times. Part of the prestige value of these slit gongs derived from the fact that an individual had been able to accumulate enough wealth, beyond what was constantly required for advancement within his grade society or societies, to pay for the making of one of these objects and for the feasting required when it was set up in the dancing ground. This brought social benefits to his entire clan, and pleasure to the community. The carved faces on both the clubs and the gongs agree in appearance with the symbolic ancestor faces on the grade-society figures and masks, so that it would seem likely that they must have had a similar significance when repeated on these sculptures.

All advancement in the grade societies of Malekula and the neighboring islands sharing this cultural characteristic carried with it an elevation not only in the social position of the individual but also in his spiritual power, which insured him a more important status as an ancestor. Thus the religious and social aspects of these institutions were of almost equal significance. Social pressures demanded that each man exert every effort to advance from level to level within the grade societies or be faced with annihilation at death, leaving his

descendants without assistance from ancestral power; moreover, he would be, during his lifetime, a nonentity with no social standing or respect in his community, and this led, indirectly, to the economic aspect of the rites and their art forms. The constant press forward, from level to level, from life to afterlife, reveals that the dynamics of this culture were ever present as opposed to the dramatic but periodic aspect of the Malagan in New Ireland culture. For the peoples of these New Hebrides societies, the underlying reason for existence was that life on this earth was but an interlude, a phase in the ever-moving cycle of influences; and man strove to pass, with the support of his ancestors, through this phase and on into life after death when he would become a strong, spiritual force in the future life of the community, a link in an unbroken chain connecting the past

78-79

with the future. This drive for continuity was, therefore, a dominant feature of New Hebrides life where it received one of its strongest expressions in both art and culture among primitive peoples.

The idea of future existence as an ancestor with powers to help or to chastise his descendants was strong among many peoples of Africa and the islands of Melanesia. Numerous and varied art forms were needed to implement these ideas—so many, in fact, that many of the major motivations toward and functions of the art grew out of these concepts for use in the innumerable ceremonies. The great importance of ancestor beliefs, and the idea that ancestors were aware of all of the activities of man, were, to a very large extent, responsible for a marked and firm conservatism that permitted few deviations from the customs and practices of the past. Until after European contact, which brought with it the greater power of scientific accomplishments, this conservatism was a powerful stabilizing factor for these primitive cultures.

In various parts of Africa and Melanesia, and in other parts of the Pacific world, direct contacts with ancestors were accomplished by the preservation of their skulls or even of their entire skeletons—the skulls, especially in

25

certain areas of Melanesia, often being modeled and painted in a generic simulation of life forms. Not all of these ancestor remains were used in ritual practices, but merely served as memorials in remembrance of the dead. In Gabun, an area of west-central Africa, the Fang, in literature sometimes called the Pangwe or the Pahouin peoples, and their neighbors in the northeastern part of the country, had a somewhat comparable method of revering ancestors, requiring the use of an art form of different character.

The Fang kept the skulls of their dead in circular containers made of bark from the top of which, on one side, projected either a carved human head, a half-figure, or a full figure (Fig. 25). These carvings represented either male or female figures set in a pose of attentiveness or alertness, but carved without any attempt at individualization of such elements as scarification marks or unique hairdresses. They were apparently motivated by the desire to protect the ancestor skulls against desecration by anyone not entitled to see them, and protect persons from coming upon the skulls inadvertently, since the power they contained could, they believed, cause great harm if encountered suddenly. The well-being, security, and continuity of the peoples seemingly depended upon venerating and giving protection to the sanctity of these skulls. Periodically, they were removed from their bark containers, cleaned and oiled in what appears to have been a procedure to reactivate their latent power; afterwards they were replaced in the container. At the same time, the figure on the side of the bark barrel was also removed for cleaning and oiling, and then replaced in its former position. It seems likely that, by this action, the power of the figures was also reactivated.

The function of these Fang sculptures was to impress upon the beholder, through a conventionalized symbolic form, the ideas of danger and taboo. Based on a tensely posed human figure, the symbol had stark, hieratically conceived shapes and alert, menacing facial features. This severe, protective figure might originally have been the generic representation of a protective ancestor since the survival of such a power would account for the treatment accorded it when the skull was reanointed. The original function of these carefully shaped and finished forms—that of representing the ancestors, and so their inherent power—seems to have become modified until they became guardian figures, protecting the revered skulls in their bark containers. By the time these peoples were discovered by the Western world, the figures had become symbols. In the process of change, the refined and elegant shapes, surfaces, and lines so characteristic of these figures offer mute testimony to an ever-increasing concern of the sculptors with the aesthetic effect of their workmanship; and it is probably because these objects began to have greater and greater function as artistic forms that the powerful, expressive quality given them as ancestor figures gradually lost its force. An analogy may be drawn between these Fang sculptures and those of the Baoule. In both instances, the original significance of the carvings became weaker as the interest in their aesthetic properties grew stronger. Morphologically, the symbolic appearance of Fang skull-container figures closely resembles three-dimensional, natural form; the artist and tradition have merely combined to reduce these forms to simplified, artistic patterns.

26

The Bakota peoples, kinsmen of the Fang, also had art forms that functioned in a similar way, but which had become, in appearance, so highly conventionalized and remote from life forms as to approach the realm of abstract design (Fig. 26). The skulls and bones of their important ancestors were kept by the Bakota in rectangular boxes, one side of which was placed against an outer wall of their men's house. Into this box, a figure shaped in three or more fairly shallow, parallel planes, the surfaces of which were covered with sheets or strips of copper and/or brass, was placed in a way comparable to the Fang mortuary sculptures. These Bakota forms are without doubt analogous in motivation and function to the Fang carvings; but aesthetically they have been developed to a far greater extent. In fact, the desire for aesthetic results may well have gained sufficient impetus to supplant the original function of these works as guardian, power figures watching over ancestral bones. The change in function observable in the Fang, and to an even greater degree in the Bakota mortuary figures, is comparable to changes that occurred in the tomb sculptures of fifteenth-century western Europe, where simple, calm expressions of the dead, aimed at evoking feelings of emotional loss for the deceased, gave way to an elaborate, artistic expression of his former wealth and importance. This shift in function, and the great concern with death and its effect on the living, can be discerned in the art forms of many other primitive peoples.

The mystery of death, and the resultant severe change it wrought in the equilibrium and balance, was strongly felt by peoples of primitive cultures and frequently led to various ceremonies in which art forms were an essential factor. Many of these ceremonies were directed toward an adjustment of the disturbed equilibrium; but as has also been noted in the ritual practices of the Iroquois Indians of North America and the Papuan Gulf peoples of New Guinea, other attempts were made to avert such a displacement. The most important ceremony of the Duwamish, an American Indian people from the Puget Sound area of the Northwest Coast, was involved with thwarting the disruption caused by "death." This death was thought to be caused by the stealing of the soul of a person by the spirits of the dead, either while he slept or, during waking hours, in periods of tiredness and lethargy. These spirits could steal the soul of an individual at various times; moreover, the evidence of this was discernible in his or her conduct of daily affairs, that is, when it became noticeable that the victim was lethargic, listless, or less alert than usual. These reactions, of course, had much to do with his day-to-day behavior as a fisherman, or his conduct in whatever other activity in which he might be engaged. The only solution to such a state of affairs was to turn to a shaman, who had the ability to discern whether or not the spirits of the dead had in reality stolen his soul, and who knew how, if necessary, to recover it before irreparable damage had been done. If, upon consulting the shaman, the decision was reached that the individual was soulless, the shamans of the tribe could stage a ceremony for the recovery of the lost soul from the spirits of the dead. Although the concept of the lost soul and the ceremony enacted for its recovery were unique to this area of the southern part of the Northwest Coast of America, the basic idea of the power and recourse to ancestors was the same as that shared by other primitive peoples.

When, among the Duwamish peoples, a shaman discovered that one of his "patients" had lost his soul, he immediately instituted a ceremony, with the support of other persons who believed that they were similarly bereaved, and in company with other shamans who had the power to recover souls. These rites enabled the shamans to go in quest of these all-important stolen properties. Each one who had the power to go on such a quest had in his possession a carved figure obtained as a consequence of his experience with a supernatural being in his younger days. The carvings, it was believed, embodied the appearance of the beneficent being from whom he had received his power. From this being the shaman had also received the knowledge of songs to accompany and release his power, and of certain secondary figures which had to be painted on boards to supplement the carvings during the ceremonial procedures.

In preparation for each ritual journey, these ceremonial boards were repainted and, together with the figures, were arranged in a house to form the outline of a canoe. Within this ritual canoe, the shamans involved would arrange their figures and their boards; then they would embark upon an imaginary and highly mimetic voyage to the underworld in order to rescue the lost souls. Each foot of this dangerous journey was dramatically acted out, not only by the shamans, but also by the spectator-participants, all of whom knew what was being unfolded before them and were, therefore, very much emotionally concerned. After melodramatically overcoming all pitfalls, the shamans finally arrived in the land of the dead while the spirits of the dead were peacefully sleeping. They searched around until they finally discovered and recaptured the stolen souls—very often they recovered, as well, additional souls belonging to individuals who had been unaware of their loss. With these recovered souls in their possession, they re-embarked for the land of the living, but before doing so, they threw stones into the sleeping village of the dead, thus arousing them and bringing them into combat. Only by the bravest of efforts did the shamans escape from the savage onslaughts of the spirits of the dead. Once back in the land of the living, the souls of those who knew they had lost them were restored. Those who had been unaware were informed of their plight, and, once conversant with the facts, their souls, too, were restored. For these services the shamans received payment, and the balance of the actual and the potentially disturbed cultural equilibrium was regained. Death and the resultant disruption for the community, which would have occurred had the lost souls not been recovered before becoming acclimatized to the underworld, were thereby averted.[4]

Although the primary need behind the motivations, implemented as they were by the carved figures and the shaped and painted boards used by the shamans, was that of urgency to maintain the balance and to perpetuate the status quo, other needs, such as survival and continuity, were also involved. The shamans' performance, for which the art forms were essential, also functioned in several important ways: since supernatural power was so fundamental to the success and even to the staging of this ceremony, a religious aspect was obviously paramount; because it was performed as a communal, social ceremony in which the spectators participated, the social character of this rite is clearly apparent; further, since the person whose soul had been recovered was reconstituted as an active member of the society, a strong economic factor was involved. There does not seem to have been any stressed artistic functioning of these carvings and painted boards, since they were rudimentary in shape and style and give no evidence or indication of aesthetic evolution. This suggests that they were merely stage props so far as the performance was concerned, in spite of the fact that the shamans derived from them their power necessary to the performance of their feats.

The various ceremonies discussed above—those of the Papuan Gulf peoples, the Sulka of New Britain, the Malagan ritual of New Ireland, the grade-society rites of the Malekula and other New Hebrides peoples, and the soul-recovery rites of the Duwamish Indians—all have one feature in common: the performance of a dramatic, communal ceremony by which the entire community benefits from a ritual that acts as a catharsis. Among primitive peoples motivations and functions led to a great variety of institutions and likewise to a wide range of art objects as an implementation of these ideas. There appears to be no consistent correlation of the design and the vigor of art forms with their motivations and functions. Some art forms have an expressive character and others function merely as important symbols or as stage props in a dramatic ceremony, in which case they are of vital importance only to the actors in the drama. Among the Duwamish, the art forms seem to have functioned as symbols of the power of the shamans, and they seem to have had, for these peoples, no role as aesthetic objects.

The opposite was certainly true in the great number of representations, both large and small, of the gods as used by the Polynesians of the Hawaiian Islands (Figs. 97, 98). The motivations for these wood sculptures were an outcome of the dominating drive of these peoples to perpetuate the existing and well-defined class system, thereby maintaining the superiority of one group or social level over the other, and in doing so to reaffirm, by prestige objects, the continuity of relationships. Among these Polynesians, the figures of the gods could function in this way because they pertained only to the upper classes, the most important members of which could trace their descent to a particular god. Thus, the gods

97–98

represented by these carvings were the sole property of the upper classes who alone could participate in rituals performed in their presence. These were the great gods (Fig. 97). Others of lesser importance were possessed and petitioned by the nonnoble classes of society; the motivation for these figures is found in the need to petition for aid and protection from deities of a specialized nature who operated within a limited sphere, such as hunting, fishing, and the like. Even representations of these lesser gods, however, were given careful, artistic expression.

The function of these Hawaiian sculptures grew out of two cultural circumstances: 1) the class consciousness of this society; and 2) the highly specialized training given to the artists. Of utmost importance among Polynesian peoples was the stressing of the prerogatives of the different grades or classes into which the society was divided, and the protecting of these distinctions by strictly imposed taboos. One of the prerogatives of the upper classes, that is, of royalty and nobility, was that the finer art forms were restricted to them; hence the deity figures, whether large or small, which were made for their use were carefully carved by the most accomplished of their artists. Such sculptures served as prestige objects which indicated by their aesthetic quality that they were owned by persons of rank.

The consistently high level of artistic achievement that is shown by these figures was the result of a very long period of careful apprenticeship given to the artists, who were so highly trained and specialized that the woodcarver never turned his hand to any other craft. Surrounding this, and enforcing the extreme specialization, was a belief in the concept of mana, that is, in the existence of an innate power or spiritual essence inherent to all matter. Its power was so strong that the artist was required to have a thorough knowledge of, and familiarity with, the use of special chants and rituals in order to handle his tools and materials successfully. Their power or essence had to be treated with special care lest his work be a failure or contain a vindictive, evil force. His training included this aspect of his craft and, further, accounted for his careful creation of every work, as well as being of prime importance for the consistently excellent quality, artistically and aesthetically, of his creations.

The essential function of these deity figures was to represent, in a traditional form, a tangible object in which the spirit might, upon occasion, reside, at which time they acted as the physical evidence of the god's presence. In addition, they conveyed, by means of their form, some of the major attributes of the deity, such as his physical power and vigor, his dynamic and aggressive character. The religious functions were supplemented by one of an entirely different nature: feeding the vanity of these upper-class persons who identified themselves, directly or indirectly, with the gods and, in narcissistic fashion, saw their own prowess and vigor reflected in that of the gods. Thus their self-esteem and position were supported and reassured by the image of the deity. Because of these motivations Polynesian art, as illustrated by the Hawaiian deity figures, did not lose its forcefulness, either expressively or artistically. On the contrary, the conventionalization imparted to these sculptures through the passing years dramatized it further.

29

The prevalence of elaborate decorative art among primitive peoples, whether to wear or to possess for particular reasons, illustrates the importance of personal prestige as a force behind many examples of their art. Objects made for the adornment of the person often functioned as a badge signifying the rank or special achievements of an individual. For example, among the Bapende peoples in the western part of the Congo, each youth wore, after initiation rites, a small, carved ivory maskette on a cord around his neck. These derived in design from the larger wooden masks worn during the initiation period (Figs. 29, 30). This served as an emblem to the youth, a badge of his full-fledged membership in the adult tribal society. Somewhat larger ivory mask miniatures were worn on the upper arm of the members of the Warega tribe in the northeastern Congo region.

30

71

64

These were indications of the grades they had achieved in their secret society. In many other parts of the primitive world, small masks were carried on the person as charms or amulets, imbued with a certain power to aid or to protect. In various parts of Oceania shells were worn as decorations or as indications of rank, a particularly fine example of these shell ornaments being known as a "kapkap," and worn largely in Melanesia (Fig. 71). The kapkap consisted of a disc of gray-white clam shell, to the surface of which was affixed an elaborately contrived and delicately pierced design cut out in turtle shell. In some areas these kapkaps indicated rank or special accomplishments. Warriors, such as those of the Marquesas Islands in Polynesia, often carried lavishly carved clubs as a form of prestige, as well as of functional importance, denoting their rank, while their great chiefs wore "crowns" of clam and turtle shell.

Utilitarian objects were often richly shaped and decorated for no other reason than to please the vanity of the user. In Melanesia, for example, where betel-nut chewing was a widespread habit, the spatulas, used to transfer lime from a container to the mouth, were treated as art forms in many areas (Fig. 64); the same applied to the containers in which the lime was kept (Fig. 74). And the American Plains Indians often profusely decorated such useful objects as tobacco bags, arrow quivers, horse trappings, rawhide carrying pouches, and many other objects with bead and quill work or with painting. Although some of these decorations denoted achievements while others had limited symbolic significance, many of them were created for reasons of vanity, their primary function being to give aesthetic pleasure. Weapons, drums, neckrests (Fig. 44), bowls and platters, in wood or in pottery, are among the most frequently found utilitarian objects with purely artistic decorations.

The artistic impulse and the aesthetic pleasure to be derived from a beautifully conceived form are powerful motivating factors in primitive art, even where other motivations are involved. Art does not just happen; it

does not develop into such rich, and often luxurious, traditional styles without any inspiration from or incentive by a society, especially when it is closely integrated with all of the aspects of the society in which it thrives. To discredit it by looking upon it as a conglomeration of borrowed forms that were undergoing a deterioration is to close one's eyes to the depth of development and creativity evident in so many of the arts of primitive peoples. The forms and the elements of the designs must be studied within their own context and that of the art tradition of the area of their use; and the art must be considered as a part of the total culture from whence it sprang. It is ridiculous and meaningless to detach a fragment or a small motif from a primitive design and find it analogous to, hence derived from, another fragment or equally small motif from the design of a non-primitive work or group of works. The roots of primitive art forms lie within the depths of their culture and not in fortuitous waves of influences from the high cultures.

74

5

MEANINGS

For a more complete understanding of an art the meanings of the forms must be considered, as well as their motivations and functions. In primitive art, while the motivations may often be sufficiently discernible and the functions satisfactorily apparent, the precise meanings of the forms—what they represent in a specific sense—have often never been recorded. A distinction must be made, however, between function and meaning as the terms are used here. By function is meant what the form does when it is used, what the presence and use of it do in creating an effect or in conveying an idea. In other words, how the work of art serves to implement the

44

motivation that led to its creation. Meaning can be defined as the content or the subject matter, and also in what particular way the subject matter is presented, that is, the attitude in which it is conveyed, such as dramatically or objectively.

For example, in the coastal area of the Congo, European traders are represented in a few polychrome figures in wood. In one of these, a trader is shown wearing a ridiculously proportioned high hat and a vivid polka-dotted shirt, and holding a big gin bottle in one hand with a cup in the other. This carving did not express a desire to represent a specific trader, but to portray him through the distinguishing features of his appearance, such as the hat and the shirt, and by such "desirable" attributes as the bottle and the cup. In a figure like this, the meaning is the subject matter as understood through the observations and experiences of the carver and through his personal response to them. This does not differ from what one must understand by meaning in any art, whether it be classic, Renaissance, or Chinese. The important factor in the discussion of meaning is the knowledge of what subject matter might be portrayed and the possible relationships of the artist to it.

Papuan Gulf masks (Fig. 60), for example, have as their meaning the depiction of clan supernatural beings and, abstractly, of historic facts pertaining to them. Since the descriptions and facts were handed down by the clan elders, no personalized interpretations were possible. Meaning here was a mere transcription of verbally related, and perhaps never previously seen, subject matter.

The meaning conveyed by Iroquois masks (Fig. 117) was, in contrast, of a more personalized character, since their traditional appearance allowed for some interpretation. The Iroquois face mask, with the crooked nose, distorted mouth, and deep folds of flesh above the brows and around the mouth, represents the Great One, who, in mythological times entered into competition with the Creator for mastery of the world. In the course of this struggle his nose was broken, but as a consequence, he

60

117

20

64

57

31

was given the privilege of instructing mankind in the making and wearing of a mask in his likeness, together with certain ritual procedures to help man combat the evils of disease. The meaning of the mask is a dramatic expression of these circumstances, interpreted by the sculptor's rendering of the facial features to convey pain as he understood it. As a result, there are variations in the treatment of this aspect of the subject matter: it may be formalized to quite a degree, or it may be sensitively dramatized.

The beings represented by the Ibibio (Fig. 20) and the Sulka (Fig. 57) masks have, as secret-society property, two sets of meanings: for the nonmembers, the forms express the danger and menace of the unworldly, weird, supernatural spirits depicted by the objects and their actions; for the members they mean disguises with which the activities of the group are accomplished.

The meaning of an art object is interrelated with its motivation and its function, and this interaction makes the significance of the art form, within its cultural context, more understandable. The motivation answers the question of why the object was made; the function, how it was used, that is, the true importance of its ceremonial or practical life; and the meaning, what the form was made to represent and the ideas, feelings, and interpretations it was made to convey. The meaning, therefore, of the Bushongo royal portrait figures (Fig. 31) was to depict, in every detail, the iconography of a king: the shape of his crown; the iron ring around his right shoulder; the armlets and bracelets on each arm; the heavy cowrie-shell belt looped around his bulky abdomen; the short sword in his left hand and the stone celt in his right; the pedestal jutting out in front containing an object associated with one of his outstanding contributions to his people—all details rendered in a completely descriptive or realistic manner. These identified the subject matter of the figure. But the aura of aloofness and timelessness conveyed by the half-closed eyes, the tenseness of the pose, and the feeling of weight, give the essential meaning to the figure—the power and divinity of the king.

1

25

In contrast, the meaning of the ancestor figures of the Baoule (Fig. 1) is revealed almost exclusively by a decisive, descriptive detail: the identity of the person is given by a somewhat exaggerated rendering of scarification marks and by the mode and details of hairdress. The quality of the figure as an ancestor is presented by an all-encompassing aloofness or remoteness, comparable to the Bushongo figures, but the Baoule forms have a calm, relaxed lightness of pose that has nothing of the aggressiveness and heaviness of the king figures. In the Baoule carvings, too, the expression of the subject matter has an aesthetic meaning, inherent in all art objects but more stressed in some than in others. This is also an important part of the meaning conveyed by the Fang and Bakota ancestor-protective figures (Figs. 25, 26). In these sculptures, however, an emotional tension in the post and rendering of specific shapes, as well as in the portrayal of facial features, gives the fundamental meaning of the figures as expressions of alert protectiveness. An undeveloped portrayal of alertness appears as at least a part of the meaning of the spirit canoe figures of the Duwamish, although the primary meaning of these very simplified sculptures seems to be the mere representation of the shaman's supernatural helper and the source of his power.

Before the full significance of a work can be known, the meanings of symbolic and decorative detail must be understood. This is evident in the Malagan sculptures (Fig. 66) and in many of the grade-society objects from Malekula. The general meaning of Malagan forms as ancestor memorials, while in most cases accurate, gives little satisfaction in the attempt to understand these complex carvings more completely. Perhaps only the elders of the clan thoroughly understood all of the symbolic allusions. But this art did have another meaning that, evidently, the majority of the spectators could comprehend: this was the lavishness of its melodramatic design forms. It could be assumed that, through experiences with other Malagan objects, the spectators and participants would react and appreciate the exotic, rich

26

66

quality of new designs. Even more likely, the objects would act as an emotional stimulus toward the release of communal expressions of rejoicing at the presence of these emblematic ancestor symbols. Their appearance produced, for New Ireland peoples, a catharsislike release from cumulative restraints, oppressions, and fears. Although this aspect of meaning is found in ceremonial objects used by many other primitive peoples, it is seldom so strong or so closely interwoven with function as it is in the Malagan forms.

Somewhat comparable are the meanings of the grade-society objects used in Malekula and elsewhere in the New Hebrides group. The carved and painted symbols on these forms were of a less complex character, and probably their meaning as identifications or badges of specific grades had, consequently, a far wider communal comprehension. Thus their primary meaning, it appears, was as symbolic designs which, through their particular shapes, patterns, and colors, identified themselves as the visual manifestations of a specific grade. It seems unlikely that their more esoteric meaning as generic representations of, or allusions to, certain ancestors and categories of ancestors would have met with any widespread comprehension from the group as a whole. Since Malekula art, in general, must have had little function as artistic expression, and little motivation in this direction, it seems reasonable to assume that this art, with the exception of certain prestige items mentioned earlier, had little meaning as expressions of aesthetic intent for many of the participants in a grade-society rite. This assumption is supported by the fact that the aspirant to a higher grade had to have a sponsor who was already a member of that grade, and who, in turn, had then to arrange that another member of the grade, whether a trained artist or not, would carve the necessary figures, masks, and/or other ceremonial objects. It often happened, therefore, that the objects were made "correctly," that is, in conformity with the requisite patterns for the grade, by an amateur or untrained artist. Thus, quality in New Hebrides art, particularly that required by

97

99

the grade societies, was incidental to the other properties in the works. This does not mean that objects of genuine artistic character were not appreciated since this would be tantamount to saying that these peoples had no aesthetic responses. This is not true of human nature in general, and of these people in particular because of the highly artistic nature of their prestige-vanity objects. Because of the different cultural significance of the forms, it is doubtful if they had any meaning as an emotional release comparable to the Malagan sculptures, although something of this may have existed for some of the more sensitive participants.

It is rare to find any group of primitive peoples who completely lack a drive for aesthetic expression and artistic meaning in the creation of their art forms. Despite the stress that has always been placed on the purely practical motivations behind these forms, only the prejudiced would be unable to recognize the powerful artistic expression of the Hawaiian deity figures (Figs. 97, 99). The supreme meaning of these Hawaiian carvings is a combination of their subject matter (deities) and their sculptural expressions of power, force, and agressiveness through the aesthetic handling of forms and details. Again meaning and function are closely interwoven. The vigorous treatment of the massive, clear-cut shapes, and their organic integration, makes clear the essential meaning of the forms as sculptural statements of the might and power of the ancestors in their role as active, assertive, and controlling deities relating directly to the members of the regal class.

In the case of art objects with societal prestige importance, meaning and function usually combine and the motivation is most often clearly directed toward these ends. Some art forms of this character, however, such as Plains Indian moccasins (Fig. 120), had a symbolic meaning that was only intelligible to the maker; but their decorative effects had a wider meaning, comprehensible to all. Allusions to a more significant meaning existed in various decorative designs, as for example, on the shell kapkaps and the Bushongo cups, on drums,

neckrests, and various weapons; but in most cases the original significance of their meaning was lost, and only their decorative importance remains. Since the majority of these decorative forms exist purely as artistic expressions the meaning is, above all else, to give aesthetic pleasure.

The importance of artistic impulse in the art of primitive peoples can never be minimized in any consideration of primitive art. The old cliché of "art for art's sake" was not, therefore, without meaning for, or application to, their art. On the contrary, it existed as emphatically for them, in a motivation-function-meaning relationship, as it has, for certain periods, in many of our so-called "high-culture arts" of the Western and Eastern worlds. To discredit this aspect of primitive art is to deny the primitive artist his creative urge, and the primitive person of any aesthetic reactions or sensibilities.

120

The use of narrative forms deserves some attention in any discussion of primitive art. While in actuality its existence is limited, a narrative content can be found in examples of this art from several areas. For example, the very small, lost-wax process, bronze castings of the Ashanti (Fig. 12) from present-day Ghana which have as their subject matter: 1) genre scenes, that is subjects taken from everyday life; 2) figures or groups of figures that illustrate a particular proverb; and 3) geometric or

12

fantastic forms that have no essential meaning. The function of these small bronze weights was to measure out a specific quantity of gold dust, and they were graduated in size to perform this function. In meaning, however, they had an entity of their own. Some depicted scenes from everyday life, and thereby told their own specific stories. Those representing proverbs condensed into visual form the familiar sayings of tribal life. For the purely geometric and/or fantastic forms, only an imaginative significance can be applied. In the coastal Congo area carved wooden pot-lids depicted commonly known or easily understood proverbs and were used to bring about a desired end in certain applicable situations. Carvings on stools from Angola and incisings in American Indian buffalo robes represented various scenes or stories, and within their respective cultures, these objects functioned largely as artistic forms. The important feature of their meaning is interwoven with their function.

It would be foolish to say that all decorative art among primitive peoples was directed solely toward an aesthetic effect. The attitude that primitive art is largely a matter of functional forms having a meaning of similar nature is invalid, although in some instances, as in the treatment of weapons by certain peoples, the decoration applied to an object had a magical significance which contributed to its successful functioning. In such cases, the meaning of the decoration is closely related to the overall function of the object to which it was applied.

The decorative art forms in a culture were, with very few exceptions, in agreement with design and motives common to the art style as a whole. That is, the life forms and the geometric patterns, used with subject-charged significance on the ritual or ceremonial objects, were similar to the design vocabulary found in purely decorative art. When used in this way, however, the forms were usually handled with greater freedom, both in design combinations and in scale, and were commonly adapted to fit the form or surface to which they were applied. An excellent example of this type of artistic freedom is found on the incised bamboo lime containers from many parts of Melanesia, on the neckrests and stools from the Central Congo, and on moccasins and other articles of clothing made by the American Indian.

RESUME

It is evident that art occupied a conspicuous and important position in the lives of primitive peoples. The artist, usually a well-trained specialist in the art forms traditional to his village or area, was esteemed for his proficiency and, certainly in many regions, for his creative ability in handling traditional forms and motifs. His work was required by various organizations and individual patrons within his socety; in very few instances did he work independently of a patron or a commission. The public for whom the artist worked was often the community at large, and to them art was a necessary, even vital, part of their ceremonial life and, in fact, of the pattern of their daily life. Perhaps the most important single feature of primitive art is its complete integration with all the major aspects of existence—religious, social, economic, political, and judicial practices or events. But one must look to the fundamental requirements of each culture group for the motivations that led to the development of art as an implementation of those needs, that is, to the functioning of the art. The meanings of the objects are to be found in the religious and philosophical concepts and expressions. Internal characteristics of any art, whether Italian Renaissance, Chinese Han, Mexican Mayan, or African Primitive, are inextricably interwoven with thought patterns and experiences, and with external pageantry, all of which are manifestations of its functional aspects. In primitive cultures, then, art is one of the most characteristic and expressive of all the essential features of the societies.

The position of art within a cultural setting is revealed by considering it in the light of the essential motivations which inspired it, and by examining its functions and meanings within the cultural context. The deep roots of any art lie in its cultural heritage. Unfortunately, these roots are all too shallow, historically, due to the lack of recorded traditions and, in most cases, to meager archaeological investigations. Nevertheless, the character and quality of art expression among primitive peoples is such that a marked depth in time spans must be accepted in order to account for the uniqueness and individual peculiarities of artistic development in each community or area.

The fact that art shows such variations throughout the primitive world is of the utmost importance and will be considered in detail in the pages to come. It is equally important to note the striking differences in motivations leading to art expressions, how they functioned, and what they meant. Too much has been written about the "magical" and "strange" qualities to be found in this art, and too little attention has been paid to the fact that the needs, aspirations, and longings of mankind are similar whether one is considering primitive peoples or peoples of the Gothic Age in western Europe. It is perhaps difficult for twentieth-century man to think outside his pattern of scientific, predigested thought, or to attempt to project himself back into a time of self-sufficiency and to grapple with the fundamental ideas of subsistence and security. Yet this is necessary if he is to understand the backgrounds and arts of primitive peoples. Just as their cultures must be considered as entities in their own right, and not as ways of life analogous to certain ancient phases of Western or Eastern cultures, so their art must be examined within the context of their cultures and not by analogy to our own traditions, present or past. To gain any comprehension of primitive art, it is necessary to distinguish certain areas of art tradition, and to characterize their significant styles. Too much attention has been given to theoretical origins and relationships of various primitive arts. Without a serious study of the character and quality of this art it is meaningless to theorize on origins. It is comparable to the little fellow who tries to run before he can walk with any degree of success.

PART II

ARTISTIC TRADITIONS AND STYLES

Every art object has two aspects: 1) the objective or morphological, consisting of shapes, lines, surfaces, and colors in their particular relationships; and 2) the subjective or cultural, containing the answers to such questions as why it was made (i.e., the motivations) and how it was used, in the fullest sense of the word (i.e., the function). The subjective or inner aspect of an art form is unique to the culture in which it evolved. This uniqueness, or cultural identity, results from the numerous differences in physical and historical circumstances which separate one culture complex from another. Because for primitive peoples there was such a close correlation of art to culture, or even to their very existence both as individuals and as a group, it is essential to examine the forms as closely as possible within their cultural context.

From the morphological or objective aspect of an art form it is possible to characterize its style by analyzing the relationships and qualities of its artistic properties. In sculpture, whether it derives from New Guinea, the Congo, or Renaissance Italy, the principles by which artistic expression is achieved and the properties for which it is evaluated remain constant, as they do in all art media. There are no special principles of aesthetic judgment applicable solely to primitive art, no separate standards setting it apart from the arts of any other time or place. Hence it is possible for a non-Congolese to recognize and to analyze the artistic properties of Congo sculpture since these are comprehensible to anyone who has previously had the experience of analyzing art. This was the initial approach to primitive art. But with any art, this approach leads to only a partial, and thus insufficient, knowledge of the works, a fact especially true of primitive art for which the subjective aspects of an object are basic to any true comprehension of it. Both aspects of form must, therefore, be given full consideration.

Through careful examination of the morphological characteristics of a form or design, the particular features unique to an art tradition and commonly called its style can largely be established; to this analysis of objective content must be added the often subtle and sensitive expression, through external, formal elements, of the content and meaning of the object. Both aspects of an art form contribute to its style because style is the sum total of various factors. But a distinction must be made between the use of the word "style" as meaning the totality of relationships and qualities inherent in a given work, and the same word as used to single out the distinctive properties of the shapes and forms by which it is possible to distill its uniqueness. With few exceptions, the latter definition applies to the use of the word "style" in this examination of primitive art: that is, the elements of a style that are shared by all art forms—such as principles of symmetry and balance and obvious expressions of rhythm—are not considered as distinguishing style features in and of themselves, and so are not discussed. The intent is to make clear why the style features of a figure from the Sepik River area in New Guinea make it possible to recognize it as such, and not to confuse it with a figure from the Eastern Congo. In this sense, it is not the attainment, as such, of the universal artistic properties that matters, but the unique ways in which they are handled, that is, the way in which the forms are built and combined in the creation of a unique expression.

In its application to the realm of art, style must be defined in its broadest and perhaps fullest sense. This can be construed as the technical proficiency of an artist through which he is enabled to re-create a traditional form by synthesizing his own intuitive insight with his physical and emotional responses to: 1) his experiences with forms as they appeared and were used ceremonially; and 2) his own sensitive observations of the life forms from which traditional patterns of shape and design were derived, modified, and finally crystallized into stylistic patterns or conventions throughout a long time span. Thus, style is both the end result of the artist's creation and the force—the perception and sensitivity of the artist—through which the work was conceived and brought to fruition. The final product must consequently be a unique creation, a personalized expression of content captured in the rendering of forms and in the interrelationships of all of the component parts united in one object. These are the broad essentials of style, regardless of time or place. This definition must always be kept in mind when considering any art form.

In a more specialized sense, more practical for characterizations of tribal, regional, or even village styles, the basic components are those which consistently recur in representations of a particular type of object or design. The fundamental way in which an art tradition is manifested, through its forms and designs, is a singular development, and because this is true it is possible to isolate and to characterize the distinctive artistic features of a specific geographical area. The human figure, for example, is susceptible to a variety of interpretations: it is composed of a totality of forms arranged bilaterally on a vertical axis; of a series of horizontals crossing this upright shaft, such as the alignment of eyes, mouth, shoulders, hips, knees, ankles, and feet. The artist may stress the verticality of the human figure or the horizontality of its forms as they are arranged, cutting across or through the vertical axis. A muscular differentiation distinguishes the various shapes of the human body which are organically integrated and connected by stressed points of articulation, such as the joints. Each contains its own volume and weight, the composition of which must be so balanced as to achieve a firm equilibrium. The sculptor is free either to represent the body as it appears in nature, or to interpret its shapes for expressive purposes.

There are, however, few examples to be found in primitive art which manifest any true approximation of the scientific reality of the human form. The most striking of the exceptions to this generalization are the terracotta and bronze heads from Ife, in the southern part of Nigeria, and a group of wooden figures from one area of Bougainville, an island in the Solomons group. In the stylistic traditions of most primitive cultures, a choice was made of what were considered the most significant forms and features of the human body; these were then treated as compressed or expanded, elongated or shortened sculptural elements. Details were in some cases eliminated completely, while in others they were either minimized or exaggerated in such a manner that the total statement produced was a creative synthesis, an orchestration of forms. The human figure was presented not as a transcription of nature, but as a sculptural reality having a distinct vitality and vigor of its own. Each area, tribe, or village had evolved its own traditional preference for a method by which they could interpret the parts and details of the human figure, and from this selective method arose the singular features through which the style of each region may be partially characterized. To complete the stylistic characterization of any area, however, it is necessary to take into account the nature and quality of the relationships exising between various parts of a form as a result of the special handling of component shapes, lines, surfaces, details, and color typical of a people or an area. These elements which occur in this particular way only in objects from a specific locale, together with an innate attitude toward the subject matter, are resolved into that set of style elements which can be considered characteristic of the art tradition for a particular group of people.

Although each small area, sometimes only a village or two, had its own distinctive art style, many of these "local" styles in primitive art had such a number of important features in common that, for all practical purposes of characterization, they must be grouped together. These centers of style are obviously geographical in delimitation, and are comparable to like centers found in any time or place. Before the complex and often theoretical problems of origins can be examined, or any attempt made to evaluate or even discuss primitive art as a whole, a knowledge of the numerous centers of style, along with the ability to distinguish them clearly, must be gained. The art traditions on which these style centers were founded must be considered insofar as possible within the context of the cultures out of which they grew. This affords a solid and scientific base on which further studies of primitive art may be successfully pursued.

1

AFRICA

Of the several regions of primitive art, it is most instructive for study to turn first to Africa. The geographical limits of this vast continent may be defined, so far as the important, art-producing cultures are concerned, as extending over the region of West Africa, south of the Sahara, from the headlands of the Atlantic coast eastward to the region just beyond Lake Chad; and over Central Africa, from the Atlantic Ocean to the region of the great lakes in the east. It reaches south of the eastern Sudan at the northern limits; and extends southward as far as the Rhodesias and central Angola. This is a vast

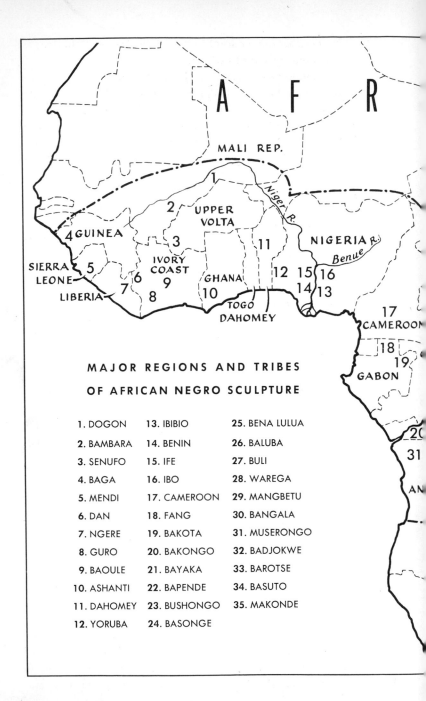

MAJOR REGIONS AND TRIBES

OF AFRICAN NEGRO SCULPTURE

1. DOGON	13. IBIBIO	25. BENA LULUA
2. BAMBARA	14. BENIN	26. BALUBA
3. SENUFO	15. IFE	27. BULI
4. BAGA	16. IBO	28. WAREGA
5. MENDI	17. CAMEROON	29. MANGBETU
6. DAN	18. FANG	30. BANGALA
7. NGERE	19. BAKOTA	31. MUSERONGO
8. GURO	20. BAKONGO	32. BADJOKWE
9. BAOULE	21. BAYAKA	33. BAROTSE
10. ASHANTI	22. BAPENDE	34. BASUTO
11. DAHOMEY	23. BUSHONGO	35. MAKONDE
12. YORUBA	24. BASONGE	

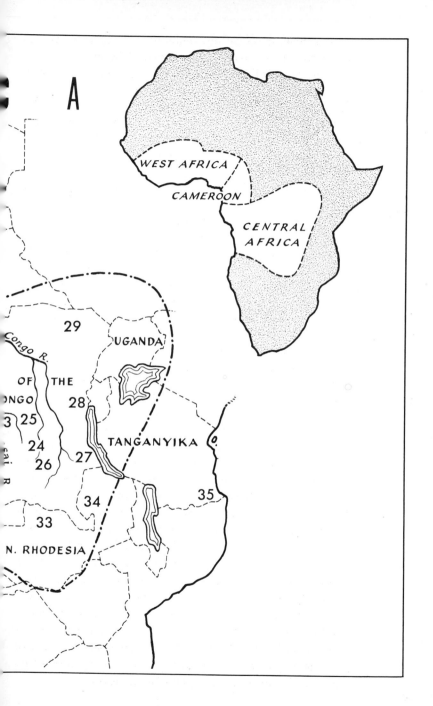

area, embracing an environmental range from tropical rain forests to savannahs, and even to semiarid regions. At the time of European contact, it was inhabited exclusively by Negro peoples who shared a number of cultural elements in common, but were differentiated by other important features. Within this great expanse of space, numerous art traditions, each with their distinctive styles, were developed. This area is one of the great regions of primitive art.

Culturally, African Negro art has, with certain important exceptions, a generally homogeneous background. Since this is so, the general characteristic patterns of life and belief that obtained for the greater part of the art-producing area, and that served as important stimuli for the art, can be reasonably postulated. Fundamental to any discussion of shared African culture traits is recognition of the family unit as the basic cell on which all larger units, such as the village, tribe, and nation, were patterned. To understand the character and the importance of this small unit is a prerequisite to the comprehension of larger social and political units. The family was organized in a simple, pyramidal fashion: the father at the apex; his wives and children in the strata below; and the slaves and retainers, if any, serving as the base. All control of a family group was in the hands of the father, who functioned as the religious leader, officiating at and directly controlling all family religious rites; he performed the necessary, controlling actions and made the appropriate offerings to assure economic self-sufficiency for the family. In addition, he was the moral leader of the family group, responsible for the behavior of them all, whether it was good or bad; and he was the social leader whose job it was to enforce adherence to all the traditional patterns of protocol. As head of the family unit, he was also a patron of the arts, since he was responsible for providing all the necessary art forms and other paraphernalia required for the various ceremonies at which he had to officiate, including all the rites of religious, social, or economic character performed on the family rather than the community level.

The position of the headman of a village and his relationship to its inhabitants was modeled on, and thus comparable to, the family unit. He now functioned as the apex of the societal pyramid, with the heads of families grouped together in the next level, followed by wives and children, the slaves and retainers again forming the base. He, in turn, had his own religious duties to perform, since the ancestors and deities to whom petitions were directed by a village were obviously of a different sort from those found on the family level. This also applied to the ancestors or spirits evoked for economic or social reasons. The tribal chiefs and the kings of nations officiated in the same manner on another, still higher, level. Art forms were required at all levels of African society, although the importance and quality of these art objects differed in each stratum; but the various ceremonies, beliefs, and institutions for which the art was needed were of a more expansive and diverse character from one level to the next. While the beliefs and the motivations behind these rites were, for the most part, similar in nature, the level to which they belonged marked a distinct difference in their importance.

Ancestor beliefs were basic to the majority of African areas, but the significance of the belief and the importance it played in the lives of the people varied considerably from area to area. Among the Baoule tribes of the Ivory Coast, for example, ancestor beliefs were of the utmost importance; and sculptured figures and masks were for use in the many ancestor rites. These figures were created in agreement with the style traditions of their locality while, at the same time, showing clearly their stylistic affinities with the larger, over-all area of the Ivory Coast as the center from which they emanated.

The features characteristic of this area are particularly evident in this standing female figure (Fig. 1), and an analysis of its style will thus serve to characterize the art of this important region. The individual parts of the body —the arms, legs, torso, and head—are distinctly separated, either by constrictions, or by long, intermediate parts such as the neck; and each part is given its own volumetric expanding shape. These shapes are related by strong, rhythmic interplays of forms, lines, and surfaces, and form a linear pattern in depth that flows around, almost caressing the shapes, and establishes a clear and conclusive three-dimensionality. Multiple small planes define these shapes and contribute to their expression of roundness, while clearly articulated joints act as points of differentiation between them. Typical of Baoule style is the remarkable organic quality and emphatic naturalism prevailing in the treatment of body parts.

As usual in these figures, the head is disproportionately enlarged and manifests a carefully detailed treatment of such elements as facial features, scarification marks, and hairdress. The stress given the elaborate hairdress, and the clean and precise rendering of the scarification marks, combine to give the figure a marked elegance; a dignity and calm aloofness, in keeping with the sanctity of and reverence for an ancestor, is established by the half-closed eyes and the pose. Further examination of these Baoule figures reveals a subtle asymmetry in the bilateral alignment of practically all the forms and descriptive details. On the right side of the photograph, for example, the knee, hand, breast, shoulder, and eye forms appear as slightly lower than those on the left; the plane of the shoulders is turned a bit to the left of the knees and body; and the head is off-center in relation to the axis of the body as well as being tilted up and somewhat to the right. The mouth, too, is not centered. The forehead, with its protruding, full planes, subtly flattens out below the eyes to form a concave facial area. The variation and refinement of parts and relationships shows a remarkable discernment of the nature of similar parts and relationships observable in human forms, and gives the figure a strong vitality of expression. The extent to this vitality is revealed when a figure, of the quality of this one under consideration, is compared with the completely symmetrical, regular forms found in Baoule sculptures made in more recent years for appeal to European taste.

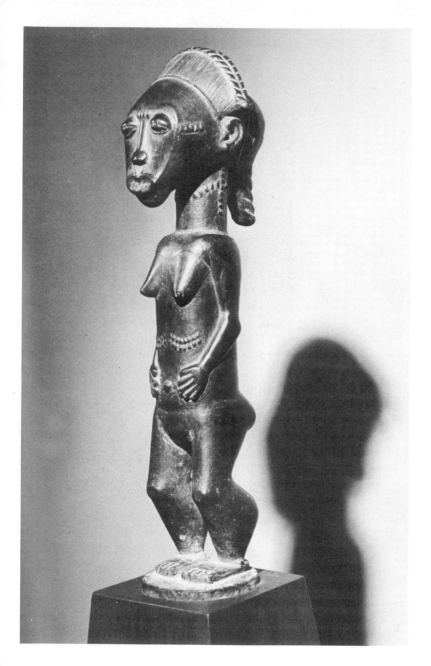

1 West Africa, Baoule, standing female figure.

2   West Africa, Baoule, "monkey" god figure.

The emphasis of the Baoule on the aesthetic accents and the artistic expression of formal relationships, already a style characteristic prior to contact with Western civilization, furthered the trade interest in this art. The fact that the Baoule were aware of, and responded to, this interest is known and poses some important questions, the answers to which are partially available by contrasting the style elements of new and old works. First, did European contacts and their expression of interest in the naturalism and elegance of traditional Baoule works lead to an increase in both of these stylistic features? If this was the case, did it carry further, to the point at which the traditional vigor applied to sculptural expressions of human form became excessively stylized and effete in quality? It is not meant by this hypothesis that all art from this area, since European contact, has been modified to appeal to buyers from the Western world—this was by no means the case. But certain examples, now reposing in museums and important collections, show how acculturation affected this strong, elegant, naturalistic style.

As with the standing female figure of the Baoule, the admirable, so-called Monkey God (Fig. 2) shows none of the vitiating influences of European preferences. It has, instead, the powerful, traditional vigor of formal expression, while the concept is clearly not indicative of any real drift toward overrefinement of forms and naturalistic statements. The traditional handling of shapes makes this work an important example of Baoule style. A wide variety of deity and ancestor masks, various types of ceremonial objects, such as divination bowls, and numerous utilitarian objects share the same style characteristics as the Baoule figures. A comparable subtlety of expression, a discernment of the variabilities of shapes and relationships in nature, is the key characteristic of this most refined of all African styles; and it is the one closest to the aesthetic ideals of Western culture.

To the west and south of the Baoule region, the Guro tribes developed a comparable style, perhaps a variant of the Baoule art tradition, with an even greater emphasis on elegance of detail and subtle changes of direction, from concave to convex, of the surface planes.

In sharp contrast to the strong naturalism and refinement of the Baoule, and of Ivory Coast art in general, is the work of the Sudan region in West Africa. This area is located between the arid Sahara lands on its northernmost fringes and the coastal, tropical rain forest to which it graduates in easy stages as grassy savannahs. On the basis of recent studies[5], it appears that the western Sudan was one of the oldest inhabited regions of Negro Africa. This antiquity seems to be reflected in its art style, which is strongly schematized and, in some examples, has designs of severely hieratic form. Animal subject matter was more predominant in the Sudan than in any other major art area of Africa, although strongly stylized human forms, especially female, occur in the majority of substyle regions, while in mask designs, human and animal forms frequently combine. Some few animal figures and masks have a firm naturalism of expression through forms relating closely to nature; but the greater part of the sculpture is heavily stylized. Both naturalistic and schematic examples of this art having creditable antiquity were brought out of the same parts of the Sudan; hence it is not valid to place the naturalistic forms earlier in time than the conventionalized ones. Both were known to exist in the same region at the onset of prolonged European contact. As representative of Sudan area art, examples from the Bambara, Dogon, and Baga tribes have been selected.

Living in a basically agrarian society, as did the majority of African Negro peoples, the Bambara tribes believed in numerous fertility-protective spirits, which they honored and petitioned ceremonially for the welfare of their crops, and in other ancestral-mythological beings, some going back to cosmogonic times, from which strength, health, and protection against unknown forces were requested. The Tji Wara Society of the Bambara is typical of the Sudan-type agrarian confraternity which had a vital role to perform in regard to the abundance of crops and, therefore, the security and survival of the group. At sowing season, its members would don masks known as Segoni-kun, which represented, or were based on, the form or head of an antelope. Wearing these in pairs, they would perform, one set at a time, their prescribed dance on the planting field.

Segoni-kun masks showed tremendous variation in treatment of details, forms, and types according to their locale within the Bambara country, yet recurrent features, distinctive of an over-all tribal style, are evident as being shared in common by all of them. Whether depicting the full figure or merely the head of the animal, they were all worn in the same manner: attached to a basketry cap that was tied on top of the dancer's head. They range in expression from characterizations of the aliveness and stylized vigor of movements in the forms (Fig. 4), to presentations of the animal in a severely schematic, almost hieratic manner (Fig. 5). In this example, the emphasis is placed on the neck, mane, head, and horns of the animal, with the body minimized to an open, rectangular form containing the heavier back and the flatter ground or base as two parallel vertical shafts comprising the four legs of the antelope. Backward and upward from one end of the simple solid shapes of the body, the slightly differentiated, void cylinder of the neck sweeps in a long, slow curve that contrasts sharply with the stiff rectangularity of the body. The mane is an open form composed of a flattened surface paralleling but expanding the arc of the neck, and separated from it by free, triangulated shapes which are then repeated as bifurcated triangles on the outer side of this curve. The contrast of rigid lines and sweeping forms and the open, pierced geometric shapes of the mane are elements diagnostic of Sudan style as a whole. Typical also is the geometric treatment of the long, thin head, and the way in which this shape changes direction sharply, from the curve of the neck and mane, to hang downward as a heavy form counterbalancing the upward sweep of the sharp horns and bringing all of the design elements into static harmony. In fact, the expression is

4 West Africa, Bambara, Segoni-kun mask.

3 West Africa, Senufo, equestrian figure.

that of a mathematical orchestration of parts and their relationships.

The second example (Fig. 5) of these Bambara mask forms shows a marked contrast with, but has many basic similarities to, the first, discussed above. This lively Segoni-kun mask is formed as a composition of sharp, angular shapes, active in direction and brought into a rhythmical relationship by curved surfaces and dynamically curving forms. The body is again a solid shape, but this time of trapezoidal form, with a more rounded volume for the back, and active angles now given to the representations of legs and feet. A rigid cylinder defines the neck: it rests on the shape of the body and affords a

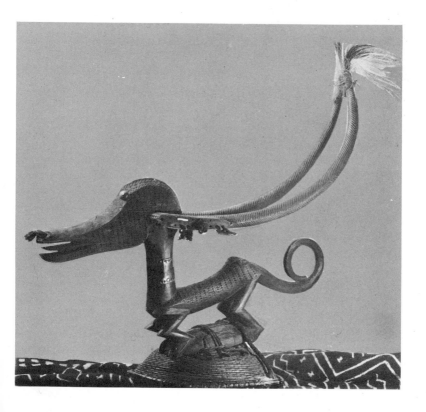

5 West Africa, Bambara, Segoni-kun mask.

springing point for the large, narrow-shaped, and open-mouthed head. As in the example just considered, the head is a narrow, elongated, stylized shape. There is one important difference, however: in more schematic Segoni-kun masks the rounded forehead area, the long, thin nose with flattened facial planes to either side, and the small, undifferentiated mouth are comparable to the head and facial shapes given to other Bambara masks, and also to many of their human figures. There appears to be, in this Bambara head-type, a degree of schematicized anthropomorphism of the animal form; the more active Segoni-kun mask, on the other hand, has a more complete, animalistic characterization. This treatment, too, is found in other mask forms.

Both antelope headpieces have a decorative treatment common to many examples of Sudan art. This consists of small-scale repeated design elements cut into the surface, and is in contrast with the more typical renderings of surface design in other African art styles, as for example in Baoule sculptures (cf. Figs. 1, 2), where the design elements project in low relief from the surface. Since the Sudan had been subjected to heavy Moslem influences from the north from the eighth or ninth century, it is possible that the Bambara method of rendering design came from Moslem metalwork. This influence may also account to some extent for the stylization given to many of their forms.

Located at the southern end of the Sudan, just to the north of the Ivory Coast, the Senufo peoples evolved a style midway between those of the Ivory Coast and the Sudan areas. The Senufo equestrian figure carved in wood (Fig. 3) displays very clearly this blending of style elements, with the strong Ivory Coast naturalism often yielding to the more expressive Sudanese stylization. This is very pronounced in the rendering of the horse's legs, which are treated as two thin vertical planks supporting the compressed volume of the body, the horse's rump and neck projecting beyond the limits of support. The head of the horse has the same conventionalizations of form found in the ox-head masks used by the so-called

Fire-spitters in the Korubla dances performed by a secret society among these peoples. It is quite possible that this resemblance is not fortuitous, but rather that it denotes the use of the equestrian figure in some Korubla ritual.

The human rider is just as drastically schematized: the legs expressed as mere dwarfed and nebulous clutching forms; the torso as two expanding cylinders meeting at the navel; the arms and shoulders as huge geometric volumes that sweep down to the elbows at which point a sharp right angle allows a thin tubular form to project as the lower arm. These are all conventionalized forms showing a relationship with natural shapes but going beyond them as schematic, sculptural expressions of form in three dimensions. The head is defined as a truncated, globular volume from which the facial area protrudes outward as a fairly thin, flattish surface. Although the facial features are obviously Negroid in origin, they are again schematized to fit within the confines of the facial area. Below the neck is a large, rectangular, block-like form with three rows of vertical, rectangular shapes, a design that may represent a container for verses of the Koran. These Islamic references are often found in the Sudan.

The Ivory Coast style elements evident here consist largely of the refinement and fluidity of surface planes and the stress on a continuity of flow. That these schematized shapes express a new, creative interpretation of life forms gives them an impact that only a prolonged examination of them can fully convey. The stylistic relationships with the Ivory Coast to the south and the Sudan area to the north, resulting in the development of a new set of forms blending refined naturalism with conventionalized elements, is evident in this and other examples of Senufo art.

More distinctly Sudanese in style than the art of the Senufo was that of the Dogon peoples who fled from the Moslems into a wild and rocky region east and northeast of the Bambara. Unlike the Bambara, however, whose art was produced by trained professionals of the blacksmith caste, Dogon art, especially the mask, was often carved by the member of a mask society, who may or may not have had artistic training and ability. The result was an art of uneven quality, which was almost always without any refinement of detail or contrived aesthetic effects, the expression coming, instead, from direct and often stark sculptural statements of shapes and forms carved in a style replete with common Sudan elements. Dogon art was, therefore, frequently one of vigorous and compelling forms presented as idiomatic, artistic statements.

Numerous figures, masks, and ritual objects were made for use in rites only partially involved in fertility and protection for crops and animals as a food supply. The emphasis seems to have been on maintaining a continuity with the cosmogonic, mythological, and ancestor personnel of the past as a source of protection and general aid, and on the safeguarding of societal balance as evidenced by the concern with rites following a death. The mask representing Andumboulou, a mythological character, and one of the "original" owners of the Dogon country, from whom they derived many benefits including the land and the cult of masks, is an excellent example of Dogon style (Fig. 6).

The features of Andumboulou are expressed within a long vertical head of characteristic Dogon shape and delineation, composed mostly of high eyebrows shown by sharp horizontals, from the center of which a high and narrow nose divides the facial area into two equal halves. The nostrils are bulky, projecting shapes that restate the horizontals of the eyebrows which, in turn, are echoed below by the curving horizontals of the lips within the protruding shape of the mouth area. In typical Dogon manner, the square piercings that form the eyes are set far down in the facial plane, just above and to either side of the nostrils. All these features are very roughly cut, devoid of any feeling for regularity of shape, size, or line. The stark and powerfully geometric rendering of the head as a whole, and of each essential unit within, brings this sculpture into the orbit of Sudan-area

6   West Africa, Dogon, mask of Andumboulou.

95

7 West Africa, Baga, standing male figure.

style. It has its own lively reality through the vigor and contrast of depths, surfaces, and forms, but the almost mathematical stylizations of Sudan art are ever foremost.

Human figure sculpture in wood, the material preferred throughout the Sudan for ritual objects, was used in practically all regions with style characteristics comparable to those already noted. By the time Western explorers reached the Sudan and established relationships with the various peoples, these forms had evidently become vestigial ancestor figures and in some areas were used as ritual objects associated with fertility cults. Apparently two varieties of ancestor figures existed among the Dogon: 1) the so-called "Tellem" figures, which seem to have been the common family votive carvings placed in the rocky grottoes; and 2) the larger forms, the most carefully carved of all Dogon sculptures, which may have been ancestor figures of important priests or personages of the region. The relative scarcity of the larger figures, and their better state of preservation, would tend to support this supposition, while the "Tellem" figures may not have been any older, but had been less well cared for, and had been exposed to the severe elements of the Dogon country. The latter figures are more summarily carved, relying for expression upon simple or dramatic poses, while the larger figures are eloquent in the severe, hieratic timelessness of their formal aesthetic expressions.

It was among the Baga, a Sudan people who had migrated to the west, that the Sudan figure-type reached one of its most dramatic statements of form (Fig. 7). The large geometrically shaped head thrusts forcibly outward to overhang the body; the neck is a nonorganic cylindrical form between the head and the geometric shape of the body, which bulges forward at the central point of an expanding, curved surface, where a peg marks the navel as though to prevent the form from bursting open. These explosive, highly geometric forms, and their nonorganic interrelationships, contrast markedly with the muscular definition and organic articulation of the legs. The latter forms strongly suggest that the western migration of these early Sudanic peoples was responsible for the fusion of naturalistic and geometric shapes.

Comparable transitional art elements to those found in Baga figures are a feature of the art style south of the Baga area, in the extreme western part of the Guinea Coast, within the present political boundaries of Sierra Leone, Liberia, southeast Guinea, and the westernmost part of the Ivory Coast. While figures, some of them in bronze, are not uncommon in this art center, it is one of the regions in the world of primitive art dominated by masks. Almost the full range of motivations for art, and a nearly complete scope of possible functions, are involved in the masks from this art area. Two societies, both more or less secret, controlled much of this expansive region: the Bundu, or Sande, and the Poro. Both were essentially initiation societies, but they varied in the details of their social position and function.

The Bundu Society, known as the Sande in some localities, was exclusively a female initiation society that held a strong position in the culture, one that in some areas, at least, partially balanced the great role of the male Poro Society. A large mask, depicting a spirit who gave power and protection to the girls, was worn by a leader of the Society, particularly at the conclusion of the initiation rites when the girls paraded through the villages. The Bundu masks differed slightly from those usually associated with transition rites from adolescence to adulthood, since they were motivated by the need for protection against the overwhelming force of the men, and functioned as a symbol of the spirit who supplied that needed power.

Although they differ somewhat in proportions and interpretations of detail, Bundu (Sande) masks are shaped in one essential pattern, that of a helmet mask fitting completely over the wearer's head. The sculptural emphasis in these masks is on the expression of the expanding volumes of the head (Fig. 8). This is either stated, as in the excellent example here, by an exaggeration of the natural dome of the head or, as in carvings from other regions, by delineation of the cranium as a

8 West Africa, Mendi, Sierra Leone, Bundu mask.

stylized shape that tapers toward the top. The facial features of all Bundu (Sande) masks are placed as compressed, small-scale elements at the lower front surface of the head mass; in some examples, as in the one illustrated, these features are descriptive in a naturalistic sense, while in others these elements are stylized to a degree that is strongly reminiscent of Sudan conventions of style. It is in these stylized examples that the transitional relationships of this art area with the Sudan are evident. Even in the representation of hairdress marked stylizations occur.

Aside from the expression of volume, Bundu masks have a number of symbolic details. Around the lower part of the face and head, for example, a series of folds symbolize fat which, in itself, stands for wealth, a possession of the spirit which, it is hoped, will be transmitted to the initiates. Wealth is also symbolized by the elaborate hairdress which differs in its degree of stylization according to specific locale. The expanding volume of the head and face, stressed by placing the features at the lowest part of the front facial plane, and the exaggerating of the volumes by placing the hairline at a very high position, are also used to emphasize the expression of expanding space, or fat, the equivalents of wealth. Technically, this is achieved by a smooth, undifferentiated handling of surface planes, and by sharp rendering of details in the neck rings and the hairdresses. Despite their differences in detail, however, or in the degree of stylization versus naturalization of form, there is but one kind of Bundu (Sande) mask.

Masks of the men's Poro Society have, in contrast to those of the Bundu, a wide range of types. While some of them from the west manifest a degree of Sudan-like stylization, the majority of them are based on naturalistic human or animal forms, or on expressive interpretations or combinations of them. Unlike the women's initiation masks, the type and shape of the Poro mask does not reveal its motivation, function, or meaning. The motivations for them were rooted in all of the possible human needs; but the forms they assumed were often so

standardized that it is impossible to associate morphological elements with the object's **raison d'être.** The
same was true in regard to the meanings of these masks,
which, in fact, seldom had much to do with their form.
Masks related in sculptural character with those of the
Poro Society were also used among the Dan and related
tribes in the eastern part of Liberia and the westernmost
section of the Ivory Coast; but the motivation, function,
and meaning of these masks differed from those of the
Poro Society.

Poro masks were derived fundamentally from ances-
tor-type traditions, although they relate to a remote
ancestor who had held a position in the Poro Society
equal to the one for which the masks were used. The
doorkeepers of the Poro lodge, for example, wore masks
representing early ancestors who had performed the
same function for the Society long ago; and, in the same
way, the wielder of the scarification knife wore a special
mask based on the generic appearance of the original
user of that instrument in the Society. Multiple functions,
some known only to its members and restricted to its
secret limits, others enacted publicly, for the benefit of
all, as certain social functions, were performed by this
Society. These masks are still being made for use in a
few areas; but in most of this region acculturation has
set in and the masks no longer function as cultural
elements.

Morphologically, a wide variety of Poro masks are
derived from, or based on, human form. A typical example (Fig. 9) shows obvious Negroid features which are
often regularized or stylized. Other features, such as
the eyes, the dome of the forehead, the shape of the
lips, and the volume of the nostrils, are dramatized to
bring out the expressive possibilities of these features.
References to anatomical elements of human skull structure can frequently be seen in these masks: the lines of
the frontal sutures down the center of the forehead and
the nose, and the reference to bony and fleshy structures
in the cheeks. A highly stressed expression of the tense
membrane of the skin that covers the bony and fleshy forms

is often found in these masks, an effect achieved by the tight and highly polished rendering of form-enclosing surfaces. In Poro masks these were frequently embellished or otherwise obscured by the time a mask was fully indoctrinated for ceremonial use, since the sculptured form was only a basis to which other materials and substances had to be added or appended if the mask was to achieve its full significance. At times these appendages gave a very different appearance to the carved

9 West Africa, Dan, mask.

10 West Africa, Ngere, mask.

form, and, in fact, largely interfered with the original artistic effects (Fig. 10). In many of the more sensitive Poro and Dan masks a marked stylistic feature is the refined handling of the ebb and flow of surface planes and of the way they fuse or melt into one another. But always, in these masks, the dynamic expression of form and the manner in which it sinuously changes direction, together with a monumentality in the scale of individual parts and features, demonstrate the exceedingly dramatic potentialities of the creative use of human features.

Many Poro masks are animal as well as human in form, some a blend of human and animal elements, while others grotesque or dramatic representations (Fig. 10). It is always possible in these seemingly grotesque forms to find one or more solid bases in nature for their shapes or details, which, however, are often treated in a reversal of reality to achieve the desired aesthetic effect. In this mask, for example, the planes of the face are recessed, in opposition to naturalistic handling, while the eyes protrude as telescopic tubes from within the depressed facial area; the nose and mouth are rendered as heavy, projecting sculptural forms. When combined, these forms extend as entities, the volumetric setting of the facial area. Earth paints applied over the brow and other features, red cloth wrapped around the protruding forms of the lips, tin discs attached to the rims of the tubular eyes, and the carved wooden appendages hung around the face as a full beard contribute to the dramatic effects, but are extra elements in relation to the carved forms. The ultimate effect of this type of Poro mask is of dramatic quality but doubtful aesthetic character, although from the standpoint of function and meaning the extraneous materials are of the utmost importance. There is a wide disparity in artistic quality between Poro masks of the type just considered and those of the Dan tribes, with their more subtle, naturalistic expressions.

Much of the sculptural strength characteristic of Poro-Dan masks comes from the full-volumed integrity of the tight, smooth forms and the sureness of the planes by which they are defined. A distinguishing style element found in many of these masks is the hard, polished, almost enamel-like blackness originally given to the surfaces. Dan masks, in particular, are admired for this quality, which, in combination with the subtlety of modulations in the form-defining planes, creates a feeling of elegance and refinement. This style is transitional between the more dramatic forms to the west, and the Baoule and Guro styles in the central and southwestern parts of the Ivory Coast.

104

Among the Ashanti peoples of Ghana, wooden masks and figures were not used ceremonially, with the consequence that masks were not carved at all, and only one type of wooden figure was created. This was the Akua'ba, a small, full-length or half-length figure that was carried as a charm by pregnant women in the belief that it would ease the birth, protect the women, and assure a perfect and beautiful child (Fig. 11). The figure is so

11   West Africa, Ashanti, Akua'ba figure.

strongly stylized that it suggests Sudan influence. The head was rendered as a large, round, disclike shape, with the facial features simply carved on one side in high relief, and incised lines indicating hair on the other. A continuous, double-curve, relief ridge represents the orbital line, from the center of which a narrow, square-shaped, pendant relief form defines the nose; eyes are irregular ovoid forms carved in relief, while, far below, a small incision indicates the mouth and still further down a jutting knob marks the chin. These facial features vary in the degree of their relief projection, stylization, and/or approach to naturalism. The disclike heads, however, are common to all of them, together with a long, geometrically ringed neck which attaches to the back of the head in such a manner that the heads hang freely in front of the neck which may be either slightly tapering and cylindrical in shape or composed of a short, cylindrical form ending in a rounded point.

The older Akua'bas seem to have been half-figures. In these, the body is rendered as a slightly differentiated columnar form, tapering a bit at the top and terminating in a cylindrical base of somewhat greater diameter. On the surface of the body column, relief knobs represent breasts, nipples, and navel. The full-length figures (which have legs) are usually articulated and basically naturalistic in form. Some of the figures have a dark-brown coloration and others a dark red-black; and the majority seem to have been carved in a close-grained, fairly hard wood, so that from handling and use they have acquired a smooth patina. The flattened head shape derives from the practice, common among these people, of molding the head of each infant into their ideal of perfect form. The Akua'ba seems related to the stylized small figures found among the Bambara peoples of the Sudan and usually designated by them as twin figures. Aesthetically, the nonorganic starkness and the variety of shapes and schematic detail give these small figures an intensity of sculptural statement that creates an artistic entity. A design with these properties must have developed from Sudanese influences. The motivation and function were

12 West Africa, Ashanti, gold weights.

here combined to produce an object with protective force; but its aesthetic appeal must also be included as an aspect of its function. The meaning is purely symbolic, the carving being equated with the ideal of perfection of form and beauty desired by the expectant mother for her unborn child.

In several of the style centers in West Africa already considered, objects of bronze were produced. While in each case they are stylistically characteristic of their own area, none were as important artistically for their respective areas as, for the art of Ghana, were the small bronze figures used by the Ashanti peoples for weighing gold dust (Fig. 12). The main reasons for this are: 1) the Ashanti gold weights are distinctive and well known; and 2) they are unique to the Ghanaian art area in their particular style character. Also, these small metal objects, because of their importance among the Ashanti as creative art forms, must be considered as indications of westward extension of the strong centers of African metal art found particularly to the east, in Nigeria. They were first molded in beeswax, and then directly cast in bronze by the method known as the lost-wax process, or **cire-perdue.** The small castings were graduated in size and weight according to an established system of monetary weights and measures. From this custom, already in practice before the era of western exploration, came the original name of this region: the Gold Coast, a land of gold dust.

Apparently the artists were free to interpret subjects based on observed reality in these castings and were little bound by traditional practices. Similar subjects, it is true, have a clear relationship of style elements, but the spontaneous naturalness of each representation is unique. The gold weights of Ghana are more closely related to impressionistic art expressions of nature than is usually found among primitive peoples. No attention was paid to refinement of the form as it came from the mold; rather, the essential vitality in the original wax rendering, of the vigor and reality of the forms, was completely retained. It was necessary, however, that these weights agree with the established scale, so that if a figure was a bit too heavy, a little of the surface was filed away; if it was too light, a little more bronze was pelleted on. Perhaps, because of the motivation and function of these small castings, one must consider them as outside the pale of subject-significant art; but they should not be considered minor art forms. Aside from the motivation behind their practical function, they had, by their expression, a certain prestige value. Artistically, these gold weights are vibrant expressions of life; they are sensitive renderings of pose, figures, and relationships that must be considered as free, artistic expressions of reality.

To the east of this area, in Dahomey, was another center of metal art. In this region art expression was culturally divided between the upper classes, that is the nobility and royalty, and the people at large. The best known of Dahomean art forms, although not necessarily the most significant, is the art that was developed and cen-

13 West Africa, Dahomey, brass figures.

tered in the capital city of Abomey. It was, with almost no exceptions, a prestige art consisting of fine cloths appliqued with genre scenes, elegantly incised calabashes, and a plenitude of small brass castings. While these did not have the utilitarian function of the Ashanti gold-weight castings, they shared a common, genre-type of subject matter, with that of the Dahomean works being more inclusive than that of the gold weights. Hunters with their dogs, women beside their water jars (Fig. 13), and a wide range of other subjects ranging into the realm of fantasy, such as crocodiles with humans in their jaws and fantastic, hybrid animals, can be found among these pieces. One important difference between the Ashanti and Dahomey metal castings is that the Dahomean figures are cleaned and chased, that is, the detail is sharpened up by cleaning and/or by cutting after the figures are removed from the mold. As a consequence, the Dahomey brass castings are more elegant and refined in their final appearance; they are also a bit more stylized in their rendering of natural form. They were often mounted on a wooden base to form a composition, such as a chief being carried from one place to another with his complete retinue in attendance. The figures were made by a particular guild within the royal compound, and their products were available only to those of rank who could, by virtue of their economic and social position, afford to purchase them. Hence these works must be placed in the category of prestige objects having sociological significance. One of their primary functions was to create aesthetic reactions and give artistic pleasure, if only to a limited audience.

One of the most important art-producing areas of Africa developed in what is now the Commonwealth nation of Nigeria. The best-known, but by no means the most aesthetically important, art forms from this area are the bronze objects from the old kingdom of Benin and from the religious center of Ife, both in the southwestern part of this region. Monographs have been written on the art of Benin, and could be written on that of Ife. Both arts appear, by present standards of chronological definition, to be of a decidedly earlier date than the art forms current in this area at the time of persistent European contact. On the basis of all of our present knowledge, the fullest realizations of the classic styles, in both Benin and Ife, occurred prior to any regular contact between them and Western cultures.[6]

Benin art is well represented by the royal ancestor head (Fig. 14), which was made to be placed on the ancestral altar. Expressively, this head agrees with natural form, even though certain features are somewhat schematized. The full volumes of the head are represented by the carefully modeled planes which define its surfaces and areas. In subtlety of naturalistic modeling, this head is beyond the range of stylistic features found in any other area of African art, except neighboring Ife. The recognition of these alien style characteristics has led to various theories of direct influences from external sources as being responsible for this art style. As archaeological work in the Niger-Benue river valleys progresses, however, it would appear that the style which became crystallized in the Benin area had widespread antecedents in the north and northeastern sections of Nigeria. In fact, present chronological knowledge of the

14 West Africa, Benin, bronze head.

art to the north places it at such an early date that Benin art would seem to have developed from, and actually represented, the final stages of development and maturity of an early, naturalistically inclined art; and the dating accepted for the most classic Benin works is given as during the fourteenth or early fifteenth centuries when contact with the Portuguese is known to have occurred. It is evident from the remaining heads, figures, and groups in the round, and from the relief plaques, that the technique of lost-wax bronze casting was handled at that time with such accomplishment as to produce works comparable to those of any known time, place, or civilization.

According to tradition, bronze casting as an art came to Benin from Ife, the hypothetical date of the late thirteenth century being given to this event. A number of Ife heads, largely in bronze and terra cotta, have come to light since 1910. The finest of these, and they all manifest a remarkably high level of achievement, could well be included among the most sensitively modeled, naturalistic heads found in any art. They have the variation of shape, proportion, definition of features, and rendering of planes characteristic of personalized portraits (Fig. 15). The way in which the subtlety of modeled planes is handled as form-defining and character-revealing is so accomplished as to suggest a depth of background in agreement with the theoretical traditions of Benin, and this, through researches already in progress, may some day be established. That they differ radically from the general character of Negro African style does not mean that they, any more than Benin, were imported in the full flower of development, as shown at the time of Western knowledge of this art. At the moment one can only classify the art of Ife and Benin as strong, independent styles which appear, on the basis of archaeological investigation, to be related to a very early and possibly inclusive style that reached a high point of development in the south-central part of Nigeria at an early date.

The significance of the arts of Ife, and also of Benin, for the more traditional style developments throughout Nigeria, is that a number of features were dispersed among them. This does not mean that, although Benin was a royal art and Ife a restricted, possibly religious, art, the other style areas of Nigeria must be considered as provincial offshoots or reflections of them in one aspect or another. Very strong and clearly distinguishable regional styles exist throughout Nigeria which have only slight references to the art of Ife and Benin, some showing no affinity whatsoever.

15 West Africa, Ife, terra-cotta head.

The extensive Yoruba region of central, western, and southwestern Nigeria contained some of the most prolific art-producing tribes in Negro Africa. They lived in various large urban centers such as Ibadan, as well as in smaller rural areas, and tended to develop somewhat individual art styles. These have, however, so many features in common that it is readily possible to characterize a Yoruban style. The degree of variation between a more stubby, naturalistic figure style, and an elongated, somewhat more stylized representation of human form makes so little difference in the incidence of important features that the shared elements of Yoruba style are immediately evident.

A typical example of Yoruban wood sculpture is the kneeling female figure holding a bowl (Fig. 16). In this work, squat, heavy proportions prevail; and in the geometric head shape, with its characteristic expression of the forehead, upper eyelids, and other facial forms, a clear reference to Benin style is evident. At the same time the particular creative mode of these forms has a naturalism of its own—characteristic of Yoruba art. Volumes expand from within the tight, carefully carved, and separately defined areas and features of the head; blending with this and emphasizing the naturalism is the monumentality of scale and integration of the body parts. Another feature characteristic of this style is the genre-like interpretation of such cult objects as this bowl. The Yoruba had a great number of socio-religious rituals organized around the over four hundred deities, major and minor, in their vast pantheon of gods. One or another deity, or "orisha," had special control over every province of human activity, with the resultant need for cult objects providing the artists with constant patronage. Numerous iconographic details, centering around the orisha, are common to many Yoruba objects, such as the small kneeling figure supporting the bowl, and figures of comparable size nestling against the upper arms of the figure.

In substance the elements of Yoruban art style consist of: genre-type backgrounds for subject matter and its

16 West Africa, Yoruba, cult bowl.

115

17 West Africa, Yoruba, Gelede mask.

interpretation; enlarged heads with a gashed type of
facial scarification indicating the local or subtribal origin
of the figures and forms; an expression of the mass of
the human body and its various parts, or an interpretation of its volumes and verticality; and the exaggeration
of Negroid facial characteristics, with nostrils equal in
width to the mouth, the large, everted lips, and the dramatic statement of the heavy upper eyelids.[7] With these

constantly recurring style elements must be included the patterned and rhythmical manner of depicting important, selective details. In the example, the sides of the hairdress are rendered by the use of wavy, parallel grooves, and in the sharp crest that moves from the front, over the top of the hairdress, by close, chipped, parallel grooves on each side. Strong fillets, shown as parallel curving grooves, bind the crest to the hairdress and encircle the base of the forehead. A variation of the sculptured surfaces is produced by the incised or chipped design below the neck, and on each breast and shoulder, while on the lower segments and the removable lid of the bowl, which is shaped as the body of a fowl, a stylized pattern of designs covers the surfaces, suggesting the softness of feathers. Parallel, sculpturally marked zones are decorated with a chipped chevron design clearly related to that of the crest, but adapted to the bowl subject. The neck, crest, and tail of the fowl are defined by a surface decoration of parallel grooves. In range, surface treatment is restricted to the rhythmical variation and repetition of a few motifs. Color was also used to differentiate between decorative details and descriptive forms and shapes: in this example, only remnants of a bright blue remain in the sculptured details.

Masks were used in several socio-religious Yoruban groups, and had, as their basic motivation, the general welfare of a village or area. Of such a character was the Gelede Society, a semisecret organization which performed periodically and at the death of a member, in a traditional manner aimed at satisfaction of the balance-equilibrium needs, and in a general therapeutic fashion as well, by the staging of masked dances. The masks were created in a wide range of designs and subject matter, each one having a mythological or historical significance. They were worn at a sharp angle on top of the head, the wearers looking out from beneath them rather than through perforations in the masks themselves. One fine mask illustrative of the Gelede type (Fig. 17) seems to portray a European wearing a strange headgear with a loose chin guard. A remarkable feeling for form is discernible in the carving of the head within the depth of the headdress, and in the characteristic treatment of volumes expressing the head and facial features. The projection of the volume of the forehead, the size and scale of the eyes, and the flat, fleshy form of the nose, with its very wide and expanded nostrils, are highly characteristic elements of Yoruba style. To this must be added one other feature commonly found in objects from this area: the wide lips, extending the mouth area as far to each side as the nostrils, and the particular way in which the lips are treated, i.e., as parallel, shelflike forms which, unlike natural forms, do not meet at the corners. Masks of this type are among the most sculpturally significant art forms produced in this area.

East of this part of Nigeria, and extending to the south and southeast, the tribal styles of the Ibo peoples predominate. While these include elements of the surrounding art styles, certain elements can be singled out as unique to the art of the Ibo peoples. Since the Ibo tribes are spread over a sizable area, mainly to the east of the Niger River, their art style exhibits marked regional idiosyncracies. Certain expressive elements and concentrations on formal art features are crystallized in a fashion that clearly separates Ibo art forms and traditions from those of neighboring peoples.

In contrast to the nearby Yoruba tribes, the Ibo depended more on nature spirits and ancestors than on specialized deities for aid in moments of crises. Their rituals required masks, figures, and other objects, including a number of terra-cotta family shrines or modeled bowls with the same meaning, used for directing petitions to the deities or, most frequently, to the ancestor spirits (Fig. 18). They are unique in form, completely individualized in style, and are among the most important Ibo art forms. As in so many examples of Yoruba art, there is a strong genre basis for the forms and poses: on one side of the bowl the head of the family is depicted in very high relief modeling, flanked on his left by the factotum in charge of sacrifices; to his right and far left

18   West Africa, Kwale Ibo, shrine vessel.

are his important wives. Comparable clusters of figures appear on the terra-cotta shrines. They have a compressed but naturalistically articulated body treatment, the lower parts of the forms being adapted in shape to allow the high-relief forms to curve in and become attached to the side of the bowl. In keeping with the characteristics of Ibo style are the enlarged heads set organically on long tubular necks, the head being in proportion, about as high as it is wide. Certain facial features are analogous in some respects to those of the Yoruba, such as the shaping of the forehead. But here, a high-relief line marks what can be associated with the frontal suture of a human skull; the nose is a more fleshy and less differentiated form than in Yoruba style, while the long, partially open mouth and the small chin have a slight prognathism in the thrust forward from a shallow or depressed facial area. The small, deep-set eyes, and the pattern of raised scarification marks are also in contrast to like details of Yoruba sculpture. A typical feature of the figures on these modeled Ibo bowls and shrines are the semicircular depressed disclike ears that are set at right angles to the side of the head and give even greater width to the already wide heads. These terra-cotta bowls and the shrines are unique to the Kwale Ibo who live in the trans-Niger region in the west-central part of Ibo-land. This is probably one of the strongest naturalistic art styles in West Africa. The adaptation of natural forms to nichelike spots on the side of a bowl is a unique interpretation of form and space. In this instance both form and pose are of complete reality.

Throughout the entire area of eastern and south-eastern Nigeria, one of the most important art forms, required by a variety of ceremonials, was the mask. Numerous dance rites of social and religious significance were performed by the Ibo and Ibibio groups from this region, many of them requiring masks of a particular kind. The motivations for these rites were of the security-survival and continuity-stability types; and related to them as subject matter was the very important content of mythology. Many of the "characters" represented by the masks were drawn from mythological lore, functioning as semisymbolic forms, in rites that have been denoted as "plays." This is a rather unfortunate term since it implies that the ceremonies are all of a purely social nature with an entertainment content. On the contrary, these "plays" were of a socio-religious character which was an outgrowth of mythological concepts and religious beliefs. In some cases the entire community contributed toward the ceremony; at other times a particular group staged the "play" for the benefit of the community as a whole. The Ibo employed various types of masks in these ceremonies, the most important from an artistic point of view being the carved wooden face masks. Although these differed according to the particular features of their individual or local style elements, forms characteristic of Ibo art traditions are, for the most part, evident.

In contrast to the Kwale Ibo terra-cotta ancestor groups, which have a plasticity of form in keeping with the modeled medium, the majority of Ibo wooden masks have a carved definition of form and detail with a hardness and tightness indicative of the harder, more resistant material (Fig. 19). Planes are sure and strong as they project, recede, and meet in resultant lines or sharp edges to create a precise statement of facial shapes and features. The angles of the hairline are connected and emphasized by a downward curve, which is flattened and reversed to indicate the orbital structure and is then restressed in the short curves of the upper lip; the heavy downward curve of the thick lower lip re-echoes that of the hairline. Rows of vertical, rectangular projections flanking the eyes describe the scarification patterns which, among the Ibo, differ from subgroup to subgroup. Remnants of white paint form a light-colored facial zone that extends as a continuous surface from the narrow bridge of the nose to the outer edge of the face, marking off the facial area below the brows and contrasting with the darker color of the geometrically shaped nose and the slightly prognathous mouth and chin area. Included in the white surface are the sides of the upper portion of the nose, reducing the apparent size of this feature at the top segment by leaving only a narrow strip of darker color; this widens as it proceeds toward the nostrils, allowing this otherwise absorbing facial part to draw the focus of attention away from itself and down to the large-lipped half-open mouth which thus becomes one of the most expressive features. Typical of this art style is a controlled reality of expression that is dramatic and intense, but seldom becomes melodramatic. The Ibo used, and still use in some regions, a great number of varied mask forms in their secular and religious cere-

19 West Africa, Ibo, mask.

122

monies ("plays"), as do their neighbors, the Ibibio, to the east and south.

The Ekpo Secret Society masks (Fig. 20) are characteristic of the more dramatic Ibibio masks. This representation of a creature from the underworld, probably derived at least partially from a large-eyed, lemurlike animal, attracts the eye at once to its primary centers of interest, the weird, out-size eye forms. These consist of heavy, sculptural shapes that project from and occupy most of the small facial surface. A small, sharp nose emerges below the eyes. Under that, a wide, open oval represents the mouth, with three large teeth above and below. This serves both as a terminating form for the lower end of the facial area and as a secondary center of interest. The eye area is composed of a pair of open tubular forms surrounded by and set off-center within the deeply concave interiors of two large, thick, concentrically circular shapes. A vibrant color balance is applied to each eye form: on the right, the concave interior surface of the larger form is painted a delicate mauve-gray, with the very rim of the open tubular form colored a gray-white; on the left, these colors are reversed, with the small open rim painted in the mauve-gray and the surrounding concavity in the gray-white. Similarly, the upper teeth are gray-white, and the lower ones mauve-gray. The remaining surfaces are almost black, apparently soot-encrusted. The disposition of two colors in this manner is a skillful device used to create an optical tension between obtrusive and recessive tonal sensations. The application of this device to both eyes and mouth results in an optical tension in both areas. The sculptured eye forms and the rows of upper and lower teeth gain a greater intensity of expression because of the dramatic use of color. This and other Ibibio masks must be considered among primitive art's most creative combinations of sculptured and polychromed forms integrated in an optically and tactilely expressive design.

Various Ibibio "plays" used small wooden figures in a manner comparable to marionettes (Fig. 21). These

20   West Africa, Ibibio, Ekpo mask.

sculptures are powerfully rendered interpretations of
human form that show little actual transcription from
reality. The scale stresses the bulky upper part of the
body and the large neck and head, with the lower legs

124

21 West Africa, Ibibio, standing figure.

125

and feet reduced to compressed, balancing, and supporting members. While the articulation of forms is vigorous and in part organic, the full force of sculptural expression comes from emphasizing the contrasts in projection and recession of the shapes and parts of the human body, thus expressing them as sculpturally dynamic elements. From any angle, the profile is marked by sharply irregular, broken contours, the forms expanding and diminishing, but always wholly in three dimensions.

Shapes are essential sculptural statements, without refinement of surfaces or details, since the purpose of the artist was to present, dramatically, the dynamic potential of the human figure poised for action. This he accomplished by interpreting the forms as thrusting shapes which combine with the pose to give the figure a rhythmic unity of form through the purposeful artistic treatment of component parts. The shaping of the forehead, for example, is a sharp, forward-thrusting, almost geometric form. A repetition of this can be seen in the nose and in the large, heavy lips of the open mouth; it is re-echoed by the slightly changed direction of protrusion in the chest and by the pyramidal shape of the abdomen. The conclusion of this appears in the angle of the genitals and knees. Balancing these forward thrusts is the backward directional force of the tablike ears. This is stressed by three greatly enlarged geometric scarification marks in front of each ear and by the pulling back of the shoulders, which intensifies the vigorous reversal of thrust. Accents that highlight this reversal are found in the flexed elbows and the backward protrusion of the buttocks, which balances the projection of the abdomen. It is weakly restated in the calves of the legs. Neither the hands nor the feet are shown naturalistically, the fingers and thumbs being mere suggestions, but rendered in such a way that the grasping character of the hands forms an important expressive element in the content of the figure as a whole, while the feet are carved sculpturally to convey their function as the base and stabilizing support of the figure.

Art was, and to some extent still is, a highly significant and important cultural element throughout the large, well-populated country of Nigeria. Many stylistic elements from each of these important art areas were shared by one or more of the other traditions, and certain general features are common to all of them. Of the "ancient" art of Ife and Benin, some examples suggest a relationship with the archaeological art of the Niger-Benue to the north, in the analogous or comparable treatment of naturalism in the human form. Benin has numerous points of analogy with Yoruba wood sculpture in such elements as the scale of facial features, the size and shaping of the eyes, and in many examples, the stressing of the aspects of mass and volume. Ibo and Ibibio art, in common with that of the Yoruba, exhibit a strong tendency to interpret human forms and details in expressively sculptured shapes, rather than to render them in a stylized or schematic manner. The attempt to translate into sculptural terms the vibrancy and vitality of life forms evident in much of West African sculpture south of the Sudan reaches a high point of development in this area, particularly among the Ibibio. This tendency also serves as the primary basis for the art of the Grasslands area of the central part of the republic of Cameroon, to the east of Nigeria.

Cameroon Grasslands art is more homogeneous in style than that of any other large region of Negro Africa. This area is inhabited by many small tribes which are not clearly differentiated by culture elements. In the past these tribes were frequently hostile toward each other, but markets were held in common in a sacrosanct region outside the towns and were in operation whether or not the tribes were at war. The interchange of products sometimes included art forms, so that there was a good deal of diffusion and influence of one tribal style on the other. Although it is possible to characterize the style of certain tribes, the elements are seldom unique—they are but variations and combinations shared by the numerous other styles and differ mainly in degree. Wood was the most commonly used material and was usually given a

22 West Africa, Cameroon, stool with figures of animals.

monochrome color of either light red ocher or flat black;
but pipes and some ritual objects were cast in brass or
modeled in clay and given a maroon or black coloration.

Two distinct traditions may be recognized in Cameroon
art: 1) a vigorous and direct interpretation of life forms
in which the refinement of surfaces, shapes, and detail
was eschewed in favor of the textural quality in the creation of forms (Fig. 22); and 2) an expression of dramatic,
sometimes grotesque, designs based on human, animal,

or hybrid forms in which the shapes, surfaces, and details were handled with a greater refinement and self-consciousness or aesthetic effects (Fig. 23). Other examples combined these two traditions. It must not be thought, however, that in the first of these traditions, no conscious thought was given to artistic values, or that sculptural vitality is lacking in the second mode of expression. Rather, these expressions were achieved in each tradition by the employment of methods appropriate to the over-all treatment of forms. Both traditions must be taken together to reveal the full quality of Cameroon art style.

The forms of this region, in whichever tradition, include a variety of different types of sculptured objects: masks of many kinds, ritual bowls with figures or animals, small figures for ceremonial use; large, architectural carvings of doorframes, poles, and lintels; and stools with prestige function. The small stool, supported by six carved rabbits, is of the latter category (Fig. 22). It belongs clearly to the more naturalistic tradition, although some evidence of stylization may be observed in the way the backs of the animals fuse in a common mass beneath the top, at the center of the free space. Each rabbit helps to support the top on its two long ears, while its forelegs rest on the open ring of the base. The importance for this art of alternating, rhythmical modes and variations is highlighted here by the manner in which every other head is marked by a sharp, medial ridge, a slightly expansive, snoutlike mouth, and topped by two, acutely angled ears. The heads between lack the central ridge and have as a substitute wide grooves that curve down from the top of the head, going over and under each eye; the mouth is narrower and the lips more widely opened, while the ears stand more erectly on top of the head. Also, one foreleg of each rabbit extends farther forward on the rim of the base than the other. Thus a rhythm is established between the two interpretations of form and pose which enriches the total expression through the alternating sets of detail and contributes to the greater vitality of each of these little forms. Such a treatment is not unique to this stool, but is a feature of Cameroon art style.

In rendering, these rabbits are very roughly defined in shape, surface, and detail, the tool marks being clearly evident and contributing a quality of vibrancy to the surfaces. A sense of vitality and aliveness is characteristic of sculptures done in this tradition, whether stools of this type or ones with human figure supports, freestanding figures or mask forms. In some cases, the figures, animal or human, are elongated; in others, compressed into heavier forms. Color seems to have been used sparingly on the carved stools to pick out certain details, as in this example: the mouth and eyes; the grooves on the head of each alternate rabbit; and the interior of the ears.

As with other ceremonial or prestige objects, such as long-necked gourd containers, drums, and costume masks, the entire outer surface of many of these stools, especially those with grouped figure subjects, was covered with beads, strung, and then applied with a resinous substance. The older of these objects were covered with tubular Arab beads, acquired in trade, of soft coral, off-white, dull black, and tan colors. Later, small European glass beads of wider and more garish tones were used along with a few of the older type. In both cases, cowrie shells were used in combination with the beads. The sculptural quality becomes obscured in these examples, giving way to a less pleasing, more colorful effect.

Masks were common to almost every group in this Grasslands territory, many of them attaining an aesthetic quality and expressive effect unsurpassed in any other primitive area. These masks (Fig. 23) were ceremonially worn by members of semisecret societies, perhaps better described as confraternities, which banded together for socio-religious activities, frequently under the aegis of a "totem" animal. These are totems only in a highly specialized way: they were felt to be protectors and sources of power; but they were not symbols or signs of ancestors or kinsmen around which many taboos were erected. The motivations back of these institutions included most of the human needs generally implemented by art forms. The masks used were of several types: face masks, helmet masks, and, as in the example

23 West Africa, Cameroon, mask.

being considered, the type worn on top of the head. Expression ranges from generic, human, facial forms to dramatizations of human features, some of which approach the grotesque; from fairly naturalistic, animal forms to a highly creative interpretation of an animal head.

The basis for this animal form (Figs. 23, 24) seems uncertain. It seems to represent a chimpanzee, perhaps

24 Side view of Fig. 23.

used in the powerful confraternity allied to that animal. But as strongly as this is suggested by some of the elements, it is denied to some degree by the large, horn-shaped forms that sweep up so effectively from the back of the open ring base, coming to rest atop the head between the sharp ears. The end product is a hybridized form basically inspired by the chimpanzee, but enriched and altered by the addition and integration of imaginative combinations of other animal forms. From the front, the head seems to be surmounting a thick neck beyond which it projects as a smoothly concave, diamond-shaped plane from which all of the striking facial features protrude in very high relief. The eyes are treated as wide-based, conical shapes, the bases of which intrude upon the sides of the nose; the nose itself is given a wide, triangular form bisected by a low, dark ridge that repeats in linear fashion the concavity of the facial area, ending in a high point to either side of which the nostrils expand to meet the facial plane. These are defined by a narrow, dark line crossing the vertical, central ridge of the nose and combining with it almost as an arrow, pointing out the very high projection of the wide, open, irregularly shaped mouth with its inner ring of sharp, dentated notches as teeth.

In profile (Fig. 24), the forms shift so that the head rests as a plastic shape molded to a wide bridgelike form spanning the open ring of the base. The "neck" seen in the frontal view becomes an illusion of the organic form which in reality does not exist. Attached to the back of and looping from the base at either side of this bridge are the sweeping "horns." From either front or profile views, this mask is a sculptural tour de force, with suggestions of surrealistic double images evident in the different forms and the combinations of shapes.

An aesthetic analysis of this form is both rewarding for itself and revealing of the expressive nature and quality of Cameroon art. Frontally, the design is dominated by sharp angles established by the ears, the diamond shape of the face, the flat triangles of the nostrils, and the dentates in the open mouth. Only a few curves are used to relieve these angles: the horns; the shape of the eyes; the mouth area and lips; and the illusionistic, curved volume of the neck. Attention is focused almost equally on the mouth and eyes through the bisection of the facial diamond with the strong horizontal line of the nostrils; and the mouth, the most aggressive and arresting feature in the lower area, is enlarged and stressed. In the upper portion of the face, attention is drawn to the eyes through the sharp directional angles of the ears. In profile, the sharp angles of the facial design are replaced by heavy open curves, the "horns" acting to lock the mask or to hold it in place. Remnants of a thin, white, earthlike pigment remain against the light brown of the wood, and it is unlikely, on the basis of other examples, that it ever had any polychromy. All of the shapes are dynamically welded into an expressive unity. Although an outstanding masterpiece in itself, the artistic character and the vigor with which design concepts are handled, together with the integrity of dynamic expression, are characteristic of this tradition of Cameroon art. In contrast to the rougher, naturalistic tradition, the forms and design elements are here given an accomplished refinement of shape and surface which contributes to the more deliberate creation of an aesthetic effect. This abets rather than vitiates the originality with which these forms are interpreted.

Three major expressive-artistic trends have thus far been observed in African Negro art: 1) the naturalistic, 2) the stylized, and 3) the dramatic-grotesque. The distribution of these modes of interpretation in West Africa, based on the frequency of their occurrence, may be charted as: 1) the stylized or schematic interpretations appearing largely in the western Sudan, with some evidences of its influence on the art styles of the northwestern and northern regions of the Guinea Coast area; 2) naturalistic tendencies, appearing most strongly in Ghana, the Ivory Coast, Dahomey, and certain regions of Nigeria and the Cameroons; and 3) the dramatic-grotesque expression most commonly found in Liberia-western Ivory Coast, southeastern Nigeria, and the Cameroon Grasslands. Only in the "ancient" art of Ife and Benin does naturalism refer to a close approximation of natural forms. Instead, it is applied to the use of generic or nonindividualized shapes and details to interpret, sculpturally, the character or quality of natural forms. For this reason, the component parts of the total figure or mask created in this naturalistic tradition do not duplicate like parts or forms in nature, although they usually interpret those forms poignantly or revealingly. In the stylized or schematic approach, the elements of the forms are also derived from nature, but may be distorted into almost abstract patterns or symbols which agree with the traditional conventions in treatment of specific forms so that the entire figure will serve as a schematic or almost abstract symbol-reference to forms in nature.

The dramatic-grotesque expressions are less closely allied to natural forms. A shape derived from natural form may be greatly distorted or treated in a basically creative manner. This may be combined with one or more similarly inspired forms, producing a unique hybrid design to which are often added startling, nonnaturalistically derived, abstract shapes. The total effect is spectacular, arresting, or even terrifying. The subject matter of such a work can thus be treated with reference to its aggressive appearance and to its attributes of power, strength, or ferocity. In the Gabun region to the south-southeast of Cameroon, in what one can consider the northwesternmost part of Central Africa, elements of these three West African art trends combine in varying degrees.

The mortuary-guardian figures of the Fang and Bakota peoples come from this Gabun territory. In style the Fang sculptures range from a relative naturalism to an almost cubistic interpretation of human form (Fig. 25), the variations signifying local or village differences in the rendering of commonly held style elements. Basically, the style defines each separate body shape as a distinct entity, and as a structural or functional member that relates to the figure as a totality. These relationships may be established organically or rhythmically. The head shapes vary only slightly, but facial forms, both in shaping and in expressiveness, differ considerably. The majority of Fang figures have a monochrome, deep-black finish applied to their refined surfaces, which are then highly polished. Details such as fingers, toes, scarification marks, or hair delineations either are omitted entirely or, in a few instances, are summarily rendered.

The Fang figure from the Basel collection (Fig. 25) expresses, in one of the more cubistic examples of this style, power and force held in a contained state of equilibrium. All the essential parts of the body are marked off as self-sufficient, geometric shapes. The feet act as an undifferentiated, flat base; the lower legs as heavy, semispool shapes with considerable expansion at what corresponds to the knee, expressing the heavy, supporting function of these forms. In contrast, the thighs are irregular, semicylindrical forms unrelated organically to either the lower legs or the body. They act as lateral body supports and help to transmit weight to the lower legs. Generally cylindrical in shape, the body fits down into a saddle created by the form of the upper thighs. From this point it extends upward, expanding slightly at the navel, and flattening out as it approaches the chest and shoulder areas. Flanking the upper part of the chest and in part related to it, the shoulder area is sharply marked off by constrictions comparable to those separating the leg parts and the body. In a similar manner the upper and lower arm are treated as separate entities while the hands are indicated by abstract, cylindrical blocks marked off at the wrist by a deep indentation.

A large cylinder, in nonorganic association with the body or head, supports a somewhat enlarged and geometrically shaped domelike head. This flattens out and reverses direction as it flows into the markedly prognathous face, thus creating a sinuous movement of surface planes. Within the facial area, the eyes and nose are treated as large-scale forms occupying much of the

25 Central Africa, Gabun, Fang figure.

space, with the wide, closed oval of the mouth placed at the very end of the facial zone. Several devices are prominent in the design and shaping of the head. First is the heavy, flattened, geometric form of a hair crest that extends back from the crown of the head, flanked by irregular, flatter forms which, sometimes with an extension of the central crest added, extend as short pendants. All of these simulated hair forms are treated as smooth surfaces or simple grooves. Second is the carefully rounded, smoothed dome of the forehead that expresses controlled and expanding volume. This is picked up and restated by the forms below, making it the key element in the expression of power held in tense repose. Also typical of these sculptures is the fluidity of planes and ridges marking the directional changes of surface forms. These are frequently subtle, as is the double curve over the eyebrows, which continues around the side of the face to the narrowing chin, creating a heart-shaped design framing the face.

Analogies to the naturalistic-dynamic character of Cameroon style appear in the Fang figure in the manner of separating parts by severe constrictions, although here the balancing and the stolidity of the pose do not express actual movement. The active aggression conveyed by the Cameroon sculptures is held in abeyance here, again by the pose and by the simple expedient of representing the mouth without the menacing teeth. In a way similar to Hawaiian figure sculpture, the power of the broken profile and the force of the relationships of geometric shapes impart a vibrant quality to the form.

In contrast to the vitality of Fang figures, the Bakota mortuary objects are among the most stylized, near abstract sculptures in Negro Africa (Fig. 26). These metal-covered forms have the severity of a Byzantine icon, although they are even further removed from reality. Some of them, in fact, have the quality of a psychotic nightmare image. With regard to their impact, they can only be related to forms outside of Africa—to the Melanesian areas of New Britain and the south coast of New Guinea. They can, of course, also be compared in their

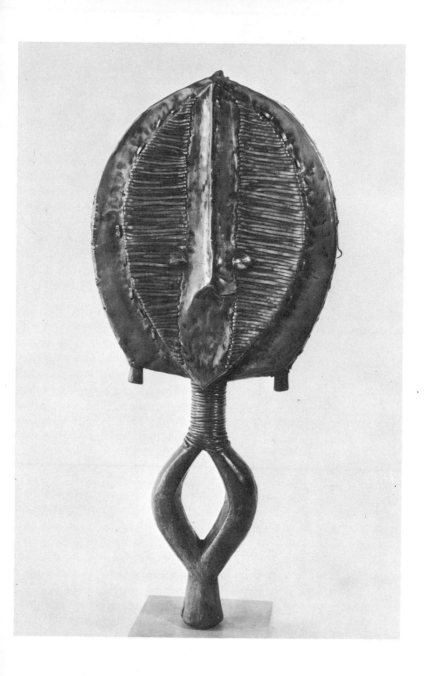

26 Central Africa, Gabun, Bakota figure.

mode of representation to certain twentieth-century abstract paintings in which the three-dimensionality of form is represented within a few shallow two-dimensional planes on the canvas. Bakota figures were evidently intended to be seen from the frontal or near-frontal point of view since they were placed against a side wall of the men's house. As a consequence, the back is seldom defined to any degree, and only a few are double-faced.

These forms appear to represent the neck and head of a figure as it was visible above the ancestor bone box in which it was placed. Some, however, seem to be busts, since the upper half of the open diamond form below the neck is also visible in some examples. The upper part of the figure is usually designed as a somewhat flattened, wide, oval shape that contains few projecting planes; in some examples a crescent form, set in a plane parallel to the back surface, tops the design. In all of these objects the entire upper form seems to represent a three-dimensional head that has been bisected and flattened, the two halves depicted in a conventionalized manner to either side of a median line or ridge. In this interpretation, the central and most projecting of the several flat planes serves as the facial area, and the flanking forms can be equated with the sides and back of the head, conventionalized and reduced into a single plane. The crescent form, appearing atop many Bakota figures, would thus be an idiomatic statement of the hairdress crest turned at right angles and shown in a single plane. Any part of the figure that appeared above the rim of the box was covered on the outer face with brass, copper, or a combination of the two.

A wide metal strip extending from top to bottom was the usual method by which the oval face, with its slightly concave surface, was divided. Further division was accomplished by a horizontal strip of metal running from side to side at eye level. The eyes were contained within the horizontal band, while any nose or mouth forms that were used were set in the vertical one. The four quadrants were often decorated with additional strips of copper or brass. At variance with this norm, the Basel example has the face area, with its sharp-pointed oval shape, divided into two halves by a vertical strip, the upper two thirds of which project as a central ridge terminating in a nostril-like shape. The lower segment of this vertical strip is flattened and intended to suggest the mouth and chin area, neither of which is actually shown. Two pointed brass discs represent the eyes and are placed near to, and on either side of, the lower end of the raised ridge of the central zone. Narrow strips of copper, more or less carefully arranged horizontally, cover the two halves of the facial area from the top to the bottom. The outer, depressed area around the face, in all probability depicting the sides and back of the head, is covered with a plain sheet of brass; the small wood pendent forms terminating the outer zone seemingly depict a pendent type of hairdress.

Below the head the columnar neck is covered with strips of copper, twisted to give them a thicker form than those covering the sides of the face. The neck area is usually found with a covering made up of strips or a sheet of metal similar in type to that used on the upper arms of the open diamond. In this example, the open form has three-dimensional arms that fuse to form an oval on the outer side; and a flattening of the inner surfaces creates the diamond form. No part of the shapes which define this open area ever seem to have been covered. It is rare, too, to find this part, together with the neck and the terminal support below, given such a volumetric treatment.

The expression as a whole is less schematic and decorative in this example than in most Bakota figures. The verticality of the head is stressed; and there are greater variations between the rounded and the flattened shapes and the expression of depth. A vibrancy of relationships and design results which is manifested in the conventionalized and hieratic figure by a commanding vigor of appearance.[8]

To the south of the Gabun area, along the lower reaches of the Congo River in what has become known as the Lower Congo region, one of the strongest naturalistic-expressive styles prevailed. Of the various objects carved in this region, including ritual staffs, a few masks, and utilitarian forms, the seated commemorative ancestor figure is the most representative. The greater number of these had a mother nursing her child as the subject (Fig. 27), although some were of seated male figures and others of kneeling female subjects. Of the various tribes in this region, these sculptures are most often ascribed to the large Bakongo group. The motivation, function, and meaning of these forms are classic examples associated with the commemorative ancestor figure.[9]

Carved from a single cylinder or block of wood, the limits and often the shape of the original piece appear in the circular or square plinth on which the figure is seated, tailor-fashion. The figures have full-volumed forms that increase in size and scale from the crossed legs to the body, arms, and shoulders, with the heavy neck and large head as dominant forms. Full articulation appears throughout these sculptures, along with an organic integration of the shapes unmatched in other parts of the primitive world. On the lap of the figure, so arranged that the left hand of the mother always supports its head, while the right hand rests on its lower legs, the child reposes and suckles the left breast. With the exception of the outer surface of the low plinth, descriptive or identifying, but not merely decorative, details are characteristic of this style. For example, there are the necklace, bracelets, and ear pendants found on most examples. The half-open, full Negroid lips display the mutilation of the teeth common to this area, and on the back of the shoulders and body elaborate scarification marks are carved. Both details are identifying elements of the subtribe in which the carving was made or of the individual it was intended to represent.

Another characteristic feature of this style is the pose of the figure: the body inclines forward in a frontal pose; and the head is turned to the side and inclined slightly upward, breaking the strict frontality. This particular attitude is one of respect and dignity, appearing consistently in both seated and kneeling figures, and even

142

27　Lower Congo, Bakongo, mother and child figure.

143

on the ends of ceremonial staffs. Often associated with this position, as in this example, is the expression of a calm remoteness conveyed largely through the heavily drawn upper eyelids.

While completely defined, the forms, either singly or in their organic relationships with other forms, are not usually given a smooth, polished, and flowing surface. Instead, there is a slightly textured quality, the tool marks being visible on the carved surface, especially on the body. In rendering the full physical character of each part, the sculpture is very close to natural form: the musculature is given in the arms, legs, and neck; the rounded bone structure of the forehead is distinguished from the heavy, fleshy forms of the cheeks, the thin membrane of the eyelids, and the softer flesh of the lips; and even such details as the finger joints and the fingernails are defined. The only forms that are nonnaturalistic are the large blocky ears. Typical of this Lower Congo style is the completeness with which the figure exists in and utilizes its complete volume of space: with the exception of the legs, the body parts are cut free, moving forward and backward, as well as laterally, in space. This is evident in the shift in position and depth of the knees in contrast to the shoulders and head. The firm outline of the forms moves around the figure and freely establishes the spatial and the formal relationships. The figure is contained within its cylinder of space: no lines or shapes break its quiet, compact pose; even the angles of the face are kept within the design by the restraining value of the half-closed eyes.

It has been thought by some that the descriptive naturalism of such Lower Congo figures was the result of long-established European contact, going back to the fifteenth century, and that the predominance of the mother-and-child subject matter was a consequence of Christian missionary influence. But the same theme is found in other parts of Negro Africa, and the naturalism of this style is, in the interrelatedness of its parts, more closely allied to the concepts of naturalism in other African styles than it is to any naturalistic European mode.

This naturalistic style reappears in the central and eastern parts of the Congo, but immediately to the east, in the Kwango River area,[10] a more schematized and dramatic style appears in the arts of various tribal groups who carved masks, figures, ritual objects, and utilitarian forms. An important type of figure in this, as well as in the Lower Congo, area is the so-called "fetish" figure which is often of doubtful aesthetic quality.[11] Among the Bayaka tribes along the Kwango River, however, magical substances were used sparingly (Fig. 28).

Stylistically, these figures were far removed from the ancestor carvings of the Lower Congo area, since they have a geometric form and a distinctive, stylized handling of certain details that separates them from any naturalistic affiliations. In general, Bayaka figures are a composite of rhythmically and expressively, but nonorganically, related shapes. The legs and undifferentiated feet serving as a wide base are acutely articulated and handled as vigorous, sculpturally cubistic shapes; the bulk of the body is treated as a geometric form that fits into the spreading upper parts of the thighs in a manner reminiscent of the Fang mortuary-guardian figures. In many examples, the arms are rendered as completely nonorganic and unrelated sculptural bands in high relief that encircle the body, going around the back of the form and terminating in small, mere suggestions of hands. These are attached to the body, as is the whole of the arm band, in a purely schematic manner. The shoulders are flat-surfaced shapes that do not integrate with the long expanding tubular shape of the neck on which the head rests. The head is presented as an irregular globular shape broken only by the large, looplike ears placed almost at right angles at either side. A fairly shallow, high-domed forehead dominates the face with its features set close together and consisting of large, ovoid eyes, a small, tight mouth, and, one of the most distinctive traits, a nose that terminates in an enormous, almost right-angled hook. The significance of this feature is not known, despite various conjectures. A further peculiarity in the treatment of Bayaka heads should be

28 Western Congo, Bayaka, standing male figure.

noted: a wide borderlike plane, possibly indicating a full beard, extends from the hairline down the sides of the face and meets under the nose; it is a feature of style found on most carved heads.

With the exception of the head, which is generally carved with care so that the surface and facial details are clear and precise, the figure shows vigorous tool marks that contribute an essential vitality to the work. Little color was used on these figures, although all Bayaka masks were highly polychromed.[12] The life-size male and female figures which flanked the entrance to the initiation house were also polychromed, and in a realistic manner. (Due to the color treatment of the Bayaka masks, they seem to be related, at least to some degree, to the central Congo polychrome mask tradition.) The geometric shapes and sharp angles of the legs which are characteristic of Bayaka power figures express through their bold technique the dynamism of natural forms, while the tensions of shape relationships between the arms, body, neck, and head, together with the powerful facial features that are centered around the grotesque nose, add to the nonnaturalistic force of expression in these forms. This same quality appears in the variety of ceremonial and utilitarian objects given sculptural form or decoration, such as neckrests, ceremonial whistles, and cups, most of which are carved in the typical shape of the head with its Cyrano-like nose.

Bayaka style bears testimony in a number of ways to the differences in attitude and expression between the art forms of West Africa and those of Central Africa. An outstanding style characteristic common to the entire region is the conventionalized treatment of natural form which is, at one and the same time, more remote from reality and more expressive of the permanent and inherent attributes of its force, power, and movement. The artists strived to create shapes that would express the dynamic essence of natural forms. This goal is fundamental to the comprehension of most Central African sculpture.

147

Similar elements of Central African style are evident in the art work, particularly in the mask forms, of the Bapende tribes, neighboring the Bayaka peoples in the Kwango region. Of the masks used by the Bapende, the semihelmet type was shared with the Bayaka and Basuku peoples: the unusually small face type was unique, being often only five or six inches high (Fig. 29) and stitched to an enveloping costume that allowed the wearer to look either through eye apertures in the mask or through slits in the costume below the carved face. These Bapende face masks are among the most sensitively carved of all Central African masks. The head, a wide oval, tapers sharply to the narrow chin, the width at eye level becoming greatly extended by tabbed, animal-like ears which project at right angles to the sides of the head. Within this oval the area between the temples bulges out in a narrow form, its defining planes changing direction to establish the depth of the eye area and the shallow volume of the features below. The facial forms themselves are emphatically stated, but have only a partially organic integration within the volume of the head. The eyes, for example, are carved as projecting geometric shapes that act as balancing agents between the angles of the upper lids and the sweep of the restraining lower lid. A grooved and painted design stresses the depressed sweep of the nose, beginning at the bridge and continuing down nearly to its tip; the lower end of the nose is then formed as a comparatively naturalistic rendering of a moderately flaring, Negroid-type form. Of the accented features, the open mouth is of extreme importance. From the lower third of the facial zone, it projects as a tight, oval form with sharp, irregular teeth and an emphatically aggressive expression.

Bapende masks were motivated, as were most such initiation objects, by the desire for continuity and stability. In function, they were symbols of the ancestral and mythological power and support with which the initiates were ceremonially brought into contact, and which were revealed to them at this time. The meaning of these masks was the tangible conveyance of the vigor of these

29 Central Congo, Bapende, wooden mask.

aloof, mythological-ancestral beings. In design, they are accomplished, artistic combinations of curves and angles, of rounded surfaces and flattened forms. There is a clear expression of the anatomical character of the human face, not as a transcription of reality, but as a creation based on knowledge of the forms. The rounded volume of the shallow forehead flows unbrokenly around

149

the sides of the face; and over the depressed areas of the facial planes it is interrupted only by the incision of the eyebrows and the grooved relief design of the nose.

Several sharply angular accents create a balance of curvilinear and rectilinear elements in the projecting, ovoid plane of the face. The angularity of the large eye forms is particularly significant. Of a shallow volumetric nature, the eyelids are formed by the rectilinear bisection of irregular, rhomboidal forms; their angularity is then denied by the smooth, curvilinear shape of the lower lid. A minor rectilinear accent is found in the treatment of the inner ear, which has a sharp triangular shape. Other elements of angular or rectilinear stress appear in the striations between the eyes and down the nose, and in comparable forms below the eyes and mouth. Along with the treatment of the eyes, these vertical elements are the most important forms to develop in opposition to the curvilinear character of the mask as a whole.

Bapende masks vary not only in size, but in shape, ranging from the sensitive, naturalistic form of the British Museum example to a triangular design wide at the forehead area and tapering to a sharp chin. In another version, the design is a diamond shape, tapering at the chin and at the crown of the head, and extending in breadth at the eye level. Some of the naturalistic masks have an angular projection at the lower part of the face, giving the over-all form a quadrilateral shape. This serves as a beard, and its surfaces, along with the sides of the face, are given a geometric, cofferedlike treatment in simulation of the texture of a beard (Fig. 30). The more naturalistic forms, with or without a beard, are most commonly found, in miniature, in the distinctive and remarkably carved ivory maskettes used as initiation badges. All of the sensitive Bapende style elements appear in these small forms, masterfully shaped in the hard substance of elephant ivory.[13]

Color was an important aesthetic adjunct of these wooden masks, although the range was quite limited. Among the Bapende of the Kwango area, a light red ochre was the basic color, with white and/or black and

30 Central Congo, Bapende, ivory maskette.

white used to pick out a few details (Fig. 29), while in the central part of the Congo region, another group of Bapende peoples, living to the south and west of the Kasai-Sankuru area, employed a wider range of colors, including a rust-colored ochre, on naturalistic masks and on many small horned animal masks. Eastern (or central) Bapende style differed little from that of the Kwango area. Among all these groups, the most significant stylistic feature is the blending of curvilinear and angular shapes to give these masks an expressive character typical of the Central Congo style, but handled in their unique fashion characterized by a fusion of naturalistic and geometric renderings of the natural forms.

Of the art from the Central Congo, Kasai-Sankuru region, the most important and extensive development occurred among the Bushongo (Bakuba) tribes. The classic example of their style is the representation, as a royal commemorative portrait figure, of Shamba Bolongongo, the Nyimi or king who reigned about 1600-1620 (Fig. 31). He is rendered as a massive, completely articulated figure seated tailor-fashion on a low base or plinth. The sculpturally descriptive form is suggestive in pose and proportion of a Lower Congo commemorative ancestor figure (cf. Fig. 27). Unlike the latter, however, the pose of the Bushongo king is completely frontal, with stresses laid on the regal iconography, and on the bulk and weight of specific body parts as they combine to press down upon the pedestal base. The scale is impressive, although less naturalistic than in Lower Congo figures, the Nyimi being rendered as very short and comparatively thin from the hips down, but massive in the upper body shapes and bulk.

Typical in style of the relatively few surviving figures of this type is the ovoid head which is the most conspicuous part of the figure and conveys the sense of heaviness pressing down on the supporting neck and on the bulky form of the body mass below. The method by which the hairline sets off the facial area with a delineated, shallow-grooved line that describes a flattened curve over the forehead and three sharp angles over the temples is not only characteristic of the royal figures, but is found on all Bushongo sculptures depicting the human head, including effigy cups and masks. The facial features of Shamba are schematized in such a way that they function very nearly as superficial relief forms. Thus, they emphasize the mass and volume of the head, rather than penetrating it to diminish the surface pressure. The eyebrows, for example, are carved as a low-relief band of shallow, parallel, incised lines; the oval shape of the eyes, divided nonnaturalistically into puffy upper and lower lids by a narrow horizontal slit, are outlined by a narrow space that

1 Central Congo, Bushongo, figure of Shamba Bolongongo.

merely establishes a surface setting for the eye. The nose is a heavy, projecting mass, with only a suggestion of the nostrils delineated at the sides, while the low-relief pattern of the mouth and its association with the heavy shape of the nose is another style element of Bushongo art. The bone structure is clear in the forehead and the cheekbones, while the jaw-line is subservient to the fleshy bulk of the cheeks. As previously noted, the expression is that of the aloofness, omnipotence, and oppression of divine African kingship.[14]

These royal portrait statues are composed of a balanced, almost static, set of related shapes and forces which thrust forward and backward in space, but are devoid of the linear patterns that give the Lower Congo figures such a complete sense of three-dimensionality within a prescribed space. An axis is emphatically given to the design by the mass and projection of the base, balanced by the bulk and thrust of the head, and by the crown placed directly on a line with the base. To either side of the rigid mass of the body, the cylindrical volumes of the upper arms serve as equilibrating relief forms, while the shorter left arm, and the hand holding the short sword—symbolic of the king—are asymmetrically balanced by the slightly lower and sharper backward thrust of the right arm in concert with the lower and more forward placement of the right hand. These style features are consistent in all the extant Bushongo statues, suggesting that a figure-type had been evolved for some time prior to the carving of Shamba Bolongongo's portrait. The wood used for these forms was an exceptionally heavy and hard variety, and was given a fairly smooth surface treatment with a high, mahoganylike polish, not as smooth or fluid, however, as on many Baoule and Fang figures.

Bushongo royal portrait figures represent one of the several so-called court styles developed in Negro Africa,[15] all of which had, as the ostensible motivation prestige and aesthetic refinement. But other motivating factors are involved here, such as security-survival, continuity-stability, and fertility, since the Nyimi, or king was believed to be the great ancestral source through which all of these benefits derived. Although the slight individualization of the Bushongo figures make them more than generic portraits, they must nonetheless be considered as highly symbolic sculptures charged with potent meaning in their highly significant, formal patterns.

According to oral history, the idea and type of royal ancestor figure was established by Shamba, who had been influenced by his experiences while traveling in the "west." As a result, he introduced both the commemorative figure and the art of raffia weaving.[16] The textile art was highly developed by these people, with the men weaving a plain cloth from the raffia-palm fibers, and the women embroidering it with characteristic, complex angular designs. The textile designs also appear on the elaborately shaped and decorated wooden cups made especially for the drinking of palm wine. These utilitarian objects had distinct prestige-vanity significance as aesthetic forms.

The numerous and varied wooden cups carved by the Bushongo can be roughly divided into two categories: those of geometric shape which are covered with rich, surface designs derived from embroideries; and those shaped as three-dimensional human heads, the so-called effigy cups,[17] which also have the neck and base frequently decorated with the embroidery designs (Figs. 32, 33).

Effigy cups have not only a wide range of design, but also, on the basis of the many examples in museums and private collections, exhibit a very wide range of artistic quality. The effigy cup in the Stockholm Museum (Fig. 32) is an exceptionally fine one. The head, in shape and in handling of facial features, is a classic Bushongo object: the balanced shape of the sharply ovoid head and the flaring base of the neck are completely harmonious; so too is the proportioning of the head to the neck and its shaping, as it fuses into the base with a finesse so often lacking in other examples. Although slightly less commanding in scale, the facial features agree in form with those of the portrait figures. There

32 Central Congo, Bushongo, effigy cup.

appears to be a bit more integration of the eyebrows with the nose form, thus drawing all of the facial forms into a stylized pattern. In comparison with the portrait figures, the head form is wider above the temples, and the surfaces of the face are smoother and more fluid, with none of the marked bone structure. A crosshatched design decorates the top of the head and marks it off both from the facial forms and from the narrow cylindrical mouthpiece of the cup which develops and is shaped atop the head. The neck is smooth-surfaced, with a median area below marked off by a series of soft concentric rings; at right angles to the rings a number of deep vertical sections, alternately decorated with parallel horizontal and vertical grooves, terminate the base. Carved in a dark close-grained hardwood, the cups are often given a deep, reddish-brown stain and a high polish that is accentuated by constant use.

Geometrically shaped cups also have a varied range in shape, size, and quality. Like the effigy cups, they are carved in stained and polished hardwood, with similar principles of decoration (Fig. 33). The base and the top of the cup are marked off by decorated zones separating them from the major body of the container, which is considered the main decorative field. In the effigy cups, too, the base and the lip are established as distinctive parts, and the head, as the container portion, is the major carved form. Typical of Bushongo cup decoration is the plasticity given to the motifs by defining them as wide bands lying in the surface plane. The area between is filled in with lightly crosshatched, dentated, or parallel-line elements creating a textural quality in depth. In the Stockholm example, the textile designs, dominated by the large-scale, angular interlace, are perfectly adjusted and proportioned to the wide central zone of the cup. Irregularly shaped inlaid discs of bone add to the enrichment of textures, while the alternation of crosshatched zones and horizontal bands of dentates between the decorative segments of the base and top further show this to be an exceptional cup.

The fitting of the design to the space and the use of alternating zones are not always such conspicuous features. Often the neck and base of the effigy cups, or the large central zone of the geometric ones, are decorated with whatever portions of an over-all embroidery design the space can accommodate, the complex angular patterns being cut off at the upper and lower edges rather than, as in the Stockholm examples, being completed patterns. A textile-derived design treatment appears also on the sides and lids of the carved wooden boxes which are as characteristic of Bushongo art as the cups. They were made in various sizes and shapes, seldom exceeding twelve inches in length, and were mostly used as containers for blocks of tukula.[18] Among the most common shapes are the crescent, the square, and the rectangle. Small drums and a few other objects were also decorated in this manner. The concept of design, whether used for textiles or carved objects, is based on an unlimited repetition of a variety of elements.

Another feature of Central Congo art was the consistent use of dramatic, stylized polychromed masks Created in this tradition are the Bayaka masks of the Kwango area, the eastern Bapende forms of the fringes of the central area, and the masks of the Bena Lulua and Basonge peoples just to the east in the Lualaba-Lomami River region. Masks of this tradition are often composed of spectacular, weird large-scaled forms, arresting in their vibrant contrasts of shape and color. Various shades of red-orange, yellow-green, black, and white were combined as surface designs or as nonnaturalistic emphases of carved shapes. Although not as highly polychromed as some, a unique semihelmet type of mask made by the Basonge and known as a "Kifwebe" is characteristic both sculpturally and expressively of Central Congo style (Fig. 34).

Kifwebe masks differ considerably in shape and in the precise renderings of features; but they are all dominated by one particular motif: wide parallel grooves covering the entire surface and painted in contrasting colors of white and black or red and black. The forehead

3 Central Congo, Bushongo, carved cup.

159

is usually described as an expanding, heavy, cowl-like form below which massively hooded eyes project still farther. In this impressive example from the Basel Museum, the triangular, cubistic nose is carried upward to the crown of the head as a high, crested form, while the mouth, set closely below the nose, is shaped as a hollow, protruding rectangle. Attention is concentrated on the massive facial features by their placement, and by the medial and directional line of the crest. All this is stressed by the lines of the surface design which lead toward the central facial forms with a distinctly rhythmical flow.

The representational associations of these Basonge masks, apparently made up of combined human and animal forms and features, have little to do with the dramatic power of their expressive sculptural shapes. There is almost an auditory element in such a mask that seems to come from the dark, mysterious shadows of the eyes and the blatant forward thrust of the mouth. The qualities of sound and rhythmical movement suggested by forms, and particularly evident in these Congo masks, have special relevance for primitive art since not only the masks but many of the figures were intended to be used and/or viewed with the accompaniment of drum rhythms, vocal chants, or songs. These and other forms were often used nocturnally, when the flickering light and shadow of open fires contributed to the sculptured, dramatic effects.

Although the motivation, function, and meaning of the Kifwebe masks are only known in a speculative way, it is certain that they were more than "masks used in ceremonies to welcome guests" or "masks used in important secret rites."[19] Certainly masks of this aesthetic quality were not merely trivial objects with an entertainment character only. They must have had, at one time, a vital cultural significance that was, most likely, of a socio religious nature and origin. But, because of European contacts and influences, their original importance seem gradually to have been dispelled. Such a hypothesis is more than substantiated by the potent formal and expressive elements of the mask forms.

34 Central Congo, Basonge, Kifwebe mask.

The power or so-called "fetish" figures, so characteristic of this eastern central Congo style, also agree with this aspect of Basonge art. They range in size from only five or six inches in height to some of more than life-size. The subject matter, however, regardless of

35 Central Congo, Basonge, standing figure.

size, is always the same: a full-length standing figure with very flat and extremely large feet which cover the entire surface of a moderately sized base of angular construction. The body shapes are schematically and nonnaturalistically articulated, and there is seldom any convincingly naturalistic, organic integration of forms. On the contrary (Fig. 35), there is a formal organization of a geometric, even cubistic, character built up from component parts of similar nature.

Basonge power figures were motivated, like all fetish figures, by the need to control the forces that held sway over illness and other adversities. The dynamic expressiveness of these forms conveys in dramatic, sculptural fashion the implementation of such needs by an abstraction of physical and spiritual forces. Because of its function as a power figure, the head is horizontally exaggerated so that the cranium would provide space for the insertion of magical materials. In some few examples, the protrusion of the abdomen provided additional space for this. Aside from the additives just mentioned, a number of magical forms and substances were attached to or suspended from the carved forms. Aesthetically, such substances were of no value, but functionally, they were of great significance.

The sculptural quality of these objects is particularly dynamic: the head thrusts forward vigorously and is repeated in form by the bulge of the abdomen and the large, flanking hands; the stylized aggressiveness of the facial features, marked in the projection of the eyes, the geometric nose, and the vigorous open mouth give the features an active expression. Strict frontality of pose prevails in these Basonge carvings, along with bilateral symmetry. In this example, the cleanness in handling of details and the smoothness in surface refinements emphasize the independence of the parts rather than their organic co-ordination. Figures of this type are embodiments of the characteristic emotive force that abounds in Central Congo style.

This divergence from naturalism of Basonge figure and mask style crystallizes certain of the differences

163

between Central and West African developments of style traditions. While West African art forms are handled either as stark conventionalizations of natural form, or as robust, naturalistic versions of reality, those of the Central Congo, except among the Bushongo, are treated as geometric stylizations, at times creating a remarkable but nonnaturalistic reality in sculptural terms. Basonge style, created in the idiom of Central Congo style and within the larger context of the Central African vocabulary of forms, has a dynamic energy that clearly stamps it as among the most vigorous of African art traditions.

Located between the Basonge and the Bushongo style areas, the Bena Lulua peoples created art forms which, in many respects, may be considered the epitome of this nonnaturalistic and emotive sculptural tradition in Negro Africa. The motivation, function, and meaning of the Bena Lulua figures are not fully known. It would appear from the earliest sources of contact in this area that the figures might have served either as commemorative ancestor sculptures or as protective amulets. They are free-standing, and have a fairly rigid stylization of pose and proportions (Fig. 36). The forms move up from the short, heavy, functionally supporting feet and lower legs to an elongated body, neck, and head, all of which are set in an ostensibly strict frontality. In the more classic examples, however, as in this one from the Hamburg Museum collection, the frontality is specious. Close examination of the object reveals a subtle shift in direction from the hips to the shoulders; the head is turned at a slight angle from the frontal plane. All body parts in these Bena Lulua sculptures are separated from each other, and are shaped in such a way that each form is removed from reality and can only be considered as an expressive stylization. The torsion and movement of forms, and their individualistic nature, are clearly evident in the nonnaturalistic shapes and relationships of the profile. Unlike the Bushongo and Basonge objects, these figures, as a whole, give no evidence of scale. They are, in fact, often very small, ranging from about five to fifteen inches in height.

36 Central Congo, Bena Lulua, standing figure.

Bena Lulua renderings of the human form, whether as figures or masks, are distinguished by a particular type of surface treatment which seems, according to historical accounts, to have had only a slight basis in the traditional scarification patterns. While it is known that the Bena Lulua performed extensive scarifications on both the face and body, they were meager in comparison to what appeared on the sculptured objects. There is every reason to believe that the sculptural patterns were, as in other instances of African art, amplifications and exaggerations of the actual practices.[20] These surface designs—for example, the heavy scarification patterns—give the forms a vibrant quality. The majority of these figures, however, were so heavily rubbed with tukula powder that, in many instances, the surface designs were almost totally obliterated.

In these figures a vigorous and mobile outline creates a force of alive expression in keeping with the general mood of neighboring Central Congo styles. These figures are, in many respects, the most representative of the entire Central African area: in their creative-versus-naturalistic relationship of form; in their vitality and expressive rhythm; in their assemblage of descriptive and representational details. They also demonstrate further distinctions between the styles of West and Central Africa in that forms and details, such as facial features, are less associated with naturalistic origins, tending toward a schematic or symbolic interpretation to an even greater degree than did the art forms of the Sudan; and further, the northern forms are more hieratic and less alive than those of the Congo styles. As a consequence the Bena Lulua figures, along with the other Central Congo art forms, require more in the way of understanding and interpretation, aesthetically and compositionally, than the more easily read Sudanese objects.

By comparison, the style developed by the Baluba peoples, who inhabit the eastern and southeastern part of the Congo area, shows a far more naturalistic orientation and mode of presentation. The territory inhabited by the Baluba tribes extends toward Lake Tanganyika and into the Katanga region and was divided, artistically, into several substyle areas. There was, however, an over-all style of which the subgroups were variants. Together, they evolved one of the very strongest sculptural and aesthetic art traditions of Negro Africa; and in the numbers and variety of objects created, they vied with the art production of the Bushongo peoples. Their art work included seated or kneeling figures with bowls, figures that supported small neckrests or larger stools, free-standing figures that functioned in either a utilitarian or a ceremonial manner; and a type of mask, partially related to Central Congo forms but devoid of polychromy.

For the sake of convenience, the Baluba style tradition can be divided into two major substyle categories: the central or classic Baluba style; and the Buli style of the eastern sector. Central Baluba art is well represented by the crouching female figure holding a bowl (Fig. 37), from the collection in the Museum in Florence. This style is one of the most organically integrated in its creations of shapes based on, or derived from, natural forms to have arisen in Negro Africa. In the Florentine example, the female figure is proportioned to the pose and to its expressive possibilities. Although the parts are each distinct and specifically defined, they are also completely integrated so that the total form presents an organically unified expression but an ill-proportioned figure. The legs of the kneeling figure are greatly elongated and folded back so as to form a sufficiently long and stable base for the sizable bowl held between the knees. The figurative shapes are all defined as bony representations of the various forms which are arranged as a balanced expression of full and attenuated volumes and meager, emaciated shapes. Heavy abdominal scarification patterns extend below the breasts and well around the sides in high relief, and are typical of both the major Baluba styles. Also characteristic of the two style categories is the elaboration of the hairdress, which has varied local styles of design, and the low forehead sloping back in an elegant flattened curve to the very high hairline.

37 Eastern Congo, Baluba, figure with bowl.

Head shapes in the central Baluba style tend to be irregular globular forms usually extended deeply at the back by the hairdress. In the Florentine bowl-figure, a very wide fillet crosses the head at the hairline and is paralleled by a high crest extending from ear to ear; the hair is twisted to form a large rounded shape that extends sharply backward and low down on the head. The fillet band, defined by a narrow border, is decorated with shallow, parallel, vertical grooves, while curving parallel incisions indicate the manner in which the hair is twisted and tucked into the ball-like terminal form of the hair-dress. A comparable wide band of decoration, composed of similar grooves, encircles the brim of the bowl. Of the facial features, the low-bridged nose and the full-lipped, partially open mouth are naturalistic and organically integrated elements; the sharp ovals of the fairly large eyes, however, are carved as surface-relief forms that project considerably farther than the very low-relief delineation of the eyebrows. The ears are large and somewhat conventionalized forms of great importance because of the emphasis they place on the horizontal thrusts of the head.

The expressive and aesthetic success of this carving depends upon the sensitive relationships between forms of similar shape but varied size. The subtle balancing of parts gives a vibrant vitality to the work. The most strongly established and readily apparent set of relation-ships in the design is the pattern of forward-thrusting horizontals. Of these, the base form is established by the legs, which create a firm framework for the upper forms; almost parallel with them, the long arms serve as stabilizing elements and carry foward to embrace, with functionally enlarged hands, the sides of the bowl. Thus, the bowl is incorporated into the design by its placement on the knees in a manner that makes the actions and pressures of the arms requisite to its balance and support. On a slightly higher level, the breasts, together with the protrusion of the navel, serve to pull the volume of the body forward in three conical thrusts that parallel the horizontal positions of the legs and arms, but are variations of their shapes. The head is the crucial directional and balancing form in the composition as a complete unit. It reaffirms the horizontal thrusts below, and presents an important relationship to the globular shape and volume of the bowl. It is also marked off as a forward projection by the lateral design of the hair crest. Thus, the jutting forms are restated in varied shapes, volumes, and accents. A solid anchoring mass rises from, and is integrated with, the legs as a moderately heavy body, which is of vertical importance. This is continued in the heavy shape of the neck. A relationship exists between the rounded shapes of the bowl, the head, and the back of the hairdress. The backward thrust of the hairdress plays the subtle role of bringing the bowl form into a satisfactory state of equilibrium with the other balanced elements in the design. Surface planes are strong and continuously fluid but, as the profiles show, without modulation. The work is carved in a moderately light wood, and given a dull, dark-brown finish.

This type of figure, whether kneeling, seated, or in some instances squatting with a bowl, represented a benevolent mendicant spirit. The Baluba were motivated by the need for protection at times of crises, such as during the later stages of pregnancy or at childbirth, when a woman was unable to work in the fields. At that time, the bowl was placed in front of her dwelling so that passers-by could put objects of value in it to help the family over their time of difficulty. Out of respect for the spirit for whom it was made, it was used in comparable ways at other times as well, and functioned as a symbol of need or of beneficent spirit help.

Standing female figures, some of which serve as decorative adjuncts to utilitarian objects (e.g., the central shaft of a bow-rest, or as in this example, as the support for a small mortar set on top of the head), also display central Baluba style (Fig. 38). By comparison with the bowl figure, this small sculpture, even though generally organic in concept, has certain schematizations, particularly in the shape of the looped arms, the hands, and the pattern of the facial features. The proportions are those often found in standing figures in Negro African art: heavy, short legs; a long body with short arms; a heavy neck; and an enlarged head. These Baluba figures often have the strict frontality broken, as here, by a twist in the length of the torso and a slight turn of the head. In other respects, however, this object agrees fully with central Baluba style.

170

38 Eastern Congo, Baluba, standing figure.

A distinctly local style, possibly coming from one particular atelier, has justifiably been recognized as the Buli style, named for the site where it is believed to have been localized.[21] The majority of examples of Buli-type

39 Eastern Congo, Baluba, Buli-style stool figure.

figures are now in the collection of the Musée du Congo Belge at Tervueren, although this figure from the Linden Museum compares favorably with any of them (Figs. 39, 40). Buli-style figures appear as kneeling, mendicant forms or as supports for stools. They usually represent a very thin, almost emaciated, elderly woman with very long legs, a short body, long arms terminating in extremely large flattened hands and fingers, and a very large head. They are carved in a relatively heavy hardwood which is given a dark-brown finish.[22]

40　Side view of Fig. 39.

Characteristic of Buli style is the stress placed on the hard bony construction and on the meager fleshy forms between the bones and the loose covering of skin. The slightly textural rendering of surfaces is used with great success to depict the skin quality. While the expressive concentration is, as usual, on the head, there is a complete integrity in the over-all expression of an aging woman. The head shape is distinct from that of the central Baluba style, sharing only the low and receding forehead as it slopes back to the high hairline. But this form is more acutely flattened in the Buli heads. The head shape is long and juts out sharply over the body; the cheekbones are prominent, geometric shapes which continue to the nose and have, as their upper limits, the sharp edges formed by the sunken eye area. The eyebrows, carved as thin, high-relief lines, are set well above the eye area, and curve abruptly downward on either side of the nose, while the eyes, as small, ovoid relief forms, are expressed in organic association with the facial depth, and are shown with the upper lid almost closed. The nose, long and concave, has its origin at the margin of the forehead surface high above the eyes; it terminates in a sharp form, and is flanked on either side by differentiated, expanded nostrils. Two thin-lipped shapes projecting abruptly in a nonnaturalistic manner above the meager chin represent the mouth.

In characteristic Baluba fashion, an elaborate hairdress, marked by a decorated fillet at the hairline, balances the overhanging chin by its reverse projection into space. The Buli hairdress, well illustrated in this figure, is distinguishable from all others by its four huge petal-like shapes which define, by their outline, a circular area at the back within which is inscribed an equalarmed cross. This motif is created by the use of forms representing strands of hair pulled from side to side, and crossing from top to bottom. Another conspicuous element of this style is the great exaggeration of hands and fingers to increase their functional significance as supports for the sides of the stool top, the central part of which rests on the axial line of the figure, on top of the hairdress.

The numerous Baluba substyles show varying degrees of influence from these two major style classifications of Buli and central Baluba. They lack, however, the organic integration, the meaningful balance and sets of relationships between the forms, and the often subtle refinements of composition that are so much a part of central Baluba style. Also, they fail to create the expressive power so sensitively rendered in the concordance of physical forms and the spirit of their content which mark the achievements of Buli artistry. From this failure to comprehend the essential elements of these styles, came a tendency either to exaggerate or to omit their significant features, some of the works produced by the substyle groups being blocky, geometric attempts at comparable forms.

The distinctive, strongly sculptural, and aggressive art style of the Badjokwe tribes suggests certain relationships with the Congo region. It is an historical fact that these people, who inhabited the territory south of the Central Congo area, in the northeastern part of Angola, at the time of European contact, had at one time penetrated into the Central Congo and lived in the southern part of the Kasai-Sankuru region.[23] From their contact with the cultures of this region, they must have absorbed, and perhaps exerted, some influences. The most important aspects of their style are apparent in the free-standing figures which may have functioned as ancestor and/or power figures (Fig. 41). Frequently moderate in style, the Badjokwe sculptures are impressive in scale and vigorous in their interpretation of an aggressive, dynamic reality. Each part of the figure, from the feet to the head, is conveyed by a bold, active shape that is well integrated with its neighboring part to construct a formidable and energetic figure. Even the few defined details are established as comparably large and vigorous elements; so too are the oval loops which mark off the eye and mouth areas. The hairdress, with its lateral loops and the shapes extending to the back, is rendered in the same bold scale. Also distinctive of this style is the flexion of parts such as the ankle, knee, and elbow joints, and the sharp angle and twist of the head which, together, add up to an explosively powerful quality. There is an obvious unity of approach in the treatment of body parts and the handling of facial features; the aggressiveness of the latter, at times appearing to have an animalistic quality, refers to the power of the Badjokwe warriors as portrayed by stylistic traditions.

The wood used in these sculptures was hard and close-grained. To this they gave a textural quality by not refining the surfaces to remove the tool marks. Any handling of this type of wood is bound to give it a surface polish; but these figures seem to have been additionally stained to a very dark color, and the surfaces polished further by constant handling. The vigor and power of these figures, though not their forms, relate Badjokwe sculptures with both the Kwango River and the Central Congo style areas. But, at the same time, they establish this art tradition as an independent style.

The relationships and influences of any style center can become vitiated and considerably modified in the art forms of marginal areas. This was certainly true of the art tradition developed by the Warega[24] peoples of the eastern to northeastern Congo area near Lake Kivu. Their style shows, in combination with distinctly northern features, what might be called provincial reflections of certain aspects of Baluba style; but these are admittedly minor and appear only in certain shapings of the facial area. The stylized, almost cubistic renderings of form, whether on masks, heads, or full figures in wood or in ivory, are shaped by a style unique to the Warega, despite the borrowings and blendings of other elements. The stunted body repeats, in a slightly enlarged, angular shape, the form of the head, as in this example (Fig. 42), while the body parts are, in typical fashion, roughly and abruptly indicated. The legs fuse on equal terms with the body, and the huge arms dangle down in a non-organic, expressive manner which establishes the character of the torso and main mass of the sculpture. The head conveys, by the rendering of its facial features and their relationships, an intensity of expression that is further developed by the design treatment of the body. The work, in its total form, is an abstraction; but it contains a directness of shape expression that results in a strongly sculptural appeal of very northern flavor.

Warega style thus partakes of both the Baluba expressive traditions and the simplified and variegated form developments of the northern Congo area. It is the essence of simplicity combined with a remarkable feeling for the relationship of parts. All the features and details

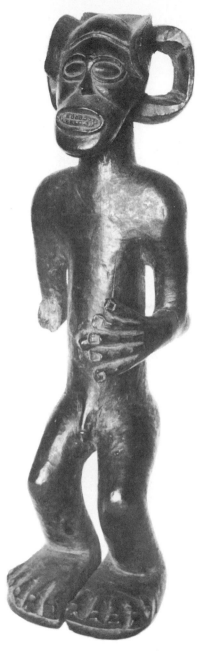

41 Southern Congo, Badjokwe, standing figure.

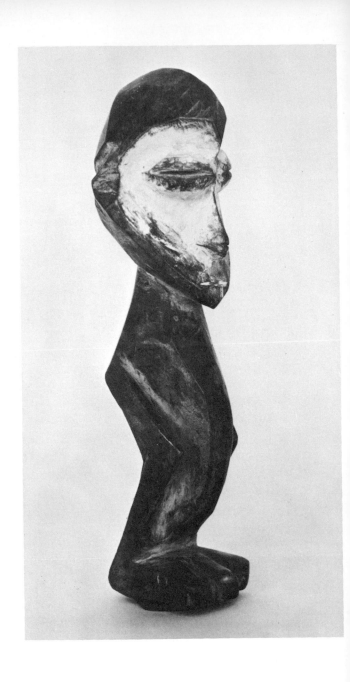

42 Northern Congo, Warega, standing figure.

of Warega figures are thus heavily stylized so that they contribute to a dynamic expression of nonnaturalistic form. This quality is heightened by the general roughness in handling of surfaces, in contrast to the few smooth and polished areas or shapes. Implicit in their style is the quality of reality in nonreality, of form expression through schematic designs. This is important because it imparts to Warega forms a vibrancy symbolic of reality.

In the northernmost parts of the Congo region, pockets of generally undeveloped local art styles are found, an exception being that of the Makere tribes, better known by the name of their leading clan, the Mangbettu. Much of their art, however (including large and elaborate pottery jars of geometric and effigy type, freshly made ivory objects, anatomically modeled figures, and wooden heads used as decorations for knife hilts and for the key arms of harplike musical instruments), reflects a strong European influence and acculturation or shows a purely decorative intent. One of the most satisfying of their decorative objects are the musical instruments, the key arms of which are terminated with a carved head, in typical northern fashion. The long and tapering cranium is shaped in accordance with the practice of the Mangbettu peoples of deforming their heads by binding them from birth on through adolescence. Some of these instruments have the entire key arm carved as a thin, attenuated human figure with small legs and feet projecting from the end of the sound box. Their neighbors, the Azande, had a comparable type of musical instrument, similarly decorated with a carved head. But, as the Azande did not practice head deformation, their sculptures are rounded and full-volumed.

Musical instruments of this type, decorated in a similar manner, are found among peoples as far west as the Fang tribes of Gabun and, in the northwestern part of the Congo region, among the Bangala. The art of the Bangala is typical of its area in the simplicity of shapes and detail. This is exemplified in a variant form of the harplike instrument of the region (Fig. 43). In this example, a carved human neck and head are attached to the top of the sound box, and the key arm springs from this form in a long, irregular curve. The neck and head are nonorganic, cubistic shapes; long, vertical, facetlike planes define the form of the neck; and the head is an ovoid shape, truncated by a sharp horizontal plane forming the lower portion. A concave plane cuts into the surface to provide the facial area. In characteristic fashion, a horizontally notched ridge carries from the crown of the head almost to the tip of the nose, suggesting a conventionalization of the frontal and nasal suture lines. The facial features are small, and defined in a typically Bangala manner. There is a suggestion, in the shaping of facial planes and features, of some relationship with the art style of the Fang to the southwest and of the Bambole to the southeast. But these analogies are, general at best, since Bangala style is far simpler and less sophisticated than that of the two southern groups.[25]

East of the long string of great lakes in east-central Africa, and north of the Congo limits proper, relatively little plastic art was produced. Only in a few remote fringe areas, which suggest long fingers of influence from the Congo, were any crystallized sculptural styles developed. Important among these are the arts of the Makonde tribes of the most southeastern part of Tanganyika, and of the Barotse and Basuto peoples of Northern Rhodesia. Aside from the Badjokwe, whose art style has already been discussed, and the Muserongo, whose work is at least partially related to the traditions of the Lower Congo area, the art of Angola has a decidely provincial flavor, an awkwardness of form, and an unsureness of expression.

Carved neckrests, common to the art of the Congo, especially in the central and eastern regions, also appear among the sculptured works of the Barotse in Northern Rhodesia, and are among their most accomplished art forms. As was usually the case, these decorated utilitarian objects were, in motivation, function, and meaning, of a personal-prestige significance. While some of them are purely geometric in design, others, as this fine

43 Northern Congo, Bangala, musical instrument.

44 East Africa, Barotse, neckrest.

example from the Florentine Museum of Anthropology and Ethnology, combine animal forms with geometric elements (Fig. 44). Although the water buffalo was the animal most commonly used by the Barotse, the animal subject of this work appears to be either a horse or, more probably, a zebra. The animal is rendered in highly stylized, geometric, decorative shapes: the legs, body, and neck, and the head in particular, have little reference to the shaping and articulation of natural forms. Simple oval outlines are incised to define the eyes; the head and neck are surmounted by a flat, curved crest to indicate the mane; and a deep groove at the end of the head equals the mouth. These details are of expressive importance only. To complete the entirely functional design, three vertical slats extend upward from the back of the animal to support the elegantly curved top of the neckrest, with two decoratively grooved pendants near either end. Carved in a hard, moderately heavy wood, the object was given a dark, brownish stain and polish. Aesthetic pleasure in this work derives from the variety of forms and from their relationships within the finely realized structural entity. The great volumetric shapes representing the legs satisfactorily enact their function as the main support, and in addition, the forms have clear relationships with the tapering volume of the head and with the relatively thin slats above, which carry the weight down to the supports. The balancing of the pendent forms underneath the top with the shape of the head and, to an extent, with the tail of the animal, and especially the fine pattern of negative spaces that exists between, below, and around the forms, also illustrate the principles of style which characterize these Barotse sculptures. This is a work of purely artistic aims, and even a brief analysis of it shows to what degree these aims have been successfully fulfilled by the forms and designs typical to the art traditions of the Barotse peoples.

2

OCEANIA

In 1947, just after World War II, the mention of primitive art turned the thoughts of many back to the Solomons, Lae, Hollandia, and Rabaul. At least one individual in almost every group had recently come from firsthand experiences in these areas, and had even seen or acquired some art object. Just a decade earlier, any one of these areas would have been difficult for most persons to place geographically. In the early years of the century, it was just as difficult for most people to place

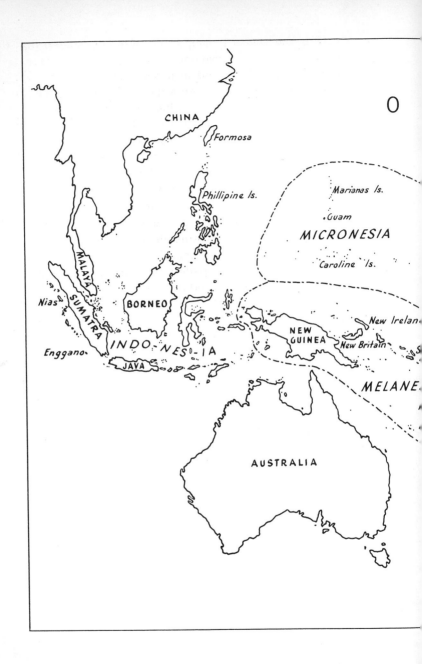

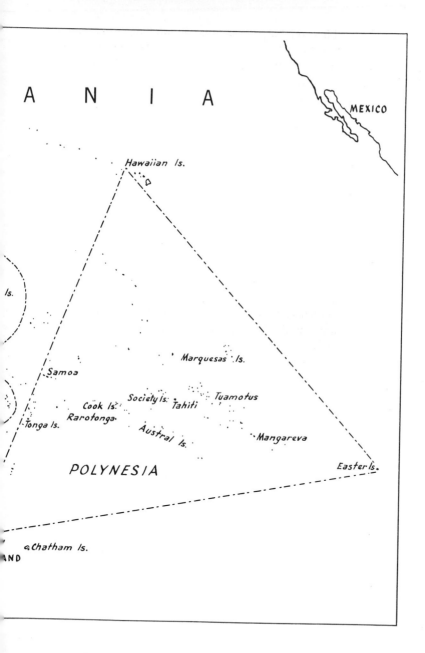

ANIA

MEXICO

Hawaiian Is.

Marquesas Is.

Samoa

Society Is. Tahiti Tuamotus

Cook Is. Rarotonga

Tonga Is. Austral Is. Mangareva

POLYNESIA Easter Is.

Chatham Is.
AND

Is.

the great island of New Guinea or the long chain of the New Hebrides Islands. Historical circumstances, although often grim, have therefore frequently had a bearing on common geographical knowledge.

Unlike Africa, the far larger area of the Oceanic world contains many heterogeneous cultures. This diversity extends even to its ethnic groups, of which there are five. The land masses, when divided according to distribution of these ethnic groups, can be charted as: 1) Indonesia, which, for our concern, includes only those island areas off Southeast Asia showing pockets of development little influenced by the great Asiatic civilizations; 2) the mostly large and mountainous islands to the east of Indonesia which have been called Melanesia because of their dark-skinned populations; 3) the subcontinent of Australia with its distinct ethnic group and culture; 4) the small atoll islands to the north of Melanesia, known as Micronesia; and 5) the many islands, both large and small, of the central, southern, and eastern Pacific, known as Polynesia. In this vast area the cultural variations make it nearly impossible to offer any valid generalizations.

The multitude of diverse societies encountered in Oceania at the time of European contact in the late eighteenth and early nineteenth centuries was obviously the result of the intermingling of the various waves of peoples who had for thousands of years spread eastward across the Pacific from south and southeastern Asia. Different physical stocks participated in these prolonged migrations: Australia was peopled by an ancient, dark-skinned Caucasian stock, possibly related to the Dravidians of India and the Ainu of Japan; the population of Melanesia derived from two Negroid groups, the Papuans and the Melanesians. The migrations to the Polynesian islands brought mostly Caucasian peoples, with some admixture of Negroid and Mongoloid blood; while the inhabitants of Micronesia were basically of Mongoloid stock but with admixtures from other peoples. In all probability these different physical stocks came from specific locales in Southeast Asia. The migratory groups were relatively small, and the process of populating the Oceanic islands occurred over long periods of time. This means that the cultural elements brought even by peoples of a common stock were by no means similar. It was the intermingling of these peoples in the Pacific that was responsible in part for the multitude of diverse cultures found by colonists, explorers, and missionaries from the Western world. They also found that, throughout the course of many centuries, the peoples of Oceania had developed an amazing variety of unique and arresting art styles. In fact, the only major cultural phenomenon shared by many of these island groups was the existence of an art tradition, despite extreme stylistic variations, with a rich repertoire of objects ranging from fragile shell pendants to huge stone carvings, and from near-naturalistic portraits to grotesque and fabulous forms.

Throughout this vast and variegated Pacific island world, five basic modes of expression are discernible in the plastic arts: 1) a two-dimensional, incised or low-relief carving or painting on a flat surface; 2) a three-dimensional, sculptural expression stressing planes and volumes; 3) a polychromatic rendering of designs or areas within a work to represent ideas or relationships other than those of the carved forms to which they are applied; 4) a compositional expression of life forms, carved and/or painted, and arranged either vertically or horizontally; and 5) an expression involving designs and forms, often of a pierced character, creating an aerial effect suggestive of actual existence and movement in space. Some of the Oceanic art styles combine two or more of these modes while others employ only one. A consideration of the art in terms of these modes of expression is one way to give some unity to a discussion of the multiplicity of Oceanic art styles. In a general examination of this sort, it seems advisable to concentrate on the two major areas of Melanesia and Polynesia, and to relate these in brief to Indonesia, Australia, and Micronesia.

187

Scientific evidence makes it clear that all the important and basic aspects of Pacific island culture came from the west, that is, from the Asiatic mainland, either directly or by way of the island archipelagoes off the coast. This statement is not meant to suggest that all fragments of Oceanic art style can be directly traced to mainland origins, since, as will be considered later, there are far too many indeterminables. It is important to note, however, that all of the basic modes of art expression found in Oceania can be seen in the art of the Indonesian area to the west, although these modes of expression were not necessarily peculiar to or developed there. Some can be traced to other inland areas, and others shown to be modifications of influences from still different sources. It is in these Southeast Asian island areas, in fact, that the diffusionists are able to find spurious suggestions of historic relationships. On a closer examination it is clear that such "historic" relationships are actually analogies common to the entire area. It is obvious that some elements would persist in one form or another in the majority of Southeast Asian art styles. They may in fact be considered endemic to the art traditions of the entire area of Southeast Asia, and so cannot be confined as influences from one particular locale. A few art forms can be localized to some degree, thus allowing for semispecific strains of influence to be traced into the eastern Pacific area.

Of the five major expressive modes common to Pacific island art, the three-dimensional, sculptural type appears in many "primitive" Indonesian regions: in the ancestor figures of Nias, in the sculptures from the island of Leti, and in works of other areas as well. It also appears in a sculptural fragment of a house carving from the island of Enggano, off the southeast coast of Sumatra (Fig. 45). The energetic figure is expressed almost in the round; only the back of the head and shoulders, the buttocks, and the feet connect it with the plank background. All expression here is in terms of sinuously active, quasi-organic shapes which exist as potently expressive, sculptural forms. The power of the whole figure is obvious

45　"Primitive" Indonesia, Enggano Island, house carving.

from the explosive qualities of the component parts. It is an exceptionally fine illustration of the three-dimensional mode of sculptural expression. Examples of relief carving abound in almost every area; while the poly-chromatic mode of expression is particularly well repre-sented in the vigorously carved and painted gable ends of Batak houses in Sumatra. Red and black, the only colors used in most of these carvings, have nevertheless an important coloristic effect. White was occasionally used in some of these and other Batak architectural decorations including, for example, the very special houses.

The other basic modes of expression also appear in primitive Indonesian art: two-dimensional expression is evident largely in the decorative, sculptured forms of almost every area; Batak shamans' staffs and various other objects from this area illustrate clearly the compo-sitional mode of expression. Pierced or aerial forms appear in various art manifestations throughout Indone-sia, for example, on the Batak staffs, where there is usually an accomplished handling of vertically oriented design, and in comparable examples of both horizontal and vertical design arrangements used to decorate Borneo shields. Not all of these forms are aerial compo-sitions. The latter mode of expression is mostly found in house finials from Indonesia and in other decorations of magical or emblematic significance, all of which have a pierced character. The influences from Indonesia are thus readily discernible in various art expressions in Melanesia, particularly along the northern coast of New Guinea.

a MELANESIA

Melanesia comprises hundreds of islands, large and small, high and low, the most important of which are New Guinea, New Britain, New Ireland, the Admiralties, the Solomons, the New Hebrides, New Caledonia, and Fiji. Certain generalities pertain to Melanesia and not to the whole of the Pacific area. The islands lie close to the equator and have a hot, humid climate and rich, luxuri-ant flora. Throughout the area, the economy is based on a small-garden type of agriculture, supplemented in

190

several regions by fishing. The people lived in small villages near their gardens and, with few exceptions, were loosely organized socially and politically into small village and tribal groups. Characteristic of Melanesia was the intervillage and tribal warfare which tended to isolate each small group from its neighbors. Many of these peoples were further isolated by the customs of head-hunting and cannibalism, which prevailed sporadically in a number of regions. A factor further abetting the isolation of these groups resulted from the great number of different languages and dialects spoken throughout Melanesia. These cultural differences and variations certainly accounted for the small local culture complexes, each with its own distinctive art style and tradition.

In this large area, as in Africa, the art forms were closely related to social customs and religious concepts. All aspects of life and afterlife, it was believed, were under the control of supernatural, mythological, and ancestor spirits. Prolonged ceremonies were often performed. These might be enacted as memorials or as propitiatory or dedicatory rites to honor a variety of spirits and to insure their benefactions. Obtaining a control of the unknown forces of the universe also gave rise to certain magical practices. In all of these elaborate and dramatic Melanesian ceremonies, an extensive variety of art objects was required. Some of these objects were made anew for each ceremony, while others were refurbished and used again and again. The art form in either case was usually dramatic or spectacular in appearance, and of strong, expressive quality.

Immediately to the east of Indonesia lies the thirteen-hundred-mile-long island of New Guinea. In some respects, the art produced there, especially along its western and northern shores, is a continuation of the basic art traditions found in the primitive areas of Indonesia. For a considerable span along the northern coast, and in the islands to the north and west, the most important art forms are the ancestor figures. These were objects made to contain the spirit of the ancestor after death. Parallels for these sculptures existed in many

46 Melanesia, North Dutch New Guinea, Geelvinck Bay,
korovar figure.

192

areas of Indonesia where the concept also prevailed that, after death, the spirit of the dead could be contained within a receptacle, such as a figure, which had been made for that purpose.

In the Geelvinck Bay district of northern New Guinea and its adjacent islands, ancestor figures were very common. These forms diverged greatly in stylistic particulars, but they all shared a few characteristics in common. Given the transliterated name of "korovar" by the Dutch, these ancestor figures (Fig. 46) have a huge head, often rectangular in over-all shape, into which, in some types, the entire skull of the deceased was fitted. In other types of korovar the actual skull replaced the carved head entirely, and was attached to the comparatively small carved wooden figure. The example from the Leiden Museum illustrates a particular variety and style common to certain of these figures. This type represents the main form as standing behind and firmly gripping an open grill-like "board." The lower-central segment of this board is occupied by a small carved standing figure clutching it at either side with outstretched hands. In common with the majority of other korovar sculptures, the technique is vigorous but unrefined. Both figures have a blocky, cubistic shaping of summarily differentiated parts combined in such a way as to create a tense, almost aggressive pose. The heads, particularly large in proportion to the main figure, have an exaggerated, blocky shape; and the way in which the face juts forward creates the impression that it is independent of the volume of the head. A low and abruptly receding forehead; the wide, concave facial planes below the high, blocky eyebrows; and the lack of chin development are all typical of this style. They are found together with a high, narrow nose that joins with the eyebrows and terminates in a long point that sometimes overhangs the mouth and that is flanked by massive nostrils. As in other examples of this style the mouth is shaped as a long, narrow oval extending across the entire width of the lower portion of the face; and just within its seemingly fleshless rim, two rows of pointed teeth are tightly

193

clenched. The larger, main figure may, because of the skull-like treatment of the head and the way the mouth is represented, have been intended to depict the deceased in his nonphysical, spirit role.

The rendering of the body and, particularly, of the open, bilaterally balanced scroll patterns of the grill-work board in front of the figure, both show a close Indonesian relationship. It is indisputable that these motifs, as well as the concepts of the korovar figures, were diffused along the northwestern coast of New Guinea from Indonesia together with various other design elements, house types, and probably the compositional and aerial modes of sculptural expression. These elements, it would appear, came into Melanesia by various routes and then combined with other elements and underwent numerous local adaptations over a long period of time. These created a totally new context within which the modified elements became scarcely recognizable. To credit Indonesia or other areas of Southeast Asia with paramount influences in the development of Melanesian art is only partially valid, since the elements that had diffused were so recombined and re-created to meet local needs and concepts that no single style can be said to owe even its basic character to these infiltrations of influences from the west. Geelvinck Bay korovar figures, for example, cannot certainly be considered a provincial form of Indonesian art. They have a different quality of expression and a considerably modified design character from like ancestor figures in Indonesia.

There seems little doubt that the Leiden figure functioned as a carving infused and permeated with the spirit content of the ancestor. Since early days of European contact, accounts from this region relate that at certain important functions the korovar figures were passed from hand to hand around the group, so that everyone present had physically touched them. By this means of physical contact, the ancestor spirits would be brought into personal participation in the function taking place.[26] In such instances, the spirit power once there was constantly present.

47   Melanesia, North Dutch New Guinea, Lake Sentani,
mother and child figure.

To the east of Geelvinck Bay, from the Lake Sentani
area of the north coast of New Guinea, the numerous
sculptural forms reveal a strong center of developed,
individual style. Figures such as the Basel Museum's
mother and child were used as architectural sculptures
(Fig. 47). The various art expressions from this area

195

include ovoid bowls, finely carved on their outer surfaces; numerous free-standing figures; and a number of crudely made but Miro-like, painted bark cloths depicting clan totemic insignia. All of these art forms are unique to the Lake Sentani region. Although carved in wood, the Basel example and others like it have a soft, ceramic-like, modeled appearance. The strange shaping of the jaw-line as it meets the cranium, the rubbery looplike arms, and the treatment of the lower leg and foot all suggest a modeled, ceramic technique. While the wood is moderately soft and easily worked, the technique is not that of wood carving; and the figures or figure compositions do not have the appearance of wood sculptures. All detail, such as the facial features, the hair indications, and arm decorations, is very tenuously incised on the surface. Compositionally, the figures have a naive awkwardness and an extremely tense, friable quality. The relationships between volume and volume, shape and shape, line pattern and line pattern are all close and bring the component parts of the composition together into a unified whole. Characteristic of Sentani style, and appearing in various other objects, including lime spatulas and ceremonial staffs, is the treatment of the head. The facial area is rather vaguely indicated. A straight horizontal cut defines the brows. Two incised circles represent the eyes and flank the nose, which is given as a flattened, uncertain form. An incised crescent, placed sometimes erratically near the end of the rounded chin, describes the mouth. There are other typical gaucheries in this style, such as the rendering of the long, animal-like feet. But Lake Sentani style has a consistency and sincerity of statement and an insinuating appeal in its artistic character.

Again along the north coast of New Guinea, but farther to the east, one of the richest of all primitive art areas centers in the region along and near the Sepik River. This art area may be roughly defined as extending to the north and south along the coast, from the mouth of the river and to either side of its banks for a long distance upstream. The repertoire of forms includes architecture, sculpture, painting, basketry, and clay modeling. They are among the most conspicuous features of the cultures in this region. The profusion of objects carved in wood by these peoples shows remarkable technical and expressive proficiency. They made free-standing figures ranging from only a few inches to over six feet high; numerous masks of almost the same size range; canoe prows carved with crocodiles; ceremonial stools supported by a large human figure, the upper half of the body extending above the seat as a back; vividly painted strips of bark and palm spathe; finely made large and small basketry masks; and many, many other types of carved and fabricated objects. Even bone, both human and, especially, the large leg bones of the cassowary bird, were carved in the round and incised. In this area probably more than in any other primitive art region the total effect of an art object depended heavily on the appending of extraneous materials to the carved or fabricated form. It was frequently necessary that shell, seeds, feathers, animal fur, grasses, and flowers be added to give the object its full significance. Various earth and vegetable pigments were used in much the same way. The art was, therefore, luxuriant and colorful.

It is possible to characterize Sepik River art style on the basis of numerous features that give it a certain homogeneity. Probably the most conspicuous common feature is the expression of spirit content in the forms. Although there is always an obvious basis in reality, the shapes are often combined in a weird or fantastic way to create arresting and dynamic effects. All of these Sepik forms have an outstanding originality of composition and expressive vigor. Typical, too, of this art tradition is the predominance and utilization of color for both descriptive and decorative purposes, with some vestiges of a symbolic color tradition being apparent. The homogeneity discerned in Sepik River art forms is thus of a qualitative nature rather than an artistic character. It appears in the way naturalistic forms are interpreted, dismembered, and then reassembled to form a very often dramatic, and always powerful, aesthetic expression. A wide range of earth and vegetable pigments was used to define and to describe details, and to depict symbolic designs on sculptured surfaces. This art may be said to be, in general, of strongly three-dimensional, sculptural nature, although all the major modes of artistic expression appear singly and in various combinations throughout the region.

The Sepik River area, despite the qualities of homogeneity, is a mélange of local or regional styles. However, in view of the deficiency in scholarly attempts to collate documented examples from specific localities, it is difficult to define or clearly separate the important local subcenters of style. From current knowledge available in literature, in records, and in tangible objects, it is clear that a good deal of diffusion of style elements occurred between the several areas. It is also evident that there were deep pockets of local style development. There was, for example, a coastal style, or perhaps a number of them, near the mouth of the Sepik, to the north of it, and to the south, including the area around the mouth of the adjacent Ramu River. Another subcenter in which at least one and very likely many styles evolved was situated in the middle reaches of the Sepik district, along the banks of the river and for some distance inland; while in the off-river areas such as the Keram and Yuat River regions, and in the Washkuk and Maprik (Prince Alexander) Mountain area, additional local centers developed. From an evaluation of illustrative examples from these major areas, an idea of the art style of the Sepik River region as a whole can be obtained.

A free-standing ancestor figure of the commemorative type, from the Hamburg Museum collection (Fig. 48), is an unusually fine illustration of the lower river or coastal style. This is, in every sense of the word, a descriptive work: all anatomical points of articulation such as the ankle bones, knees, and so forth, are clearly defined. Moreover, there is a description of musculature that appears to hang loosely on the bony armature of the emaciated forms. This interpretation, together with the

198

stooped shoulders, the angle of the head, and the rendering of facial forms and features, conveys a remarkably sensitive expression of age—of a tired and elderly man. Commemorative ancestor figures were usually, at best, generic portraits, but in this example, the head (Fig. 49) is so skillfully modeled that it has a strong, personalized expressiveness. Stylistically characteristic of this area of the Sepik is the exaggerated design and the deep, roughly defined relief carving of the scarification pattern which appears on the upper pectoral region and on the shoulders, a motif derived from common practices. Other details of the body, such as feet and hands, are suggested in a blocky, non-naturalistic manner. Also characteristic of these figures is the rough-textured finish given to all of the surfaces, particularly those of the body. This textural treatment was a matter of choice, since in certain parts of Melanesia, the surfaces are more smoothly finished. But it should be noted that all Oceanic sculpture made prior to, and in fact for some time after, European contact, was carved mostly with stone tools, supplemented in some areas by shark and rat teeth, and by shell. Various abrasives such as sand and sharkskin were used in a number of regions to achieve a smooth finish.

The pose of the Lower Sepik ancestor figure is typical. It is substantially frontal and rigid, but a few slight refinements should be observed which relieve both the frontality and the rigidity, notably the slightly lower slope of the left shoulder and the placement of the left hand a bit higher than and slightly further back than that of the right hand on the thigh. This creates a slight pull away from frontality, and the angle of the head, very slightly turned, further relieves the rigidity of the pose. There is in this figure a fine unity of expressive elements. It is in the head, however, that the aesthetic qualities, which raise this work to the rank of a masterpiece, are evident (Fig. 49). The hard, bony structure of the forms, covered only by a little flesh and the loose membrane of skin so typical of an aging man, is magnificently defined. Even the suggestion of the frontal suture on the forehead is

49 Detail, head of Fig. 48.

48 Melanesia, New Guinea, Sepik River, standing male figure.

200

delineated. Such bone structures as the orbital area, the cheekbone (zygomatic), and the thin, hard bridge of the nose are explicity stated. Naturalistic features, as the pierced nasal septum, with the resultant prolongation of the end of the nose, and the protruding, slightly off-center lips, add to the personalized quality of this sculpture. The entire surface of the facial area is modulated in a manner suggestive of a descriptive portrait. The carved flange around the face, with its roughly pierced holes through which some threading of cane is still extant, was intended, together with the tipped, conical headpiece, for the appendage of various extraneous materials such as leaves, shell, and feathers. These were attached to the carving when it was originally set up in commemoration of an important ancestor. At that time, red ochre of a full and rather dark shade was rubbed on the entire surface, giving a rich patina to some areas, particularly to the facial zone. Masks of similar form and treatment as well as figures and masks with a birdlike prolongation of the nose were also common to the coastal Sepik region and the lands adjacent to the neighboring, eastern Ramu River.

Of paramount importance to the entire Sepik territory were the great men's ceremonial houses. While several designs were developed for the architecture of these houses, they had a number of features in common. All were raised above the ground on heavy pilings, since the areas were flooded during the rainy season; and all had lofty front gables, some as much as fifty feet high, which frequently had distinctive sculptured or painted decorations attached. These buildings were particularly notable in the Middle Sepik area, and in the Maprik Mountain district to the west-northwest of the Sepik River. In the Middle Sepik, the great houses of the Iatmul peoples often had deep saddle roofs and asymmetrical gables, the front one sharper and higher than the rear one. A large, carved, and highly polychromed wooden mask was placed near the top of the front gable. The Maprik houses of the Abelam tribes were of a triangular ground plan, with a high, triangular front façade. The

50 Melanesia, New Guinea, Sepik River, Mundugumor mask.

upper three quarters of this was covered with sheets of Sago-palm bark, which were painted with alternating zones of stylized faces of clan spirits and geometric decorations. The basic colors of red-orange, white, and black, with some yellow, make these among the most colorful and spectacular of all primitive art forms.[27]

In both areas, the Tambaran cult was responsible for these fabulous houses and it is therefore necessary to understand something of this cult before the art of the region can be comprehended. Tambaran has been described as a mystery, barred to women, that embraces or is bound up with "tradition, community, ancestors, and the dead."[28] The Tambaran house is also the men's house, and only those who have undergone initiation rites into the cult and into the status of manhood are allowed to enter it.[29] The Maprik spirit figures in the house will be considered later.

Of the tribal styles in the Middle Sepik district, that of the Mundugumor, who inhabited the lands to the east along the Yuat River tributary, is highly distinctive. It embraces figures used as tops of sacred flutes and numerous masks, both of which were kept and used in the Tambaran house. Representing spirit beings of both ancestral and supernatural character as the spiritual sources of power, strength, and vitality, Mundugumor masks are among the most vigorous plastic creations of the Sepik area (Fig. 50). Heavy, explosive shapes describe the eyebrows, nose, and expansive open mouth. These are re-echoed by large protrusions on the sides of the forehead and small knobs above the corners of the mouth, while a high-relief area hangs below each eye and curves upward to the ears. These dramatic shapes are further stressed by being painted in a bright red-orange ochre; the other, similarly inflated area of the face and head are painted white. A teardrop-shaped relief form flattens the nasal ridge and ends at the bridge of the nose, which is sharply notched under the heavy, beetled protrusion of the eyebrows. From the bridge of the nose the relief area, painted a bright red-orange, moves up across the forehead, swelling into an irregular triangle that supports the rim of the hairdress cup with its clipped raffia filling. From the surface of this triangular form projects an ellipsoid area, depressed in the center, rimmed in black and painted with a white surface. The tuft of crisp, clipped raffia at the top of the mask, and the small bits twisted and depending from the ear area, are all that remains of the raffia and net costume once attached to the carving, the net covering the upper part of the wearer's body.

The aesthetic quality of this mask derives from the rhythmic relationships between powerful, dynamic, sculptural shapes and strong accents of color. The shapes are vigorous interpretations of human facial features, supplemented by enforcing, echoing forms such as the ridges over the eyes, the knobs near the mouth, and the ovoid shape at the top of the head which has an expressive relationship with the mouth. Seeing this mask for the first time, in the uncertain light of a Tambaran house, must have been an experience to remember forever.

Another example of the variety and aesthetic quality of Middle Sepik masks is well illustrated in the large sculpture reputedly from Kanganaman, farther up-river from the Yuat region (Fig. 51). In all probability this was a "spirit mask," that is, a face that was not shaped, pierced, or intended to be used as a mask. Rather it was suspended along an interior wall of a Tambaran house. It is painted a light red ochre with details picked out in white, and cowrie shell inlays in the eyes. Dominated entirely by a series of full and reverse curves that flow smoothly from one into the other, the large form (thirty-nine inches high) is particularly striking for its extreme narrowness from the frontal viewpoint. It expands from only a few inches at the lower part to scarcely six inches at the widest part of the head. The representation is typical of objects used in Middle Sepik Tambaran houses: a fabulous and expressive creation based on the fusion of human and birdlike features. The elongated upper jaw of the thin and tapering humanoid head is presented as a curving form that flows con-

51 Melanesia, New Guinea, Sepik River, Kanganaman mask.

tinuously until it meets the fairly straight prolongation of the lower jaw. Then it reverses direction, carrying the form out and down in a beaklike extension of the mouth area. The head of a hornbill is carved in the round at the base, and is attached to the loop formed by the conjunction of the upper and lower jaws and beaklike forms. From within the mouth a narrow tongue flicks out and down, producing yet another important curve in this striking medley of curvilinear patterns, until it joins the inner surface of the lower jaw. A single high crest curves out from the top of the head and is adjoined on either side by low, soft, flanking forms that move fluidly up from the sides of the head. Deep V-shaped incisions are used in various combinations as decorations for the front loop of the beak and for its back surface, as well as for the designs of the head crests. Finally, the high-relief carving of the eye establishes another important compositional curve, as it flicks up and back in a flame-like fashion.

The artistic properties of this mask comprise a varied, rhythmic, almost lyrical relationship of fluid but highly controlled curves that move over the surfaces and profiles to create and unite all of the shapes within one firmly integrated design. Strong accents of red mark the prolongation of the jaws, the crest on the head, and a small round dot on either side of the forehead, as well as a loosely hanging motif below the eyes. There is thus variation in the color definition as well as in the use of curves. It is one of the most striking of Sepik River masks, and a major work of primitive art.

The commemorative ancestor figure from the Lower Sepik expressed life forms strongly and entirely within the sculptural mode of interpretation. The two Middle Sepik masks, on the other hand, combined in a meaningful harmony the sculptural and the polychrome methods. The other modes previously discussed also appear in numerous art forms from this area, either singly or in varied combinations. Two objects, presumably used in dance or ceremonial rituals within the Tambaran house, are examples of the combination of sculptural, polychrome, and pierced modes in which various forms are assembled in a compositional whole. One (Fig. 52) is an object said to be carried in dances; the other (Fig. 53) was worn attached to a bark belt during the dance.

Fantasy in form interpretation, creation, and combination is a style element found in various of the art expressions from western Oceania. It appears in an accomplished and exciting way in the first of the dance objects mentioned above (Fig. 52). This work is composed of an attenuated human body, its arms and legs sharply flexed. The figure is surmounted by a proportionately huge and fantastic bird head, whose wide-open beak is connected by a slatted or vertebraelike area. From the end of the beak, a fish (defined in the Australia Museum catalogue as a shark) hangs downward with a grotesque, nonfishlike head; a spiky form protrudes from its mouth to terminate the fantastic design. Below the spine of the humanoid figure, a bifurcated shape connects at either side with the head of the fish form. All of the shapes in the composition are three-dimensional; that is, they exist completely in space. The whole is treated with an over-all polychromy in white, black, and red-orange, colors which animate the forms and give them added vibrancy and motion. A surrealistic weirdness and an unreality of being animates the whole form.

Comparable in the openness of its design and in the compositional integration of diverse forms, the dance-belt decoration (Fig. 53) is probably also from the Middle Sepik area. Like the ceremonial dance object it is carved in a hardwood, but in this case the color treatment is monochromatic, the forms having been rubbed in a bright red-orange ochre whose traces are still amply evident. The complex forms read, from top to bottom, as: 1) a proportionately large parrot head; 2) below this, clutching at a long, sharp hook which depends from the back of the parrot head, is a lizard, energetically moving

52 Melanesia, New Guinea, Sepik River, dance object.

upward, its tongue flicking out and its tail doubled back in a long loop; and 3) a roughly carved, very small, upside-down human head, which terminates the design by its placement beneath the bottom curved hook form. The two opposing hooks positioned at the top and bottom of the object served as the practical means for attaching the work to the bark belt. Notched designs, simulating the head feathers of the parrot and the back of the lizard, continue down both sides of the extending neck form below the bird head. In the eyes of all three heads, translucent mother-of-pearl shell is inlaid to represent the area surrounding the pierced pupil.

The forms on this belt decoration, probably of totemic significance, are rendered in the round, with superb sculptural control in the presentation of the varied shapes. The animal forms are expressed with vitality and action, and there is a fine integration of all the elements into an arresting, aesthetically exciting composition. Both these dance carvings are excellent illustrations of the artistic variety and vigor so typical of Sepik River art, qualities which, together with a sureness of technique, contribute greatly to the position accorded this area as one of the most important in the primitive world. The artistic achievements found here, as in so many style centers in the Pacific region, should refute once and for all the false idea that primitive artists created their forms in spite of poor stone, shell, and teeth tools. Rather, they achieved such quality in their work because their tools were well made and well shaped, and because of their proficiency in handling them.

In the Maprik Mountain territory some distance to the west and north of the Sepik River lived the Abelam peoples, whose art and culture should be included in the over-all Sepik River area. Within the great Tambaran houses were numerous polychrome sculptures and palm-spathe paintings depicting the ancestors and spirits from which the Abelam believed their virility and strength were derived. In some regions, the concept still prevails. Such sculptures are well exemplified by the life-size male figure (Fig. 54). The size of such objects ranges

53 Melanesia, New Guinea, Sepik River, dance-belt ornament.

from under to well over life size. Characteristic of the Abelam style is the compactness of the organic body design which is weakened by the arms as they loop forward under the chin. The large head is placed in an awkward and dubious functional relationship to the body. Typical, too, are the numerous descriptive and symbolic designs painted on the figure, the characteristic colors being yellow, red ochre, white, and black. The painting of the face, with its large central zone in bright yellow, is comparable to the face painting used for Tambaran dances.

Abelam style is an excellent illustration of the unsuccessful combination of two modes of artistic expression: sculpture and polychromy. The painted designs on these forms give them full meaning as figures representing the culture heroes, ancestors, and spirits. But while they create an intense, spiritual quality, particularly in the faces, they produce an over-all visual excitation that tends to fragment the object both compositionally and expressively. Although this is more marked in some examples than in others, it is a distinct feature that sets off the Abelam style-tradition from Sepik River art as a whole, despite numerous shared qualities.

Along the north coast of New Guinea, considerably to the east of the Sepik area, is the Tami Island-Huon Gulf region, where a distinctive, more decorative and schematic art style prevailed. Each clan in this area controlled by heritage a number of geometric and stylized designs with which they could decorate such objects as feast bowls, neckrests, and coconut-shell drinking cups, as well as depict ancestor spirits on masks and carvings for their men's houses. Black and white predominate in this area, with some red ochre used occasionally for accents. The use of color is particularly important in a discussion of Tami-Huon art because of its unique, symbolic-geometric significance for decoration of all the objects, but most especially for the masks. The mask type used in this part of New Guinea seems to relate technically, though not in form or expression, to a development found in the islands just to the north. It is pos-

54 Melanesia, New Guinea, Sepik River, Maprik, male figure.

sible that these northern islands may have provided a common source of origin for the technique; at the very least, there is some tie-in between the areas in the construction of bark-cloth mask forms.

Distinctive wooden and bark-cloth masks were made in the Tami-Huon area. Many of the wooden masks seem to have been used as spirit symbols and were placed on the roof of the "lum" or clan men's house. The bark-cloth masks, with their particular significance and important cultural association with techniques from the more northern island of New Britain, were used on Tami Island in rituals which took place every few years. During these rites, the ancestral-spirit beings would appear ceremonially. The rituals and their associated mask forms were motivated by general therapeutic aims, for which these objects functioned as symbols of a precarious ancestor-spirit beneficence. In meaning, the masks represented the tangible, physical evidences of this spirit power. The beings depicted by the masks were in the control of a secret society, and their appearance not only assured the people of the community of beneficence, but also upheld the power of the society. Thus the masks denote both a generally accepted spirit power, and a control by a special male group over the spiritual life of the entire group.

Usually a little over life size, the Tami Island bark-cloth masks (Fig. 55) were constructed of a palmwood armature which shaped the face over which a damp piece of bark cloth was stretched. When the cloth dried it became taut, and a very thin wooden nose and twisted strands of fiber representing ears was then affixed. The bark-cloth surface was painted in red and black with the designs characteristic of Tami art, including all the decorative elements, as for example: the rectangular patches across the forehead; the very typical forms around the eyes; the upward-curving designs flanking the nose; and the concentric delineations surrounding the mouth. On top of the expanding head, tufts of raffia appear, while sometimes a nose-stick of bone or wood was inserted in the pierced nasal septum. The open,

212

55 Melanesia, New Guinea, Tami-Huon area, bark-cloth mask.

aggressive mouth is represented as filled with teeth, creating a rather static quality of aggression. The expressive character of these bark-cloth masks is, in fact, in perfect agreement with the heavy quality of the figure-type used either by itself or on the neckrests.

The aesthetic expression of the masks, and of the decorative art of the Tami Island-Huon Gulf area, is one of static, stylized formal character, with an arresting, two-dimensional design applied to the surface of the sculptural forms. But the bark-cloth masks have an additional and particular importance for Melanesian art: they represent a link, by traditional accounts, with forms of New Britain, and with the geographically intermediate French and Siassi Islands art. Masks of this fabricated type, with an armature of light palmwood and a covering of painted bark cloth, are distinctive art forms, particularly of the Baining peoples who inhabited the Gazelle Peninsula on the north-northeast side of New Britain. But it must be remembered that there is a constructional relationship only; Tami masks show no real stylistic affinities with Baining masks.

Also traditional objects, in the repertoire of Tami-Huon art, are the ceremonial bowls, which have some of the most distinctive decorations in western Oceania. They are carved in a hard, gray-black palmwood in a variety of shapes and sizes. In general, they are carved as ovoids, with decorative handles at either end and a rim of decoration, continuing the line of the handles, incised along the sides. Some of them, as this fine example (Fig. 56) from the Australian Museum in Sydney, are double bowls. The two parts of the bowl, the handles at either end, and the rim around the sides, are sculpturally realized shapes. The life forms apparent in the design comprise serpent forms carved along the sides, fish-serpent motifs along the bottom beyond the handles, and an extremely stylized head form at the end of each handle. In objects of this type, not only do the incised geometric designs show clan alliance, but each clan

56   Melanesia, New Guinea, Tami-Huon area, double bowl.

artist had the right to affix his own insignia to the bottom of these bowls, this being in effect a signature. Hence these are among the few objects of primitive art which can be ascribed to a particular artist. The "signature" is usually an abstract design intelligible only to the members of the artist's clan.

Each bowl design from this area is unique, created by varying and recombining the limited designs of Tami style. The gray-black of the palmwood contrasts richly with the white lime rubbed into the incised designs, and in this respect suggests comparison with the decorated lime spatulas from the Massim area just to the east. This is substantially a very rich two-dimensional art style, which reveals the possibilities of a successful fusion of the mode of sculpture in the round with that of relief carving.

Despite the traditional cultural relationships, evidenced by the shared construction of bark-cloth masks, the art traditions and styles of New Britain are distinctly different in appearance and in formal and expressional relationships from those of Tami-Huon. The bark-cloth masks of the Baining, mentioned above, display none of the heavy or static qualities associated with Tami forms. Instead, they seem to be animated fantasies. Varied in size and shape, some are conical forms of about three feet in height; others have a large, impaled umbrella-shape measuring upwards of six feet in diameter surmounting the cone. The color range is limited to varying shades of darker brown applied restrictively to the natural tan of the bark cloth with a red ochre and/or black in some few examples.

Neighboring to the Baining, in the northern part of New Britain, the Sulka tribes evolved one of the most unique and spectacular mask forms of Melanesia. These have previously been discussed for their motivation, function, and meaning.[30] They must now be considered for their materials and style. These masks, too, are composed of a light palmwood frame, but instead of bark cloth, the outer surfacing is made from pith, derived from the reeds of the area, which is stitched together in

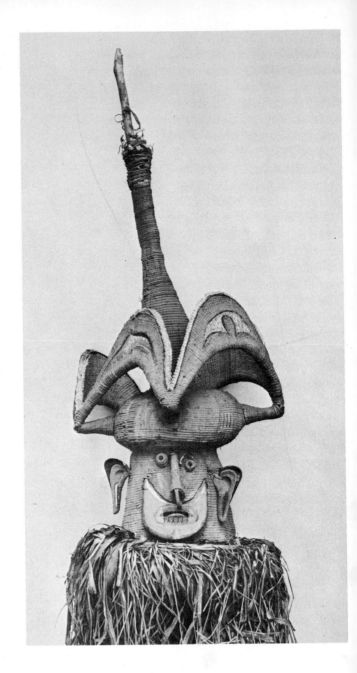

57   Melanesia, New Britain, Sulka, mask.

rows. The appearance of this pith surface frequently leads to a confusion and identification of it as basketry. There is very little to suggest any naturalistic basis of form in these masks. Rather, imaginative fantasy has been used to change the life forms into semiabstract, almost surrealistic facial or pseudo-facial features. These Sulka mask forms are among the most nonnaturalistic combinations of shapes found in primitive art. This even carries through to the use of colors: a bright, brick red is usually found in juxtaposition with an acid green. These hues, unfortunately, are impermanent and generally fade, as has happened to most of the examples currently in museum collections (Fig. 57).

Although New Britain seems to have been the original area in which the technique of composite construction evolved, as illustrated by their bark-cloth masks and those of the Tami-Huon region, the most important center for the development of this mask type is located in the Papuan Gulf district of New Guinea. This is an extremely large area, almost a thousand miles long, on the southern coast of east-central New Guinea. Its most characteristic art styles are found in the middle section of the extensive Gulf coast and around to the west in the Purari Delta region. In them, a very strong relationship is revealed with the formal traditions of the southwestern end of Dutch New Guinea. In fact, there is an almost continuous art province, with certain variations in style, extending from the westernmost part of South Dutch New Guinea through the area west of the central Papuan Gulf region. The basic character of this style is well established in the art forms created by the Mimika and the Asmat peoples who inhabit the southern part of Dutch New Guinea.

The art appears on numerous flat shieldlike boards; on ceremonial canoe-shaped dishes; on drums; and particularly on poles often more than twenty feet high. This was a highly symbolic and abstract art style for which, in each particular area, a human figure type was developed together with certain recognizable animal forms conventionalized and schematized to the point of fantasy. It was also very dynamic and powerfully charged with meaning. The various objects were required for use in initiation rights or, in some area, in rituals associated with head-hunting. In both cases the motivations grew largely out of the almost compulsive need for power and balancing of power, so that there could be a cultural security and survival, a continuity and stability. In function, the art brought alive these power sources and brought the ceremonial participants tangibly into their presence. Thus, by the process of osmosis, the necessary powers were psychologically if not actually acquired.[31] It is apparent that the significance of the symbolic-abstract content of this art was to a large extent understood by the peoples of the area.

Shields, which were used in various ceremonial ways, represent the full character of the art perhaps better than any other forms from this region (Fig. 58). They are carved in a moderately heavy wood and vary in thickness from less than an inch to more than an inch and a half; in height, from three to more than five feet. The most usual shape is an elongated, irregular ovoid with a rounded or flattened form at the top. The design suggests a nonsculptural origin for this style: the design field is surrounded by a wide border rendered in relief; within this border, the entire background field is depressed, that is, cut away in a lower relief plane; and on this depressed field, the designs are then carved with a wide outline that projects to the surface plane of the raised border. The heavy outlines define and emphasize the symbolic design elements, which are filled in with brown-tans or red ochres. This brings the symbols into the proper visual significance by setting them off against the lightly washed white of the background. Very few details, and only the most important ones, are given; and these are set within the background field in such a way that the visually arresting, esoteric imbalance of active elements yields a powerful and expressive vigor to the design. Few sharp angles appear in these reliefs, but the curves are all of a free, vibrating irregularity, most of them with an angular or tense character. In some

58 Melanesia, New Guinea, Asmat, shield.

219

designs, as in this example, bird heads, hand forms, and a few other elements seem substantially derived from a dismemberment of natural forms into separate units of shape which are then recombined and expressed in a virile, dramatic manner. The lines, margins, and details are not regular, nor are they refined in their delineation; but rather, they are roughly hewn ,enhancing the vigorous and dynamic character of the object.

Very different in form, but somewhat related in character, is the rather elaborately decorated drum with its hourglass shape (Fig. 59). An enormous, stylized lizard-monster is carved on one side of the drum and functions as a handle. It is rendered with all of the power and vigor so characteristic of this southern Dutch New Guinea art style. The animal form has such a stylization and fantastic handling of parts that it becomes an artistic creation, possibly based on aspects of natural form, but free in its interpretation from all representational restrictions imposed by reality. The hourglass drum is a type common to many areas of Melanesia; but the spidery, vibrant character of this form is unique. In meaning, it has reference to a supernatural accomplice, and thus has a singular significance.

In both the shield and the drum designs, the elements are dramatically and dynamically creative, derived from an original source in nature but re-created in the style idiom of the area. The drum is one of the most interesting and artistically satisfying designs of this type of musical instrument in Melanesia for its vibrancy of created "life" forms, the variety of its shapes, and their interrelationships. In this example, too, the strongly delineated, two-dimensional character of South Dutch New Guinea art is of paramount aesthetic importance. The subtle relief treatment used to define the forms and details is an artistically significant variation of the handling of surfaces and incised patterns; and when applied to the three-dimensional forms, they have more real importance than the free shapes themselves.

Between this region and that of the Papuan Gulf to the east, various art styles of considerable interest were

59 Melanesia, South Dutch New Guinea, drum.

221

evolved. While these show some relationship with the art of South Dutch New Guinea, they also developed individual style characteristics, particularly in the trans-Fly River and Torres Straits areas. In this general examination of Melanesian art, it is not feasible to examine all of the art traditions that prevailed. Thus, the styles of these areas, plus the arts of the Admiralty Islands to the north and west of New Guinea and various other off-shore islands, will not be given any detailed consideration. The most typical art forms of each major area have had to be selected for their representative qualities.

The most characteristic of the art styles in the Papuan Gulf region was developed in the Orokolo area to the east of the Purari Delta. The motivation, function, and meaning of this art has been discussed previously.[32] In this area, large and small masks and other ceremonial objects used in the great spirit ceremonies have a technological relationship with some of the art forms to the west, but in particular with the Tami-Huon and New Britain areas to the north, as indicated earlier. As with the Baining examples from the latter region, the large Orokolo masks, often over twelve feet high, were constructed of a palmwood armature over which dampened bark cloth was first stretched and then stitched into place and lashed to the framework. When dry, designs were appliqued with strips of cane onto the taut surface. Unlike the abstract, symbolic design forms of South Dutch New Guinea, these Orokolo patterns and motives combine angular and curvilinear elements. The lower segments of the larger masks (Fig. 60) and the major portions of the smaller masks from this area (Fig. 61) are devoted to geometric or fantastic facial features, all of which have certain expressive elements in common.

On the front surface of the large "hevehe" ceremonial masks, the appliqued design denotes historical or mythological associations with the subject of the mask. These are expressed on the lower facial area of the design. And in contrast to the practice of the western Gulf coast style, the areas or designs marked off by the stitched-on

60 Melanesia, New Guinea, Papuan Gulf, hevehe mask.

223

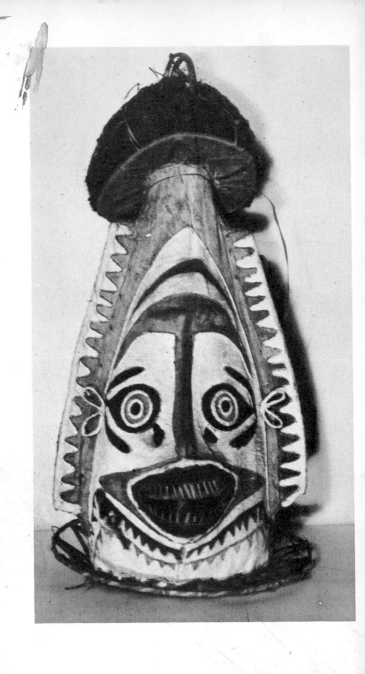

61 Melanesia, New Guinea, Papuan Gulf, mask.

224

cane strips do not constitute the limits within which the defining color is applied. On the contrary, the wide, appliqued strips are themselves painted and carry the design. The area between—that is, the background—is left unpainted in the natural, off-gray shade of the bark cloth. Color on central Papuan Gulf objects is often of a delicate, pastel shade, although some of the masks have a strong red-black-white character. Typical of these masks, regardless of size, is the apparent bilateral symmetry. Upon closer examination, however, this proves to be an illusion produced by the balancing of asymmetrical forms and design elements in a highly skillful manner. The motifs used in Papuan Gulf mask designs are limited, almost to the same degree as in the Tami-Huon style, to a few dentated forms, irregular spirals, and parallel straight or curved linear elements. Here too, as noted earlier, the design complexes are owned by the clans; and the method of combining them is a clan prerogative. The successful and spectacular achievements observable in the arrangement and assemblage of design elements are important factors in assessing the expressive quality of this art tradition, since by their particular effects the identities of clan affiliations are recognized in the objects. Thus effect and expression are requisite to function and meaning in this style area.

Papuan Gulf style is one of the most homogeneous of all New Guinea style centers. Whatever the form being created, the same basic stylistic pattern prevails. In the characteristic shields (Fig. 62) of this area, for example, the technological handling of the wooden plank that forms the object is in complete agreement with the mode of carving found in the western part of South Dutch New Guinea. That is, the outline of the design is carved in relief and projects above the surface level, so that the design elements stand out from the background. But unlike the western custom, where the areas between the design forms were painted, here it is the projecting design parts that are painted. The background falls back even further, painted as it is with a light whitewash. The shape and construction of over-all form used for this type

62 Melanesia, New Guinea, Papuan Gulf, shield.

226

of shield, with its irregular notch at the top, is of considerable importance, particularly with regard to the decoration of the two "wings." In this area of New Guinea, the bow and arrow was the major weapon. As a consequence, the shields varied in size from eighteen inches to over three feet in height. The important function of these objects was, of course, to have the visual image of a protective power spirit facing the enemy and, more important, as a tangible barrier to harm which was held in front of the warriors. These Papuan shields have, therefore, an important functional significance in addition to their artistic quality.

Also characteristic of this area are the many variously shaped ceremonial boards. Some are very small and strongly resemble the rather thin, elongated ovoid bull-roarers, so typical of this entire area, which can be twirled around and around by a cord tied through a hole in the top to emit a weird, screaming noise in the process. The ceremonial boards range from one-and-a-half to approximately three feet in height; and they generally have a snubby hand-hold at the base, and a bit of a nubbin at the top. Between these terminal points the boards swell out in various degrees of curvature, some being quite flat, while others are ovate and curve from side to side or even from top to bottom. It would seem that some of these objects were taken from ancient, famous canoes. Regardless of their sources, however, the designs were almost always composed of either a very conventionalized human figure or head. The full-figure type of decorated boards originated, in most cases, from the area to the west of the Purari Delta, although certain examples were made further to the east. The object now being discussed (Fig. 63) is an excellent illustration of the stylized full figure common to the traditional design style of the Delta region and to the west. It is carved in the same manner as the shields: all of the design and representational elements project in low relief from the surface; the ridge of the nose is here the highest point of projection. The typical facial features of central Papuan Gulf style appear in stark nakedness

against the flat white field; an inverted anchor form signifies the forehead; concentric circles with a solid center denote the eyes. The area around the eyes, in this example, hangs down as a sharp, teardrop form defined, as in the rest of the board design, by relief rims. The nose develops as a thin ridge from the top of the anchor-shaped forehead; and it is connected to a very wide oval shape containing the stressed mouth with its sharply but crudely indicated teeth. The usual delimiting facial border is missing in this example, with the rather surprising result that the forms have a more active and forceful expression than usual. Below, all of the body shapes are depicted in profile, and a crude attempt is made at indicating joint articulations. The forms of the navel and genitalia are emphasized, and the hands and feet are each given their five digits. The lack of an outline definition of the facial area is the expressive tour`de force of the carving: the face appears to be of an unreal, fluid character, moving uncontrollably and aggressively in the spatial setting of the design. Strong tones of red, black, and white are the colors employed on this as on most of these ceremonial boards.

The true use of these ritual objects is not too clearly known. It is certain that they were power sources, and that they were necessary to the handling or the control of power. Beyond that, it would seem, is mere speculation. The fact that these boards were greatly esteemed indicates strongly that, as with the Maprik Tambaran objects, they had a supernatural spirit-ancestor meaning. In function, they probably lent, by their symbolic and representational presence, access to vital spiritual forces. It is known that there was, according to the religious beliefs, a rapport between the clan members and the sources of power and aid as depicted by art objects. Recognition of this relationship, which to be effective must be constantly maintained, is essential for an understanding of Tambaran creations and other

63 Melanesia, New Guinea, Papuan Gulf, ceremonial board.

sacred art forms from this section of Melanesia. The rapport, and its constant maintenance, are somewhat analogous to the relationships which for some American Indian tribes existed between the tangible art symbols of their supernatural helpers and their sources of power and group or individual welfare.

All of these central Papuan Gulf art forms are created substantially in the two-dimensional mode of expression, and all of them serve as symbolic, abstract presentations of traditional clan subject matter. As in the art found to the west of this area, Papuan style lacks a controlled definition of design outlines, and because of that it has a powerful quality of expression that results in an appearance of outstanding vigor and an animated, creative force. It would seem, however, that the technique of creating these two-dimensional designs on the surface by the appliqueing of cane strips is more in keeping with a fabricated style than with relief sculpture. The expressively depicted content of south coast New Guinea art has that essence of subconscious force characteristic of New Britain and, to a certain extent, of some art forms from the Sepik River area. In contrast with the art of Africa and of many other areas of the Pacific, this and related styles of Melanesia are the consequence of subconscious rather than physical experiences with reality. It is important to stress this highly significant distinction between the contents or content-motivations of South Pacific and African arts. Unlike the forms of Negro Africa, which were strenuously based on reality, those of Melanesian Oceania were derived from the realm of unreality, from dreams or hallucinations. As a result, the forms were of a more creative nature, that is, farther removed from the naturalistic source of their origin, and add an evocative character to the aesthetic expression. The full possibilities of such expression are attained in this area by the blending of two-dimensionality with the polychrome mode of artistic expression.

In both New Britain and Papuan Gulf art styles, and to some extent in the work of the Tami-Huon area, the dramatic and dynamic spirit-charged content is constantly evident and dominates the objects. By contrast, the art of the southern tip of New Guinea and the various archipelagoes off the north and east coasts,[33] an area known as Massim, is created in terms of a strongly sculptural style combined with a two-dimensional surface design in a compound mode of expression of an entirely different nature.

Massim art is well illustrated by two types of objects: decorated lime spatulas and richly ornamented canoe-prow carvings. Of these, the lime spatulas, as discussed earlier, are of a purely secular, prestige-vanity significance.[34] This fine example from the War Memorial Museum in Auckland, New Zealand (Fig. 64), illustrates one of the two main types of decoration employed on Massim spatulas: the handle is carved to represent a sitting human figure. On the other type, the same part has a two-dimensional, geometric design applied to the surface. For these objects, a hard, smooth-grained, "black" palmwood was used and was given a smooth surface which achieved, from constant use, a deep polish. Surface details, as the eyes, mouth, and hair comb in this figure, were filled in with white lime, a transient substance that has disappeared in many examples. Originally, in the spatulas of both types, a sculptural, black-and-white style resulted, composed of rounded, full forms and lightly grooved or incised surface lines.

In contrast to the Papuan Gulf art style, Massim tradition is based predominantly on curvilinear forms. This is evident in the development of shapes and in the descriptive surface details of this figure; but it is even more apparent in the design motives applied to the geometric, two-dimensionally decorated spatulas. It is important to note that, in this work, the sculptural definition of the forehead of the figure, together with the extension of the nose, creates an inverted anchor-shape that bears a positive relationship with the stylized rendering of this form in Papuan Gulf art. The circular eyes may

64 Melanesia, New Guinea, Massim area, carved spatula.

also be compared with this western New Guinea art, although they lack the dramatic and expressive import of Papuan Gulf forms. The head shape in this figure is typical of the conventionalized form common to Massim art. This is true also of the rendering of the seated pose which, although simply given, is substantially of organic interpretation and three-dimensional character. The definition of parts is summarily handled; and the very crude indications of such details as hands and feet are a distinct stylistic feature. The significance of these small sculptures as prestige objects is made evident by the fact that the functioning of the handle is somewhat impaired by the size and shape of this figure in relationship to the functioning form of the spatula blade.

Canoes in all of Oceania were clearly of the utmost importance. In this area of Melanesia, they were particularly so because of an important ceremonial trade route, or "ring," which existed for the exchange of various shell objects manufactured solely for this purpose. Known as the "kula ring," the ceremonial exchange was of particular social and economic significance, since through it contacts were established whereby vitally necessary products could later be bartered.[35] The canoes of the various island and mainland areas used in the ceremonial kula-ring trading voyages were decorated in a traditional fashion. The designs employed had an important symbolic meaning, since they represented totemic beings in an area where a complex system of interlocking totems prevailed. Also, in this region, the importance of magic and magical practices was of greater import than in almost any other part of Melanesia.[36]

The canoe prow from the Woodlark or Murua Islands (Fig. 65) is a representative example of both the curvilinear art style of the region, and of the decorated kula-ring canoe decorations. Each of the two vertical arms in the Y-shaped design is composed of a modified double spiral framed within a continuous outer border design. The shape of this frame is based on that of the enclosed spiral forms. In this design pattern, then, three raised high-relief elements define the curved bands. These are separated by wide, pierced zones of a lower relief carving. The piercings in the outer zone are irregular crescents; in the next, inverted crescents; and in the

65 Melanesia, New Guinea, Massim area, canoe-prow carving.

inner band, triangular shapes. Surmounting each arm and facing outward are two birds. These forms also have their surfaces broken by relief carving. Typical of Massim style are the balanced design elements and shapes which are not, however, merely bilateral repeat patterns. Even the bird forms vary somewhat in size and shape. The finely conceived, curvilinear design is also characteristic, together with the piercings and the extremely important aesthetic quality of the negative spaces. Originally, white lime and, in some examples, a bit of red ochre were rubbed into the low-relief areas, a practice which emphasized the directional elements in these rich designs.

The elaborate designs found on canoe prows and a few other decorated objects, such as neckrests, and spatula handles, all had a specific content or meaning for their subject matter. As previously mentioned, there was in the Massim area a complex type of totemism; and in the designs, the geometric and life forms relate to these totems. They were badges of group ownership or relationship with that for which the particular object was made. For example, in this region yams were both an evidence of wealth and of complex sociological relationships. Ceremonial yam houses, which functioned during the harvest season, were erected and decorated with totemic paintings of the house boards. But it must not be thought that all of the decorated art of this region had a charged content.

In the western part of New Ireland and the offshore islands to the north of New Britain, the elaborate Malagan art has already been considered with regard to its motivation, function, and meaning.[37] This art is unique among Melanesian styles. It is a deceptive combination of the pierced, sculptural style of the Massim area and the two-dimensional, symbolic art of the Papuan area. As previously discussed, the designs of these mortuary carvings are clan-owned, just as the motifs in the Papuan Gulf art forms. But in this case, the forms are used with a different motivation, although the intent is comparable.

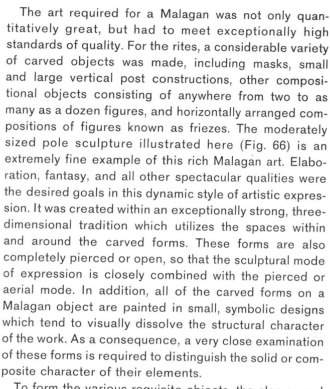

The art required for a Malagan was not only quantitatively great, but had to meet exceptionally high standards of quality. For the rites, a considerable variety of carved objects was made, including masks, small and large vertical post constructions, other compositional objects consisting of anywhere from two to as many as a dozen figures, and horizontally arranged compositions of figures known as friezes. The moderately sized pole sculpture illustrated here (Fig. 66) is an extremely fine example of this rich Malagan art. Elaboration, fantasy, and all other spectacular qualities were the desired goals in this dynamic style of artistic expression. It was created within an exceptionally strong, three-dimensional tradition which utilizes the spaces within and around the carved forms. These forms are also completely pierced or open, so that the sculptural mode of expression is closely combined with the pierced or aerial mode. In addition, all of the carved forms on a Malagan object are painted in small, symbolic designs which tend to visually dissolve the structural character of the work. As a consequence, a very close examination of these forms is required to distinguish the solid or composite character of their elements.

To form the various requisite objects, the clan-owned designs were combined by the artists under the direction of the clan elders. For every Malagan ceremony sponsored by a particular clan, these forms had to be reassembled in order to create new and exciting compositions, superior in their designs and effects to those of the rites most recently staged by another and rival clan. The basis of all of these Malagan designs is to be found in natural forms, both human and animal. But these are interpreted and assembled in a fantastic, often bizarre, nonnaturalistic manner which completely reorganizes the original shape. The resultant pierced, three-dimensional design elements are arranged compositionally along a vertical axis in an interwoven, interlocked fashion so as to combine in a dynamic and imaginatively spectacular manner. The sculptures are thus composed from weird, surrealistic fusions of strange humanoid, animal, and bird parts such as fierce, grimacing, human heads with boar's tusks; or human features may be composed of sharply projecting fish heads for the eye design, and wide-open, oval mouths filled from jaw to jaw with great sharp teeth. Important characteristics of Malagan style are the solid, sculptural renderings of the body structures to which, in their dynamic poses, these fabulous heads are so often attached; the framing of these shapes by a series of subsidiary horizontal and vertical forms which create an open, cagelike construction around the figures; and finally, the all-important painting of all surfaces, whether parts of the framework or sculptural elements, with a series of small-scale, symbolic designs, often composed of fine-line definition. These elements must be present **in toto,** as their blending is essential for the artistic expressiveness of this art tradition, and the recognition of their importance is requisite to any comprehension of these works. Perhaps the most significant single feature of this type of Malagan art is the visual import of the painted surface designs: these lead to an optical fragmentation or dissolving of the structural character of both the physical forms and the functional nature of the surrounding open cage structure. In many ways, then, this is an illusionistic art. What is seen at the first glance soon shifts or changes, sometimes melting from form to form. Many of the shapes are of that double-image character, first appearing as one thing and then as another, which so attracted the surrealists to this art. It may properly be called a fantastic type of **trompe l'oeil** style tradition.

The imaginative fantasy and visual excitation, along with the astonishing variety of forms and designs that together make up the artistic character of the "pole" Malagan sculptures, are common elements in the spectacular carved forms from the western part of New Ireland. Many weird and exciting masks were used or exhibited in open sheds during the Malagan ceremonies.

Perhaps the best known of New Ireland masks are those worn during the preliminary rites occurring just prior to the major part of the ceremonies (Fig. 67). These are the semihelmet type of mask form which fits over the head of the wearer and is used in company with a short, shredded, raffia costume. It is of partially composite form, that is, the face portion and the head armature are carved out of a moderately soft type of wood, and on top of the head-frame dyed and clipped raffia or grass forms a commanding crest. The vegetable fiber of this top piece is dyed a red-orange, with part of one side plastered over with a thick white earth. The facial structure and features are entirely pierced and have a skeletal character. In a manner typical of this style, the parts are dissolved by many small, painted, surface designs. A distinctive feature of these masks and of all New Ireland sculptures is the use of the valve of the sea snail, the operculum, as an inlaid eye-form. These inlays, known to many ex-servicemen as cat's-eyes, have a variegated yellow-green-brown striation which gives a vital but eerie and unlifelike effect. All of the combinations of fabulous, aggressive effects typical of Malagan sculptures are found in these crested masks.

One of the most characteristic style features of this art is, as noted above, the extraordinary blending of weird, semireal, nightmarish forms. This feature appears to excellent advantage in an object used by masked dancers in the Malagan ceremonies (Fig. 68). Known as a "sakabul," the symbol of celestial and other ancestors, it was held in the mouth of a masked dancer by means of a horizontal bit at one end. Totemic birds, fantastic fish forms, and various abstract, constructive elements are combined in the creation of an extremely active design. All of the above-mentioned stylistic devices are evident in this example; in fact, they are particularly developed. The piercing gives all of the forms a free reality in space; the resultant negative spaces are strong elements and contribute greatly to the artistic effectiveness of the design and to the aesthetic statements. Color is employed in the two ways which can be considered typical of this

67 Melanesia, New Ireland, crested helmet mask.

68 Melanesia, New Ireland, Malagan carving, "sakabul."

style: 1) as a descriptive element; and 2) although less in this object than in many others, as a dissolving or fragmenting force. In New Ireland art, prior to the important influences of prolonged European contact, the colors used for all Malagan sculptures were black, white, and red ochre. Since that time, however, a bright indigo blue and various other colors have had wide use. Definition of form and detail is rendered in varying degrees of relief, and in pierced forms; and in all examples, the operculum valve of the sea snail was used as an eye motive, or as an especially stressed detail. New Ireland art must be considered among the most fantastic, freely creative, and spectacular of all of the Melanesian art styles.

A type of uniquely decorated and shaped ceremonial paddle, carved in low relief and with a singularly formed, bulbous head and geometric design decoration, has been collected from the easternmost end of New Ireland. These objects, often identified in museum collections as being of "New Ireland" origin, actually were brought to that area by peoples from the Buka-Bougainville area of the farthest northwesterly tip of the Solomon Islands archipelago. Between the two areas, Buka-Bougainville and eastern New Ireland, various cultural exchanges took

69 Melanesia, Solomon Islands, carved drum.

place, including intermarriage. As a result, a number of objects such as these ceremonial paddles were interchanged by the groups. This region is of great importance in any study of the primitive world because such an interchange could occur, and because this could result in the mistaken identification of art objects. If the basic characteristics of northwest Solomon Islands style were understood, however, such a misidentification could not logically occur.

A magnificent and representative example of this northwest Solomons art style can be seen in the treatment of a small, horizontally oriented, slit-gong (Figs. 69, 70). The front side is carved near the horizontal aperture in characteristic, bas-relief fashion, with a row of four very typical heads surrounded by an also typical geometric, linear design. The reverse side is decorated with a more expansive design composed of four four-leaf motifs enclosed within irregular circles; these motifs are also surrounded by an irregularly balanced, geometric design. The extensions at each end, that is, the handholds, are graphically shaped to represent a bush-fowl, with the thin projections at the base of the neck well delineated. This object is created in one of the highly important red-black-white color styles of the Pacific. The red is a light red ochre, the black a dull, flat shade, and the white derives from a light wash of white lime.

70 Back view of Fig. 69.

They are the same colors used on the above-mentioned paddles and on all art forms of the Buka-Bougainville area. In this style there is a reversion to the two-dimensional art of South New Guinea, combined with the polychromatic expressional mode. In form, expressivity, and stylistic characteristics, however, the similarities are very limited—in fact, they are almost nonexistent.

One of the most characteristic art forms of the old German "Bismark Archipelago" area, which included New Britain, New Ireland, and the western Solomon Islands, is the so-called "kapkap" (Fig. 71). This has been previously discussed as one of the most typical art expressions from this region of Melanesia. These kapkaps consist of a slightly concave disc of gray-white tridachna, or giant sea-clam shell. In the center of the shell, a hole is pierced for the attachment of a cutout design made from turtle shell. The designs of these cutout turtle-shell forms are extremely intricate and remarkably delicate, often lacelike, in appearance; they are usually given a balanced and symmetrical arrangement of parts. These kapkap designs are among the most delicately worked and balanced examples of decorative design in primitive art; their skilled and intricate workmanship is an astounding proof of the decorative forces and aesthetic desires involved in the creations of primitive man.

71 Melanesia, Solomon Islands, "kapkap."

Other examples of art forms with a purely decorative
significance are also found in the Solomon Islands area.
Two uniquely decorated pendants (Figs. 72, 73) serve as
excellent illustrations of such objects: one an incised,
circular, pearl-shell disc and the other an inlaid, heart-
shaped pendant. The decorated shell disc is of particu-

242

72 Melanesia, Solomon Islands, carved shell disk.

lar importance because of the very finely incised, rich design motives which radiate out from the center in a variety of angular and modified triangulated forms. In the first example (Fig. 72) the design is particularly well developed; and the incised, linear design elements are brought out strongly by rubbing into them a black pigment, charcoal in this instance. The second example (Fig. 73) comes from the central-to-eastern Solomons, where a variety of decorative pendant forms were created. The heart-shaped form is carved in a hardwood, with a wide border marked off by pearl-shell inlay. The sharp, Z-shape of the inlay should be noted as a very characteristic design element of central Solomon Islands art style.

 The color and textural quality of the wood seems to have a comparable smooth, soft surface and gray-black color as that used for Tami-Huon bowls. The extraordinarily elegant and refined decorative objects created from this material have an obvious sophistication and should perhaps be classified with jewelry pieces. In this

73 Melanesia, Solomon Islands, small inlaid breast pendant.

small pendant practically all of the techniques used in shaping mother-of-pearl shell for inlay appear and are extremely well employed. This type of shell work is, as has been mentioned, characteristic of the central Solomon Islands, such as New Georgia, Florida, and Choiseul. But it is not merely confined to elegant jewelry forms: it is used to decorate and to describe certain forms on the big, head-hunting canoes. The various sculptures on these canoes and, in particular, the small head attached to the prow at the waterline, are among the most frequently illustrated of Solomon Island art objects.[38] But the pendant represents the epitome of this art tradition. It shows the delicacy and astonishingly

244

controlled technique in cutting the mother-of-pearl for inlay, and it is created in a finely balanced, elegant design. The variety of inlaid shapes and patterns and their relationship to the carved forms give to this form and to central Solomons style a very high rating in the realm of refined and luxurious art accomplishment.

Throughout western Melanesia one of the most common ways of keeping the lime powder so necessary for betel-nut chewing was in a container made from a segment of bamboo. The large stalks were cut into sections according to their natural demarcations so that an unmarred, hollow tube was produced. These lime containers are among the important decorative, rather than content-significant, sculptures found in western Melanesia. The design patterns are always rendered in an icised, linear technique, with the surface scratched in numerous rectilinear motives. In many instances the lines which carry the design are lightly burned onto the surface, producing a yellow and black design. As in the Solomon Islands example (Fig. 74), there is always a principle of symmetry. The lower portion of this lime tube, that is, the container part proper, is given two bands of decoration which are essentially alike. Balancing them is a wide band of similar motifs encircling the top section. The two vertical zones, each of which appears twice on this container, have a few well-selected design elements taken from the more decorative bands; these elements are stressed in the comparatively open, vertical field. The result of this handling of a few key motifs in an extremely sophisticated manner gives these lime containers an aesthetic and artistic quality of high standard.

In the central-to-eastern part of the Solomon Islands, the association between human welfare and the concept of continuity was often tied in with marine or fish forms

74 Melanesia, Solomon Islands, bamboo lime container.

75 Melanesia, Solomon Islands, figure.

which, it was believed, had supernatural power and control. Thus the bonito in the east-central Solomons is of great importance to the inhabitants of the area: it had a deity status and was particularly important at those times when the youth were initiated into adulthood and taught the knowledge of their people. In many instances, these marine-spirit forms were embodied, for ceremonial purposes, in sculptural objects. It is of particular significance that these forms were always given at least a quasi-human appearance. The British Museum example (Fig. 75) is an extraordinarily fine object of this type. The head is an active bonito shape, and the arms and feet terminate in lobsterlike claws. The facial area of the bonito head is embellished with active, dynamic, human features; deep-set eyes; a high, projecting nose; and a thin-lipped, sharply open mouth with a heavy, prognathous mandible or lower-jaw form. No emphasis is given to surface refinement or to form definition in these sculptured objects. All of the shapes are defined in an abrupt and strikingly dynamic fashion. The resultant forms have a complete existence in space, the shapes moving freely within and around the spatial area. The motivation for these objects resided in the need for protection, that is, in satisfaction of the drive for security and survival, and in the search for continuity and stability. The spirit content so often found in Oceanic art is strongly evident in their forms. Culturally they were of the greatest possible significance, since what might be called the motive power of the group derived from such figures. Aesthetically, objects such as this one have a visual force and a utilization of space that contribute to their important emotional and psychological statements in artistic form.

Among the highly important art forms of this same area are the ceremonial bowls (Fig. 76). Of all the objects of this type from the Oceanic area, these eastern Solomon forms have the most vibrant designs. The over-all quality of design is distinctive and artistically unique. In size, the bowls range from six inches to more than two feet long; while the decorative compositions have not only

76   Melanesia, Solomon Islands, bowl.

a genre character, but also a humorous configuration. The design of this bowl is particularly characteristic of the Solomons in various respects, the rockerlike base with the conical form of the bowl serving as a central stabilizing force and the two small figures, each clutching the bowl with thin hands and feet, functioning as balancing agents. The entire composition is one of aesthetic and expressive relationships between positive form and negative space. It is rendered with a direct vigor and sculptural statement of shapes and details, but without the refinement of an elaborate shell inlay. The small figures are particularly noteworthy. Their heads are depicted as modified fish forms, in clear reference to the ceremonial importance of the bonito. Vigorous and sure organic rendering of body shapes, along with points of pressure exerted against the sides and rim of the bowl, convey the quality of genrelike reality that is so much a part of this art style. Movement is not only implied, but is a basic characteristic of such objects as this bowl. A monochrome, dull-black coloration, typical of art forms in this region, is used on this sculpture, while along the upper sides of the rim, bonito-tail forms appear as dynamic, geometric decorative motives.

Many of the bowls from this region in Melanesia have totemic significance and are used during initiation and other ceremonial rites. The figures along the sides can easily be equated with the fish-deity forms so well illustrated in the British Museum example (Fig. 75). From an artistic point of view this work has a vibrancy and a subtle asymmetry that results in a strong vitality derived merely from its form qualities. Although no single style dominates the art of the Solomon Islands, a directness of expression is typical of all the forms; and even with the extraordinary quality of the mother-of-pearl shell inlay, it cannot be characterized as an effete or simply decorative style. Though often highly stylized, the interpretations of life forms have an aesthetic force of animated vigor.

Southeast of the Solomon Islands, the long New Hebrides chain projects in two parallel rows of large and small islands oriented along a northwest-to-southeast directional axis. As previously considered, the grade societies are the dominant cultural institutions of this area, and make the most constant demands on the artist.[39] The New Hebrides artist, however, was determined by sociological relationships rather than by being a trained craftsman, so that any person, with or without talent, might be called upon at certain times to carve and/or paint figures or masks. Thus, quality in New Hebrides art, as it concerns the forms required for the grade-society rites, has a wide range from inept to aesthetically satisfying examples. All of these sculptures were made anew for each ceremony, after which they were discarded and allowed to rot. The ephemeral significance of these objects would seem to reflect the semiartistic quality that they evidence in the majority of instances. By comparison with the equally temporary Malagan art of New Ireland, there was not the culturally dynamic pressure to create bigger and better grade-society figures and masks. Hence there was not the impetus toward accomplishment of artistic form and virtuosity of expression so important as goals in Malagan art of New Ireland.

The more aesthetically significant forms created in the tradition of New Hebrides art style lie outside the requirements of the grade societies. Such works include the big slit-gongs, for example, which were carved by skilled artists. In fact, the greatest aesthetic and artistic accomplishments of the New Hebrides are found on these gongs, and especially on the wooden mallets or pig-killers, which must be given a very high status. These adzelike objects were of comparable prestige-vanity significance to the big gongs, and, like them, they were used time and time again. Moreover, the faces carved on the pig-killers have the same quality as, and even resemble closely, those on the big gongs.

These heavy forms are carved in a hardwood, with the adze-shaped design given a perfect balance. A characteristic design element for these objects appears on an example from the Australian Museum in Sydney (Fig. 77). Both the top of the vertical and diagonal arms are carved with a large face. These seem to be pressed into the wood, so that the very large-scale features, consisting of strongly projecting and receding shapes, are softly contained within the volumes of the total form. The facial zones are markedly concave ovoids within which the large ovals of the eyes, the massive nose with its pierced septum, and the faintly indicated mouth stand out as expressive forms. On the vertical and the diagonal "arms," high-relief, spiraling, curvilinear design elements fill in the space, and bring the two faces into a balanced relationship. A multipeaked hairdress, or top piece, the outline of which is delicately serrated, is shared by both faces. The butt end of the mallet has a series of deep grooves and a sharp-angled base. All definitions of shapes and designs on this object are freely handled and give evidence that they were carved with stone and shell tools. As with the gongs, color is of no importance in these works. A dull monochrome

250

77 Melanesia, New Hebrides, pig-killer mallet.

black is the usual finish, although on some of the gongs a white and a red ochre are sometimes used.

In design, the pig-killers show a wide creative range; this is evidenced by another example, also from the collection of the Museum in Sydney (Figs. 78, 79). A single face appears on the diagonal arm or mallet head, the vertical handle fusing into this form in an irregular curve. A double manelike form develops from either side of the face and follows the swelling curve into the upper part of the shaft or handle. Facial features agree stylistically with those of the first example: emphatic and monumental in size and scale, vigorous and unrefined in delineation. The crestlike "mane" and the parallel side forms are notched in somewhat the same fashion noted in the top piece of the other pig-killer mallet. But here the notches are observably larger in scale. A dull black color, characteristic of all these objects, is again employed.

New Hebrides art, in its most vigorous aspects, is composed of powerful statements of form that are the pure outgrowth of the materials, the textural surfaces, and the concepts of expressive intent. Features of huge scale and fleshy character spread out over most of the facial zone. They are defined in what might be called an impressionistic manner, as the statements are soft and shadow-catching. Refinement of shapes, forms, and details is nonexistent, the rough-hewn quality and textures intensifying the all-important expressive power and vigor characteristic of this art style. This actively forceful, energetic quality is as evident in these pig-killer mallets as in the large slit-gongs.

Culturally distinctive of various parts of Melanesia, and frequently important to the art forms, was the preservation of ancestor skulls. In the Sepik River area the features of the deceased were built up on the skulls by clay modeling of a generic, but at times very sensitive, method and style. The objects were then painted with the designs once used by the dead person at ceremonial occasions during his lifetime. These modeled skulls were carefully kept in the Tambaran houses. Among the peo-

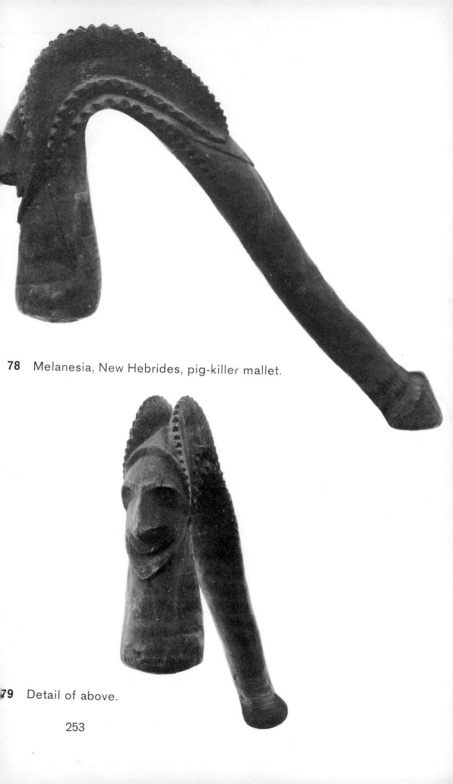

78 Melanesia, New Hebrides, pig-killer mallet.

79 Detail of above.

ples of northeast New Britain, a type of mask was modeled from a paste of crushed parinarium nuts built up over the frontal bones of the skull. The forms were then painted with the designs appropriate to the deceased and were worn at mortuary rites. Ancestor skulls were also modeled in the island area of New Hebrides. These were painted in the brilliant colors so characteristic of the grade-society figures and masks. In this area, however, the construction material was a vegetable compost; it was the same as that used in the modeling of grade-society masks and life-sized mortuary figures of important men. The modeled and painted skull of the deceased was attached to these mortuary figures; and modeled symbols were affixed to the body, along with boars' tusks, as indications of former rank within one or more of the grade societies. These figures, known as "rambaramp," were set up out of doors for a short time after death, as memorials, and then were removed to the men's houses for permanent storage and/or ceremonial use.

The use of different materials to create a particular, requisite effect or character in masks or figures was, as has been indicated, a feature of Melanesian art traditions. In New Caledonia and the offshore islands to the southwest of New Hebrides, this is again evident in the big masks representing supernatural beings (Fig. 80). A large, trapezoidal face, vertically arranged, was carved in a hardwood and stained a monochrome black. To this was attached a high headdress topped with black human hair; plaited strands of this same material hung down around the face as a full beard. A short costume, composed of dull black feathers, depended from the mask, covering the wearer down to the knees. New Caledonian masks express, in terms of heavy masses, the isolated structural and facial features. This is apparent in the forms of the huge hooked nose with its carved septum decorations, the rounded cheekbones, the forehead planes, the continuous ridge of the eyebrow curves with the solid oval eye-forms beneath, and the great open crescent of the mouth. These massive shapes are assem-

80 Melanesia, New Caledonia, mask.

bled in a bilaterally symmetrical arrangement on either side of the forehead and nasal suture lines. They are established in a dramatically important pattern of inter-relationships between three sets of conspicuous form-defining elements: 1) projecting or protuberant planear surfaces; 2) depressed grooves; and 3) ridges of varying curvilinear character. The expressive relationship of the planear surfaces to the set of cheekbone, eye, and fore-head shapes should be noted; while of the grooved ele-ments, those of the high orbital structure, the eye area, and the zone above the mouth are outstanding. Of the ridged, curvilinear forms, the most significant are the downward, strongly curved lines of the orbital ridge and the continuous eyebrow relief form, both of which are emphatically counterbalanced by the great upward-sweeping curves of the mouth definition. Unifying, con-necting, and bringing these forms into a dynamic har-mony and coherence is the spectacular curved and volu-metric form of the nose which interlocks, within the area of the mask shape, all the action of these elements. The expressive integrity in these New Caledonian forms bears comparison with those of the Cameroon area of West Africa (cf. Fig. 23). As sculptural shapes this work can be related to certain southern New Hebrides masks, particularly those few old forms from Pentecost Island.

As in all of the regional art expressions of Melanesia, these masks show regional variation in interpretation, with the southern forms being less grotesquely stylized than those of the central and northern areas. The carved ancestor figures from this region, too, display much of the expressive force found in the masks, while some of them, by the manner in which the points of articulation are constricted, again point to a comparison with Ca-meroon figures of Africa. These comparisons between artistic treatments of form are of considerable impor-tance to the appreciation of style. Not even the most rabid enthusiast of diffusionism would attempt to pro-pose a relationship between the arts of the Cameroons and New Caledonia; yet the analogies are valid and worthy of note. This does not indicate that some common

256

source of origin or historic relationship must be proved; but rather, it adds depth and clarifies aesthetic concepts or methods in primitive art. No analogy is sought in the actual forms of the Melanesian objects from New Caledonia as compared to the forms of Cameroon works, but only in the approach to formal appearances.

The Fiji Islands, lying almost due east of the southernmost part of the New Hebrides chain, are the easternmost islands of Melanesia and in many respects serve as an area of transition between Melanesia and Polynesia. Major physical, linguistic, and cultural elements link these Fijian islands ethnically with Melanesia; while certain obviously intrusive strains, such as house types, quality of tapa or bark cloth, and the shaping and decoration of wooden clubs, relate these island peoples with Polynesia. Also, the basic elements of both type and style in human figure sculpture tends to link the art forms of Fiji with traditional styles in Polynesia, particularly as found in the Tongan island group to the southeast. In this general consideration of the major style areas of Oceanic art, it is desirable to consider only the broadest characteristics of a style rather than its refined and possible insinuated relationships with other areas. In the case of Fiji, however, the art tradition seems to have developed into a style of its own by fusing the formal and expressive concepts of two major areas. Thus, it is important to establish the character of Fiji art in its own right, and to point out the elements of Melanesian and Polynesian derivation which are blended and which make this a transitional art area.

Decorated clubs, priests' oil dishes, cannibal forks, tapa designs, and carved wooden hooks together reveal the basic character of this art style. To this might be added the house types, construction methods, and materials, along with certain decorative breast pendants which were symbols of rank and position. Among the most typical of decorated Fijian objects are the distinctive cannibal forks and the shallow oil dishes from which the priests anointed themselves (Fig. 82). The oil dishes were of varied shapes, including even some formed like

81   Melanesia, Fiji Islands, club end, detail.

82   Melanesia, Fiji Islands, priest's bowl, cannibal forks.

258

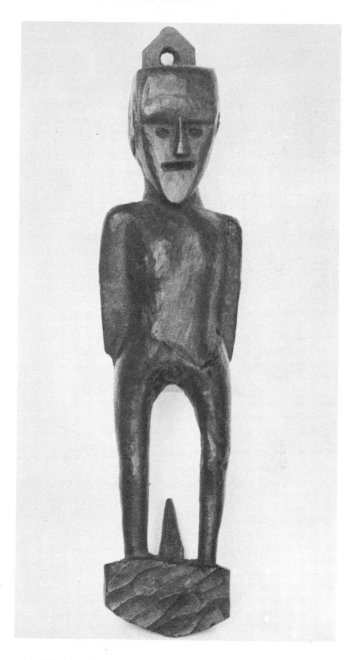

83 Melanesia, Fiji Islands, hook figure.

stamps of gingerbread men; but the most typical form was an elegant depressed oval with serrated edges, having three or four small feet underneath by which it was held, and with a large, open, rectilinearlike "hilt" at one end. Frequently, all of the forms were notched or serrated, and they were always of a dull gray-black oily surface. The cannibal forks, varying in size from a mere five inches to over a foot in length, were composed of distinct parts: a four-pronged, sharp-pointed, functional end; what might be called a short, rolled "hilt"; and a long handle, often elaborately decorated with sharp-notched designs arranged in a variety of geometric patterns. In Fiji, as in other areas of the Melanesian world, human flesh was dangerous to touch because of its well-known latent power—thus the forks, often elaborately carved, were used in the ceremonial eating of human "meat." So far as is known, no significance was attached to the type of decoration given to these implements, nor to the shape or decoration given to the oil dishes of the priests. In other words, these were important ceremonial objects that were given decoration of no symbolic or otherwise meaningful significance. They were fashioned, used, and appreciated on the basis of aesthetic quality alone, in the achievement of which they were frequently most successful.

Figure sculpture in Fiji is of particular significance for an understanding of relationships and interrelationships with the art forms and traditions of Melanesia. Numerous examples described in collections as originating in "Fiji" are clearly from Tonga; but there are a few figure sculptures, particularly those in wood, that have been authenticated as from Fiji. Some of these are single or coupled figures carved as suspension hook forms (Fig. 83). Most of these carvings have a crudity of form definition and a strength of activity in expressive implications, particularly in the flexion of the arms and in the abrupt representations of facial features. In essence, these figures have a general Melanesian conventionalization of structure and the dramatic zest of expression typical of western Oceania. Any careful study of Fijian figures clearly discloses their expressive and organic differences from Polynesian works. In spite of the marked Melanesian associations characteristic of Fijian art, however, many designs of Polynesian type—as exemplified in their club decoration—are found intermingled with other forms. It seems likely that many of the most pronounced Polynesian influences developed from the eighteenth century on, when known historical contacts existed between Fiji, Tonga, and Samoa.[40]

The fighting clubs of Fiji are numerous, but those with an elaborate, over-all decoration, such as the detail on this paddlelike example (Fig. 81), are of particular importance in evaluating the Melanesian-Polynesian character of this art. Divided longitudinally by an irregular central ridge in very high relief, the two sections of this leaflike blade are more or less symmetrically decorated. A fine, deep crosshatching of the background surface of the blade produces a series of tiny, pyramidal, high-relief sections. Within the corruscated field are four small raised areas: two in the upper part of the design, which are decorated with a horizontal, crisp, hourglass design filled in with very small crosshatched motifs comparable to those on the blade surface; and two smooth, unevenly placed, asymmetrical, solid crescent forms. Beginning at the level of the rectangular decorative forms and continuing around the lower portion of the paddle is a border decorated with interlocking, sharp, dentated designs that are alternately smooth-surfaced and crosshatched in treatment. Carved in a very hard wood, possibly ironwood, the surface of this object is clean and crisp and has a fine rich patina. Decorative elements of the type appearing on this club blade are far more typical of the design motifs used on similar objects from Polynesia than from any part of Melanesia.

It is of particular importance to note that the decorative patterns on this paddlelike form agree with the stamped Fijian tapa-cloth designs. The material as produced and decorated in Fiji has a quality closer to that of Polynesia than to the tapa or bark cloth from other areas of Melanesia, such as found in the Tami-Huon and

Papuan Gulf regions of New Guinea and particularly in New Britain. Coloristically, a dark-brown, tan, and black pattern is used to create designs similar to those noted on the clubs; while a few other patterns of the same coloration utilized very bold, rectilinear designs. The most delicate of all the Fijian tapa cloths, those used in the temples as the route by which the deity spirit entered its shrine, were often simply of the natural, light-tan color of the material, with rich disc motifs in darker brown stamped onto the strip at irregular intervals. Large blocks or boards were carved in Fiji to serve as stamps for the imprinting of designs on tapa cloth. The club motifs clearly show some similarity to these stamping blocks. In any consideration of Fiji tapa cloth, as compared to that of Polynesia, it must be recognized that the Fijian decorative style and vocabulary is, with certain exceptions, more vigorous and bold, and that the colors are deeper in tone and richer in contrasts.

The extent to which the house types of Fiji were influenced at the time of European contact by a knowledge of those of Tonga and Samoa is entirely conjectural. It seems certain that there had been some influence, just as there was in the tapa-cloth designs. All the Fijian house types were constructed of a light, palmwood frame, the supporting structural members lashed together with sennit cord.[41] The majority were of a rectangular shape, with side walls and a low, even-sloped roof. But the temple architecture at one time had been of a square or rectangular shape with very high, steeply pitched roofs. A number of the old temple walls, and even some of the side walls of present-day houses, are of a plaited character, giving an appearance of textural contrast with the thatched roofs. A typical Polynesian structural trait was the use of a double or thatching ridgepole, the ends of which projected free at either end of the roof peak. A rounded type of roof-comb was formed by the thatch being wrapped over the outer roof or ridgepole. Engravings, as well as sennit-made models of early temple structures, show that the projection of the thatching ridgepole was at times very long and

elaborately decorated with sennit cord and shell pendants. The small models served in the temples as deity
shrines.

b AUSTRALIA AND MICRONESIA

To the south of Melanesia lies the large subcontinent
of Australia; to the north is the island world of Micronesia, made up in general of small atolls, with a few larger,
volcanic islands. Both of these areas evidence some
cultural and artistic relationships with Melanesia. But
since, for the purposes of this study, the Oceanic world
must be largely restricted to Melanesia and Polynesia,
these other two art-producing areas must be considered,
at best, in only a summary fashion.

The aboriginal Australian, despite an extremely
meager cultural development, created certain highly distinctive art forms. The artistic tradition embraced
engraved boomerangs and message-sticks, polychromed
shields decorated usually in rectilinear patterns, and
designs painted on sheets of bark. There were also many
other unusual methods of ceremonial expression, such
as body-painting and the additions of feathers, blood,
and paint to carved or body surfaces, which gave the
designs or forms their full significance. In Australian
aboriginal art, these elements and the manner in which
they are utilized are of paramount significance. Artistic
forms in this tradition are, to a very large extent, of
surface, two-dimensional design character (Fig. 84).
Western Australian shell designs have much in common
with the boomerang and shield decor typical of central
and eastern Australia. The parallel, mazelike, rectilinear
patterns on these shell objects are characteristic of
Australian designs. The range of surface motifs, however, does not indicate the limits of this art expression.
Depth of relief, and variations of this depth, have much
to do with the expressive qualities of the forms. The relief
rendering, although actually slight, is given an optical
amplification by the insertion of strong color in the
incised grooves or lines. The incised patterns on the

84 Australia, northwest area, shell pendants.

shells, for example, were filled in with deep black; and on some of the shields, a red or yellow ochre was used. Even in the bull-roarers and the wooden or stone churingas — those ovate forms with incised designs of totemic significance — some color was generally employed. While some examples from each category of aboriginal Australian art show a degree of controlled regularity in the relationship of parallel lines, many of the specimens are carved with a linear irregularity that gives them a free, animated quality.

Narrow, parrying shields, as well as boomerangs and message-sticks, are often treated with a single, geometric design composed of very wide grooves (Fig. 85), which give these forms a greater degree of low relief than the thinner, incised patterns of the shell-type objects. The entire surface of this form, for example, is covered by three sets of opposing, grooved diagonals which are related as a single design pattern. Like the churingas, these shield decorations frequently have a protective, totemic meaning. Very high-relief designs of a similar geometric nature are found on the so-called burial trees as emblems of totemic-mortuary significance. In Arnhem Land in north-central Australia, and on Bathhurst Island offshore, are found some highly geometric, human figure forms and very large mortuary posts with similar high-relief carvings.

Another important type of aboriginal work is the rock art. Pecked and incised designs of natural forms and geometric motifs were engraved on outcroppings of surface rock in New South Wales, not far from Sydney, and they appear in rock grottoes and shelters in various parts of central and northern Australia. This aboriginal rock art also embraces the technique of surface painting by which fantastic totemic forms are depicted on the walls of rock shelters. In this type of Australian art, mythology, totemism, and abstract ideas are combined in the subject matter; while naturalistic and imaginative forms, together with geometric abstractions, make up the artistic content of the works. It is astonishing that a nomadic, food-collecting culture of otherwise meager accomplishments could have produced such a variety of creative and aesthetically effective art forms.

The northern Oceanic territory of Micronesia deserves special consideration in its own right for both its cultures and its art styles. The influences of these factors are clearly evident in many parts of Melanesia. Figurative sculpture is rare in Micronesia, occuring only on a few ceremonial bowls, on painted house murals, and, in small numbers, as objects carved in the round, such as the well-known figures from Nukuoro (Fig. 86). These are

5 Australia, carved shield.

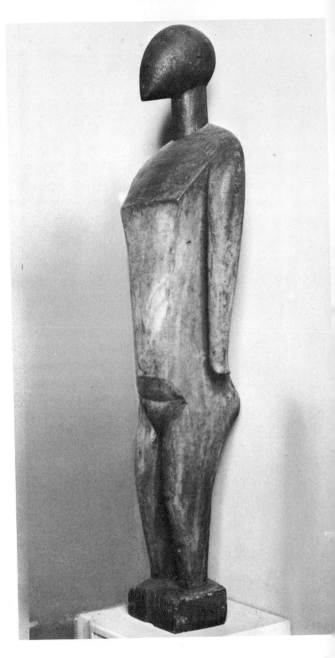

86 Micronesia, Nukuoro, Caroline Islands, standing figure.

among the most completely geometric of primitive figure sculptures. The manikinlike forms (possibly female) show but little physical "being" or animation in the rendering of anatomical parts. And there is neither characterization nor definition of facial features on the smoothly surfaced, geometric heads of purely ovoid shape. In some respects, the aesthetic and artistic properties that characterize these figures can be compared with those of early twentieth century European sculptures that were created as an attempt at reversion to the basic essentials of human form.

Form concepts in Micronesian art are principally of a strongly geometric nature. The rare examples of figurative sculpture are arrangements of shapes well adapted to functional designs. Many objects created for strictly utilitarian purposes, such as bowls, are given the streamlined, functional treatment of shape so many modern Western designs strive to attain. This trait in Micronesian art styles is also evident in the canoe prows from the island of Ponape (Fig. 87). The completely bilateral disposition of the design is clearly marked by a central segment, carved and painted in such a way as to bisect the forms. The main body of the object is surmounted on either side by a rigorously stylized tern. These bird forms are reduced and simplified in shape and heraldically set in a beak-to-beak pose. Their appearance is of geometrically shaped heads and bodies, and legs which fuse into the carved and painted low-relief band that joins the bird forms to the main body of the prow carving. The base of this prow decoration flares out below the banded middle section. Two vertical, almost parallel strips in low relief divide the form into two gently bulging curved surfaces, and an upward-pointing geometric shape at either side terminates the composition. A transient type of white and black pigment is used to define coloristically the body parts of the bird forms and the various sections of the sculpture below. The design is stark and is of particular interest for its variety of curved profiles and for the balance of horizontal and vertical elements. Such art forms are purely geometric, abstract expres-

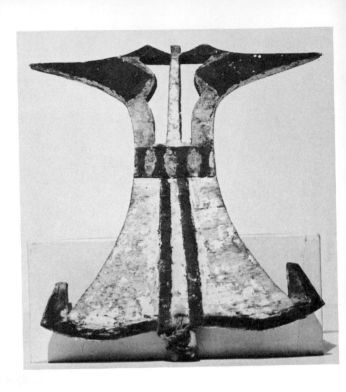

87 Micronesia, Ponape, canoe-prow carving.

sions. They have a subtlety of design and a sensitivity of balanced outlines that appeal aesthetically, for those reasons alone.

Certain masks and architectural carvings and paintings, and especially mattings of supreme quality, were produced in the Micronesian world. Influences from this island area, it is now certain, went south even into parts of New Guinea with important cultural effects. Conversely, influences from Melanesia and certainly from Polynesia were felt in Micronesia. That the art traditions and styles from the various centers in Micronesia are treated with such brevity does not mean, any more than it did for Australian aboriginal art, that it deserves only cursory attention. On the contrary, both are rich areas worthy of lengthy consideration. Unfortunately, such consideration cannot be given within the limits of this generalized discussion of the vast areas of the Pacific.

c **POLYNESIA**

In the central, north, and south Pacific, Polynesia spreads out in a vast area and is aptly described by its name, which derives from the Greek words for "many islands." Certainly the best-known part of the Oceanic world, Polynesia is also the most homogeneous of all Pacific territories. Within its boundaries, many large volcanic islands and island masses, as well as some atolls, extend along the equatorial line; the northern limits reach as far as Hawaii, while to the south the borders stretch out to include New Zealand. The easternmost extension of this triangular shaped Oceanic region is Easter Island. Ethnically and culturally Polynesia can be set apart from other areas of the Pacific. As in all other parts of the primitive world, the art is inextricably associated with beliefs and practices inherent in the major aspects of the culture. And since it is an essentially homogeneous region, certain important generalities can be expressed which pertain to the cultural context of the art forms as found in the many island groups within Polynesia.

Several concepts are of paramount importance for an understanding of Polynesia art traditions: 1) the value placed on social rank and position; 2) "mana," as the source of power and achievement; and 3) "tabu," or the force and method by which rank and mana were protected and by which those with less power were saved from the dangers of greater power. In this region social status, that is, position within the group, was all important. The cultures were socially divided into the upper class, that is, the chiefs and those related by blood with chiefly lines; and the great middle class which had certain claims to position but of a restricted nature. The slaves and retainers had no status or position, although adoption of a promising or talented slave child by persons of high rank was common practice and gave the child the privileges of blood relationships. Persons of high rank were those who could trace and recite their geneologies back to the deities of culture heroes. At various ceremonials, and for numerous other reasons, this recitation was often required as proof of an individual's position, and he had to be prepared to retrace the lengthy and complex lineage of his family without hesitation or error. The relationship thus proved to gods and demigods consequently gave a quasi-sacredness to those of great rank; while those related to them were also of importance, but of a graduated kind.

Mana, the second of the above-mentioned concepts shared by the peoples throughout Polynesia, is an inherent, spiritual essence of power, the nature of which may be likened to an electrical current or charge. It is a part of that universal power with which all things, animate and inanimate, are endowed at birth, in creation, or by growth. It can also be obtained through success, bravery, transfer from person to object or object to person. The firstborn in a great chiefly lineage, for example, had a great deal of mana by heritage, which might later be increased or decreased according to his accomplishments. All trees and living matter are endowed with some mana, and even tools and weapons contain this latent force that is manifested by the success with which they are used. Thus, all persons and things are imbued or endowed with some mana. Persons of lower rank have much less of this vital force than those of higher rank, creating a dangerous situation because of the belief that great harm would befall any who came into direct contact with a source of mana greater or lesser than his own. To circumvent this danger, the institution of tabu was devised. This consisted of controls and restrictions by which persons, places, and things could be protected against the perils of contact with the forces of mana. Polynesian sculptures not only had the mana of their original material, but gained added potency from the tools used in their creation, and to some degree, from the subject matter they depicted. This vital force could increase in proportion to the success of an object in its particular role. But it must be remembered that mana could be lost as well as gained, so that the poor performance of an individual, a low crop-yield from a particular field, the unsuccessful functioning of an art object, all indicated a decrease in mana content.

Mana and tabu are concepts of particular importance to Polynesian art because of the extent to which they fostered, even required, the development of specialization in the area. Polynesia was a world of specialists who by reasons of birth, lineage, or talent received an extremely long and intensive apprenticeship in such fields of endeavor as the priesthood, canoe-making, sculpturing, oral transmission of mythologies and of the all-important genealogies, house-building, and a considerable variety of other vocations, including that of the agriculturalists who presided over the first breaking of the soil at the planting season. These specialists were known among the Mari of New Zealand as the "tohunga"; and in various other Polynesian islands, the name was a modification or variant of the same word, as, for example, "kahuna" in Hawaii and "tahuna" in the Marquesas Islands. For any consideration of the art of this area, it is essential that it be understood that the forces of mana-tabu and the high degree of specialization have an important, interlocking relationship.

The Polynesian artist was clearly a specialist. All of the particular essentials of his craft had to be acquired through a long and arduous apprenticeship during which he was instructed, not only in the traditions of style in his particular area, but in the proper methods of handling his tools and materials. Since the mana inherent in both his tools and his materials was an important factor in his training, he had to learn the correct and prescribed routines necessary for the control of this latent and dangerous power. The concept of mana was thus involved in every aspect of artistic creation. Only a master of the practices which could avert harm was able to handle the materials of any given trade, so that a high degree of specialization was the only possible method by which the society could live. As a result of this, an extremely high level of technical and aesthetic achievement was maintained in Polynesian art. Within the regional traditions there was apparently a considerable degree of creativity possible, especially since a good deal of the art was associated with rank and prestige.

Forming an enormous triangle, geographically, in the vast area of the Pacific, with its apex at the Hawaiian Islands in the north, and its southern points in New Zealand to the west and Easter Island to the east, Polynesia can, for certain cultural reasons, be considered in terms of west, central, eastern, and marginal areas. It would appear, from present knowledge of the area, that the important migrations and expeditions for settlement fanned out mainly from Tahiti, in the Society Islands, as the focal area, after having moved east from Samoa and Tonga. Despite this fact, the most developed and distinctive art styles arose in the marginal areas: in the Hawaiian, Marquesan, and Eastern Island cultures, and among the Maori peoples of New Zealand. This does not mean that the traditions and styles of western, central, and eastern Polynesia have nothing in common with those of the marginal areas. It is preferable to say, rather, that each group of Polynesia Islands has its own particular cultural character and art style; but also, that in spite of their divergences or singularities, all the areas share many factors of art and culture in common. Some of the forms which appear in this immense region are peculiar to one small segment or island group, and can only be defined as local styles or variants; but even these forms show much in common with the general Polynesian elements or characteristics.

Samoa and Tonga, in the western part of Polynesia, have a three-cornered cultural interrelationship with Fiji that is evident in the art forms produced in the three areas. It is particularly noticeable in their tapa cloth decoration, an art tradition that still persists today. Aside from those examples available in the shops to tourists in Suva and Pago-Pago, there are a considerable number of tapa cloths to be found there which date back to the early or precolonization period. Tapa cloth has already been mentioned as being common to many Oceanic areas; but the finest quality fabric of this type is found only in Polynesia. A tree popularly known as the paper-mulberry furnishes a fine quality inner bark which can be stripped, soaked, and beaten into the gauzelike strips that are the basis of fine tapa in Polynesia. In Melanesia and areas to the west, various other barks such as that of the wild fig tree were used in the manufacture of bark cloth. Within the triangular limits of the Fiji-Samoa-Tonga area, the art of decorating tapa cloth is clearly related in certain particular respects, principally in the tan-brown color range shared by the three areas and also in the combinations of small-scale geometric designs that produced an over-all pattern. Differences in quality as well as in design characteristics can, however, be easily noted. With the exception of the white temple tapas to which previous reference was made,[42] the fabric of Fijian bark cloth frequently has a slightly heavier texture; the designs are bold, angular forms which cover a large field; and the colors tend toward the darker shades of brown and even red-brown tones. The decorations on Tongan tapa, often of a fine, soft quality, are generally given as repeat patterns of small-scale units of several shades of light tan; while the patterns on Samoan cloths, also frequently based on repeated design elements, are composed of sizable squares and relatively large-scale, rectilinear elements in a medium shade of brown and in a darker red-brown.

The pierced and relief-carved designs on the Samoan combs (Fig. 88) illustrate some of the motifs employed in tapa decoration, particularly those appearing in the upper square section of the comb at the right. The use of a single, large-scale motif fitted within a square—a decorative pattern frequently found on Samoan tapa—is exemplified here by the large design composed of parallel, crossing diagonals, with small triangular elements filling in the rest of the space. Other delicately carved designs appearing on both these combs can also frequently be seen as tapa decorations. The multiple, small, triangular or dentated patterns, with floral-derived

88 Polynesia, Samoa, wooden combs.

motifs and oval, circular, and/or rhomboidal free spaces arranged in horizontal or vertical zones, are also characteristic of the low relief and incised design elements found on the fine Samoan and Tongan war clubs.

An important art form in Samoa was (and to a degree, still is) the architecture of the large and important guest or semiceremonial houses. In this area of Polynesia the tohungas, or specialists, in charge of house construction were organized into powerful guilds. The older house-type, prevalent at about, or even before, the time of European contact, was built on a plan consisting of a large rectangular central section with apsidal ends, the ends being the most important places to seat the attending chiefs. As time went on, the sides of the houses were reduced more and more so that the appearance of the houses was altered and began to approach a short oval or round plan. This was the sociological result of an increased series of titles, which accrued from the tracing of genealogical histories through a common descent line, that is, by following the familial relationships back to one particular male ancestor. The geometric progression of titled individuals affected the architectural forms because, traditionally, all the important personages had to be seated in the apsidal ends. If the ends had been increased in size, all communication through the talking chiefs between the people in one apsidal end and those in the other would have become virtually impossible.

Samoan houses, like those of Tonga, were built with a plan-defining, peripheral structure and a central supporting framework. A row of fairly short, sturdy posts, forming the external shape or periphery of the house, was imbedded in the earth. These supported a ring of purlins or curb plates on which rested the roof beams. Down the center of the interior a line of heavy center posts were deeply sunk into the ground, and to them were lashed connecting horizontal crosspieces. Atop this long central row of post-and-lintel-type construction, several additional posts and their crosspieces were affixed. These served as the major or "king" supports for the house which essentially was "hung" on the framework. These hanging parts consisted of the heavily thatched roof and a series of thatched or plaited wall mats which could be rolled up or lowered and which functioned as movable walls. All of the structural and other timbers in the house were lashed into place with sennit cord of two or three colors, each guild having a design peculiar to itself both in the colors used and in the particular design achieved by lashing the members into place. Thus, a decorative design was achieved in terms of what amounted to a guild signature.

These buildings are large in size, often being over forty feet long and more than twenty-five feet high. "Under" the house, a stone-surfaced earthen platform was constructed, at least in recent times; such platform structures are a significant feature in many types of Polynesian architecture. In the case of Samoan buildings, however, they were unusual in that they were constructed after the house was completed. Somewhat lower than the house platform, a paved area, usually called the "paepae," was laid surrounding the whole edifice. In many parts of Polynesia, these paepae were built only in front of the houses. The Samoan architectural forms serve as excellent examples of achievements made through a controlled technology in concert with a pertinent design form. Tongan houses are very similar in plan to the older Samoan type of long oval building, although they do not necessarily have the low platform. Structurally, too, they are like the Samoan houses, with the various parts again lashed together with black, red, and natural-tan colored sennit to produce designs which are in this case, however, purely ornamental. Walls were of matting or of reeds close set vertically, and the roofs were of heavy thatch with, as in Samoan houses, the double ridgepole.

Characteristic of western Polynesia is the variety and type of decoration given to the principal weapon, that is, to the wooden fighting club. Often made of hard and heavy ironwood, the most common types are the long-handled bat and paddle-shaped clubs and the short throwing or striking weapons. Each island or island area throughout Polynesia developed its own type of club, which was usually given a unique surface decoration. In Samoa and Tonga, while various types are shared — particularly the bat and the throwing club — there are nevertheless types and decorative elements distinctive to each of these areas. Perhaps the most elaborately decorated clubs of western Polynesia are those from Tonga (Fig. 89). Of this pair, the club at the left is a localized version of the ball-headed throwing or striking club common to all of the nearby groups, including Fiji; the example at the right is again a local, modified version combining features of the bat and the narrow-bladed, paddle-type clubs. Both examples have the approximate measurements characteristic of their type: the shorter, throwing club is twenty-one inches in length; the other one, thirty-six inches long. The superior shaping and decoration of these clubs give them an aesthetically high rating among the decorative, sculptural and generally artistic achievements of western Polynesia.

The shorter club has in proportion to its size a relatively long handle which is circular in cross-section until it approaches the striking end, when it becomes an irregular hexagon. The globular head fits within the sharp grasp of this hexagon and fuses with that shape which is retained by the heavy, triangular protrusions and the sharp, spherical triangle. These sculptural motifs tie the striking end of the weapon in with the upper part of the club handle. The entire surface of this object, carved in ironwood, is covered with elaborate, carefully rendered, incised designs of geometric character. The design vocabulary, although not quantitatively great, is ingeniously utilized to produce the qualitative effect of very rich decoration. Parallel lines, framed within largely triangular elements, are the most prominent motifs, the triangles ranging in size from small and almost obscure elements to large and bold forms. The designs within the triangles are composed of linear elements, which are either straight, diagonal, or den-

89 Polynesia, Tonga, carved wooden clubs.

tated lines arranged in parallel rows. An important stylistic design feature of this short club is the manner in which the hand-hold is decorated with a long, spiraling motif developing upward from the butt end of the handle. This very finely incised decoration must be equated with the custom, shared by many peoples of Polynesia and employed also in Fiji, of wrapping the club handles with finely twisted sennit cord, often of several colors, in a variety of intricate designs. In other words, the decorations carved in relief on this handle simulated and replaced the elaborate sennit designs and wrappings. On the surface of this part of the club, within the bands formed by the spiral, irregular diamond-shaped zones are carved in bas relief, forming a rich and active pattern. Above it, on the upper portion of the shaft, are a series of long vertical zones within which the designs are arranged in irregular vertical bands. This zonal treatment, with each section marked off by higher ridges of relief carving, is common to and characteristic of Samoan and Fijian, as well as Tongan clubs; and when this type of surface treatment is rendered in ironwood, it becomes especially conspicuous since, from constant handling, the raised areas of the design acquire an extremely high polish. The manner in which the decorative zones are varied, following no strict rule or pattern, is typical to all these richly carved western Polynesian clubs. A characteristic shared by the art styles of the three group of island peoples is the scarcity of curvilinear elements in these club decorations. It is also important to observe the extremely fine quality and regularity in the deeply incised designs.

The modified bat-paddle club, the lower portion of which is shown in Fig. 89, is an even more characteristically zone and decorated club than the smaller one; it also has, in some of the sections, a few small, hard-to-identify, zoomorphs, a feature of style that may be used to distinguish Tongan from Samoan clubs. In some instances, these designs are anthropomorphic, and like the geometric design, they do not follow any particular pattern of arrangement. The shaping of these clubs is of further significance: the way in which the circular handle of the small club gradually becomes modified into a hexagonal shape that accommodates and fuses with the ball head; and the shift of forms that occurs as the circular handle of the longer club gradually changes into a rhomboidal shape when viewed in cross-section. In both objects, the shaping of the club is not merely a decorative expedient, but adds considerably to its efficiency as a weapon. These objects have a dark brown to black-brown color which is achieved in some parts of Polynesia by burying a newly carved club or other object for a considerable time in the mud of a taro patch, the color deriving from the minerals in the soil.

In the Ha'apai group of the Tongan Islands, apparently one of the few centers of figure carving in western Polynesia developed. As previously mentioned, there existed a stylistic relationship between these figures and some of those made or found in Fiji, and there is an important typological analogy in the presence in both island groups of human figures carved on suspension hooks.[43] Wood and, apparently later, whale ivory were the two materials used in these sculptures, which probably represented religious if not deity figures. The majority of Tongan figures are female, in contrast with those of Fiji which are both male and female. A hard, close-grained wood, comparable to that used for the clubs, was used for most of these carvings. Each figure was stained a deep brown or black-brown as were the clubs, and probably in the same fashion.

Representative Tongan sculptured figures in wood can, within limits, be easily characterized stylistically (Fig. 90). The interpretation may be described as a substantially organic, somewhat conventionalized rendition of human form. Proportions build up functionally from short, heavy, lower legs to long thighs and a medium-proportioned torso; the upper body expands into very wide shoulders and short, straight-hanging, often unarticulated arms; and the head is generally quite large in relation to the rest of the figure. In style, the figures from this area may be designated as rigid, formal, and

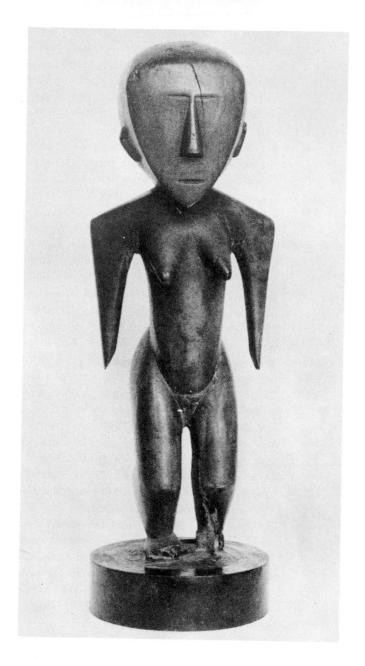

90 Polynesia, Tonga, standing female figure.

281

articulated with certain parts having marked cubistic qualities and others given a full-volumed, rounded treatment. The head, for example, has an established volume in its general shape, but the frontal area is flattened off to define the areas of the face from which the features either project or recede. Likewise, the profile of the body is composed of sharp, even acute angles which develop in space as volumetric shapes. The interpretation of the figure as a whole is one in which the forms are first flattened out, such as the planes of the back and the backs of the legs; and then they are developed as rounding out into space. This is, to some extent, an abstraction of the potentially expressive qualities inherent in the human figure. Facial features are rigidly rectilinear and have a rather tenuous actuality and implication. These works are stained with a completely monochromatic finish of dark brown or red-brown, and have a high polish. In its naturalism, this particular example is somewhat at variance with other figure sculptures from Tonga. Some of the apparently later wooden and ivory carvings have a more naturalistic expression of form, which may have been influenced by European contact. Many aspects of this type of figure can be compared with examples from Fiji.

On the basis of present research, it would appear that the original point of expansion of Polynesian cultures into the central Pacific was from and through western Polynesia.[44] However these migrations may have developed, Tahiti and the other Society Islands to the east seem to have played an important role as a dispersal point for these migrant cultures as they spread out to various other points in central and marginal Polynesia. This fact seems now to be established by various archaeological material, although future investigations may further confirm or modify the present view.

Figures of moderate size, mostly representing male deity figures, are characteristic of early Tahitian art (Fig. 91). While a few fugitive elements of this figure style can be related to the Tongan carvings, there is a basic difference in the content of formal and expressive

282

91 Polynesia, Society Islands, Tahiti, male figure.

features, which can best be related or compared with statements of form appearing in other marginal Polynesian styles. The first response to such an object as the illustrated Tahitian figure is that it reveals a complex combination of rigorously stylized, formal elements and of full-volumed, rounded parts, both of which contribute to a vigorously activated creation. In this figure the shoulders are geometrically squared off, as are the arms, with the hands resting at either side of the upper abdominal area. The head protrudes as a nonnaturalistic form which juts out over the body; the lower jaw, depicted as a very sharp, protruding line, overhangs the upper part of the abdomen. Of particular importance for comparison with figure styles in marginal Polynesian sculpture are several notable features: the way in which the shallow-craniumed head relates to the body; the squared-off shoulder treatment; the protuberance of the body area; the very short, sharply angled thighs, and the long and particularly voluminous lower legs. Expressively, these Tahitian figures are at least semi-two-dimensional, with the forms projecting from an essentially flat background. These varied degrees of projection should be kept in mind for consideration in relation to the other marginal Polynesian figure expressions.

Contrasts between the full-volumed, rounded forms and the flattened shapes heighten the active and aesthetic effects of contained power in this and similar works. An important expressive feature of this style is the dramatic statement of thrusting forms such as the head, the abdomen, and the knees. Many of these central Polynesian figure sculptures are male, with a very naturalistic rendering of the genital organs. The relationships of forms, of body parts and proportions, of contrasting elements that project and recede, are all in expressive agreement with general Polynesian styles.

As previously mentioned, many art forms in Polynesia have rank or prestige significance alone; even the deity figures, such as the one just considered, have something of that quality since they were made exclusively for use by the upper classes. Tahitian fly-whisk handles, together

with carved fan handles, are excellent illustrations of prestige-vanity art forms found in this vast area (Fig. 92). Carved with an elaborate, sculptural design, this handle consists of three distinct parts: 1) a wide, circular "guard" at the base; 2) a central section richly decorated with deeply cut parallel chevron motifs; and 3) a figure, large in proportion to the length of the shaft and Siamese-twinlike in the relationships of its body parts, which terminates the butt end of the handle. The terminal figure on this fly-whisk handle is very small and is created as a vigorous conventionalization of the larger type of Tahitian deity carving just considered. All of the features of the latter figure are exaggerated in these small carvings, being here rendered in a geometric or schematic fashion. Exemplifying this is the angularity of the shoulders and arms, the exaggeration of the short thigh form, and the shape and protrusion of the head. The Siamese-twinlike aspect of these small figures appears in the sharing of the volume of the body, and in the fusion of the shoulders with the back of the head.

It is these figures which are of particular significance, since they reveal an important tendency toward conventionalization and schematization of small decorative figures, a trend which appears in many other areas of Polynesia. The zoomorphic and anthropomorphic glyphs on the Tongan clubs, for example, are shared with a few similar designs on Fiji clubs, and appear on various objects in the Cook and Austral Islands as a particular and important feature of style, altered to suit the local traditions. Such stylizations and conventionalizations of form, as well as other elements schematized to an even greater degree, will later be pointed out in Marquesan and Cook Island art. But, despite the sharing of typical elements in this sort of carving among the art traditions of various other Polynesian areas, the particular way in which the forms are handled is unique to each area.

92 Polynesia, Society Islands, Tahiti, fly-whisk handle.

285

In characteristic fashion, Tahitian clubs are decorated with small angular designs; the tapa cloth painted with free-hand, angular motifs, as well as with designs from real leaves or flowers dipped in dye and pressed on the fabric. Nearly all the forms of Polynesian decorative art appeared in Tahiti in one fashion or another, including the practice of heavy tattooing used by the men on almost all parts of their bodies. This appears certainly to be of considerable importance in relation to considerations of the art traditions of marginal Polynesia.

The Cook Islands, which lie five hundred miles southwest of the Society group, were another important center of east-central Polynesia. The inhabitants seem to have migrated from the two major dispersal areas: from western Polynesia, or the Samoa-Tonga district; and from Tahiti, in the centrally located Societies. The art style of this island group, the larger land masses being Aitutaki, Mangaia, and Raratonga, is distinctive, and yet clearly related to other central and eastern Polynesian styles. A carving, possibly a canoe-prow board from Raratonga, serves as an excellent illustration of Cook Island art style (Fig. 93). Canoe prow and stern decorations are common in many areas of Polynesia. They have a religious-protective significance, and are marked by stylized figurative sculptures which represent deities. This transverse board from a Raratongan canoe prow is decorated with a central line of superposed figures flanked by profile rows of superposed figures carved almost in full relief. These forms are again small, and consist of an elongated ovoid head and stylistically conventionalized arm, chest, and leg forms projecting as schematized shapes. The elongated narrow head with its huge, ovate delineations of the eyes and mouth and its stubby nose is particularly worthy of note, as it agrees with the traditions of Raratongan style in almost all manifestations of its figurative art. Another characteristic style element in Raratongan art forms is the sureness and crispness of delineation. This style is one of the most conspicuous examples in which a strong, sculptural mode is successfully combined with an aerial or

286

93 Polynesia, Cook Islands, Raratonga, canoe-prow board.

287

pierced type of artistic expression. In this classic example of Raratongan art, the energetic sculptural statement of form appears in both the profile and full-face views; and a freedom within the controlled design is evident, as each figure is slightly at variance with the others. Yet each of the small design forms expresses the full power of the style. The motivation for this sculptured board lies in the primary need for security and survival. For this purpose it functioned in the usual way, giving tangible substance to the deities or spirits which were believed to protect the users of the canoe. Its meaning is inextricably tied to the function, in that the spirit beings, once represented as tangible forms, could be placed in the canoe so that their protective force could be focused and brought to bear on the boat, the men, and their mission.

It is important to note that each figure, although stylized, has much of the form and quality of the so-called free-standing fisherman's god, a well-illustrated sculpture from this area.[45] The elongated, narrow shape of the heads and the angular stylization of the body parts also appear to the same or even greater degree of conventionalization in the schematized, pierced figures of the Raratongan "district gods."[46] Cook Island sculpture, as represented by these objects, evidences a remarkable degree of design and form control.

In the southern part of the Cook Islands area, a unique type of sculpture typifies the art style of Mangaia. Here the god Tane, of particular importance for the sculptors, is represented symbolically by decorated adzes. These objects are modifications of the functional tools used by the carvers; and in shape, proportion, and over-all composition of parts, these ceremonial works show a fairly wide range. Regardless of the shapes and proportions, however, these adzes share a common decorative treatment. This is composed of crosshatched design patterns covering the entire surface, in which the diagonals are carved in a low relief; and in the middle of each resultant diamond shape, a horizontal, projecting ridge is prominently rendered. Fig. 94 illustrates a fine example

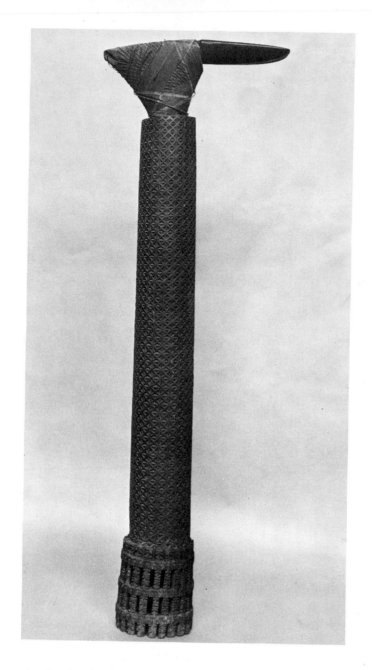

94 Polynesia, Cook Islands, ceremonial adze.

95 Polynesia, Austral Islands, female figure.

of these Mangaian adzes, even to the extent of having a good part of the original sennit lashings, used in the attachment of the blade to the shaft, still extant. It has been suggested that the geometric crosshatched design is a complex rendering of back-to-back, highly stylized, human figures reduced to a type of K-motif. This seems a bit more likely on other examples than this one. From these forms, taken along with other artistic evidences, it is clear that the Cook Island style reveals many affinities with other Polynesian art traditions.

Southeast of the Cooks, in the Austral Islands, another important center of Polynesian art arose in which three-dimensional figures and geometrically designed utilitarian objects are conspicuous. A few wooden figure carvings have survived from this area (Fig. 95). Typical of this style is the more naturalistic proportioning of parts, for example: the relationship of the head to the total figure; the treatment of the squared shoulders; the flexed arms, free of the body at the sides, with the hands resting on the abdomen; and the rounded, protruding torso area. Characteristic of Austral Island style are the chip designs over the face and body of the figure, particularly the circular elements surrounded with triangular, raylike forms. Also typical and distinctive of this style, observable in the larger-than-life-sized stone figures as well as in the wooden ones, is the unique type of headdress. Other diagnostic style characteristics are: the treatment of the rectilinear, flat forms flanking the eye-level of the face at both sides; the volumetric handling of the thighs; and the cubistic rendering of the lower legs, which terminate in blocky forms that serve instead of defined feet as a base. The finish given to these carved forms is a monochromatic dark brown.

In style, Austral figures of this type agree with the larger stone carvings of this island region and, in many respects, with other wood carvings from central and eastern Polynesia. In this female figure, a number of characteristics common to the general Polynesian figure type found in Tahiti and other eastern and marginal area styles are evident and should be noted. Outstanding among these shared elements are the backward pull of the squared shoulders, the flattened plane of the back, and the heavy leg treatment, especially the short volumes of the thighs and the massive lower legs.

Although concentric circular elements and segments of them are conspicuous motives in the vocabulary of Austral Island decorative design, they are not as ubiquitous as the patterns, often very small, composed of bas-relief crossing diagonals carved within a rectangular border and generally arranged in panels or bands. These are analogous in form to the crosshatched or K-motifs found on Mangaian ceremonial adzes. When placed contiguously over the surface of an object, the resultant over-all design shows a clear relationship to the decorative surfaces noted on western Polynesian clubs, especially those of Samoa and Tonga. In the Austral decorative art style, such rectilinear motifs are often combined, not only with the characteristic curvilinear elements, but also with short or long, slim dentates, which appear frequently as border designs (Fig. 96). While no anthropomorphs are used in this design tradition, a distinctive feature is the termination of ladle, bowl, and scoop handles, and the shafts of ceremonial paddles, by a large form around which are carved a series of tiny, grotesque human figures almost in the round, with pierced, stylized shapes and large, disclike eyes.[47] The importance of these grotesque forms is that they represent here, as they do on the fly-whisk handles from Tahiti and more particularly on many objects from marginal Polynesian style areas, a fantastic strain of figure expression. This is an important element in Polynesian art that may have come originally from the west, brought by the various migrant groups either from the art of Melanesia or as a result of other contacts made by these peoples during the long colonizing voyages.

Each of the four major areas on the outskirts of Polynesia had been sufficiently isolated from the central Pacific source or sources of migration that by the time of European contact they had developed notable forms of linguistic variation as well as other cultural divergencies, particularly in the realm of their highly individual art styles. Many, if not all, of the basic aspects of these cultures — those of the Hawaiian peoples, the Marquesans, the Easter Islanders, and the Maori of New

96 Polynesia, Austral Islands, carved bowl.

Zealand—indicate analogies among them, and strongly suggest a common source of origin. For example, the importance among these peoples, of social distinctions, and of the relationships of classes with rank and genealogies, is of the utmost significance; all are common Polynesian cultural factors. Further shared societal elements include the presence of specialists in all phases of activity including the creation of art objects, and the worship of a pantheon of greater gods who existed as the particular property of high-ranking members of the group. The majority of these, together with the customs of making tapa, of body and/or face tattooing, and of the construction of religious architectural sites, are present in these marginal island areas as they are in other parts of Polynesia. But as mentioned above, the differences between one fringe area and another were sufficiently marked as to allow a characterization of each one.

The Hawaiian Islands, as the northernmost part of Polynesia, lie something over twenty-three hundred miles northwest of Tahiti, from which point they are believed to have been settled. Possibly touched upon by the Spanish in 1555, they were finally "discovered" by Cook in 1778 and named the Sandwich Islands. From that time on there was uninterrupted contact with Europeans, in particular with the whalers and the China traders. As a partial result of this contact, the great king Kamehameha I by the time of his death in 1819 had largely fused the islands into an empire. In the same year, and somewhat under the same influence, his successor, Kamehameha II (or Liholiho as he was sometimes known), broke all the highly restrictive tabus which had been developed almost to the point of societal strangulation in Hawaii. This was an extremely significant and historic date, since at that time there was a great wave of iconoclasm; and subsequent to it, no important figural sculpture in traditional style was produced in Hawaii. Thus a terminal date is established beyond which, for this area of Polynesia, there was a rapid decline of all the traditional forms, and a virtual disappearance of figure carving. The surviving Hawaiian figures can be given an approximate date which would appear to have more authenticity than the chronological schedules applied to most areas of Polynesian or Oceanic art forms.

It was purely fortuitous that many of the extant works of Hawaiian sculpture escaped destruction in 1819. In some cases objects were given away rather than having them destroyed, and in other instances there was apparently an element of doubt as to the wisdom of burning them, in which case they were frequently hidden away in caves. Gradually, over the years, these cached art works have come to light. Such was the history of the fine pair of temple-god figures, hidden away on the large island of Hawaii, which were recovered in 1898 (Figs. 97, 98), together with a few other important figures and several carved objects. The two almost identical temple figures were created in classic style. Both measure about five feet high, and are carved on posts which were intended to be "planted" in the area around the temple or "heiau" precinct. Carved in a dense, heavy

97 Polynesia, Hawaii, temple figure.   **98** Profile view.

wood, these works are excellent examples of the figure-type created for the heiau precinct to which only the very highborn had access. Below the head, the figures have a very rigorous, cubisticlike rendering of organic and naturalistic parts and forms. The proportions are fairly close to those found in the Australs, with a typical Polynesian treatment of the thigh as a somewhat short and thrusting shape. Entirely characteristic of Hawaiian figure style is the dynamic pose of the body parts: the sharp projection of the lower legs as they meet the thigh, the forward thrust of the torso counterbalanced by the backward movement of the flexed arms, and the sloping, rounded shoulders. An important element in this style is the broad adze-marking of the surface planes and the blending of rounded shapes with sharply cubistic, defining contours. Also of great significance for analysis of the body treatment is the functional quality of the active, negative spaces between the arms and the body, and between the inner surfaces of the legs. These allow the forms to exist in space and to make their contribution to the projection and recession of parts.

Above the body, the heavy tubular form of the neck connects the torso with a grotesque head that is only a bit less in its total height than the rest of the figure. Surmounting the head is a very tall and completely aerial palettelike form. The head is of great importance, since it may be classed as in the stylized-grotesque tradition of representation of human form which has been mentioned as an underlying but significant style feature throughout marginal Polynesia. In shape, the head is a completely nonnaturalistic, heavily conventionalized form developed in a highly expressive manner. The volume of this form is shallow and almost insignificant. The nose is delineated as a high crest with heavily splayed nostrils, the mouth as an enormous, grimacing, horizontally arranged figure-eight shape with cogs or notches indicating teeth, while the eyes are not defined but merely suggested by the depth of shadow created by the heavily notched hairdress that swings out to either side from just above the bridge of the nose. A very deep and pierced, V-shaped area replaces the forehead and the cranium; it also provides a hollow into which the central shaft of the topping palette is set. This form, too, is heavily notched. The palette consists of an almost New Ireland type of cagelike structure within which abstract tubular spurs thrust to the front, to the back, and to either side. A dark brown color is monochromatically applied to the small versions of these figures, while this pair of statues is rendered in the dry, unfinished wood. But even without the coloristic treatment, the head and palette of these and other Hawaiian temple-god figures have a dynamic, vigorous expressive quality reminiscent of Melanesian traditions. And this expressiveness is combined in the same figure, with the direct and strong sculptural statements of the body parts, that is, of the forms below the neck. The body forms as they are rendered here have a closer visual analogy with elements from certain African traditions than is usual in Oceanic art. Comparable style characteristics appear in the few very large temple figures, generally about six feet high, that are still extant.[48]

Aside from the great temple gods, known as the "akua," the "aumakua," or private gods, were of such importance that figures representing them were carved for the household altars. Although these were much smaller, they frequently manifested a comparable energetically strong and dynamic quality of expression (Fig. 99). Many of these smaller figures have massively scaled proportions and are given a pose that bespeaks a powerful and active aggressiveness. These objects had, in general, less conventionalized treatment in the shaping of facial forms and features than is found in the temple-deity figures. They have an added expressive quality, however, that is derived from inlays and from the appending of extraneous materials. The eyes, for example, are carved to receive a shaped oval of pearl shell. This is held securely in place by a peg of wood having a large, round knob at one end, which is driven through a piercing in the shell and into a hole cut and shaped to receive it within the hollow eye-area. The rounded knob on the

99 Polynesia, Hawaii, deity figure.

end of this functional peg serves as the pupil of the eye. In the mouth, the lips of which are everted, slots are carved for the insertion of human teeth; and cofferlike pits were made in the head for the addition of long strands of human hair. One eye is missing in this example, as are all the teeth and a good deal of the hair. With all of these elements in place, the facial forms of this carving would have been exceedingly aggressive.[49] One final attachment should be mentioned: the loincloth of tapa which is wrapped around the lower body in traditional fashion.

Hawaiian figure sculptures of this nature are among the most notable achievements created by primitive artists. The kahuna, as the specialists of this particular island group were called, had the usual training; but they seem, on the basis of many examples, to have been particularly talented. No sculptural forms in primitive art have a more complete utilization of space; nor do any render in more powerful terms the expressive possibilities of geometric shapes and their defining surfaces to create, in aggressive sculptural statements, the potential of the organically integrated human form as a dynamic aesthetic object.

All of the major parts of the human form are actively articulated, although they can be described as being of a cubistic, creative rendering. Smooth, flowing curves are used to define such cylindrical shapes as the arms, neck, and thighs; and flat planes and angular shapes, as in the pectoral region of the body and the lower legs, are employed to create powerful, abstract shapes and contrasts in the compositional array of forms, surfaces, and profiles. The pose of the figure is one of complete flexion and tension, with the climax appearing in the overpowering force of the aggressive head. An important sculptural interpretation should be noted in the series of eight dramatic parallel horizontals which stress the vigorous projection and recession of all the dynamic expressive parts. These horizontals are in the following alignment from top to base of the form: 1) the visual thrust created by the line of the shell-inlayed eyes;

2) the equally visual, but at the same time more physical thrust of the mouth area, especially forceful when it contained all of its inset teeth; 3) the slightly receding level of the sharp, square chin; 4) the powerful forward impulse of the massive shoulders which culminate dramatically in the sharp slope of the two pectoral planes; 5) the marked line of the elbow flexions, which are accentuated by the receding and tapering chest cavity; 6) the important level of the tiny, schematic hands; 7) the jutting forms of the knees; and 8) the slight recession of the small, undifferentiated, block feet, now broken off at the front. All of these horizontal divisions are physically connected, integrated statements defined by expanding curvilinear contours, whether continuous or broken in shape. These emphatically expressive outlines emphasize the contained volumetric force of the powerful forms; and they operate strongly around and between all of the shapes. For example, the profiles formed by the inner surfaces of the arms and the body and those of the inner outlines of the legs describe negative spaces that are of great expressive importance. As previously mentioned, for instance, the small, abstract rendering of the hands is of special significance: the forward movement of the inner profile of the arms, together with that of the receding profile of the chest, creates an important area of contained space that is freed only through the narrow aperture between the hands and the parallel line of the thighs. It is this treatment of negative space that gives to the figure its most powerful visual impact, since the concept of the containment of a great explosive potential within this negative space area is apparent. This is released with great control by the careful positioning of the hands. The negative space between the legs also has an added expression of enclosed, three-dimensional space.

This sculpture, like many of the deity figures in Hawaii, was carved in a heavy hardwood, and was given a smooth surface with a deep, red-black coloration. The motivation, function, and meaning of these deity figures have been previously considered,[50] and the aesthetic expression has been analyzed here. Figures such as this must be ranked among the most powerful sculptural expressions created in any era and/or geographical locale, whether by artists of high or primitive cultures. The statement of content depends entirely upon sculptural interpretation of forms, while added materials stress the dramatic, almost fantastic strain in Polynesian art. In other words, the dramatic aggressiveness of this figure, as it is conveyed by the facial features in particular, represents a possible Melanesian strain in this art which appears, at least in the traditional Hawaiian art style, as an intensely dramatic, semigrotesque treatment of forms and composition.

Color is of no great significance in Polynesian sculpture. But it is nevertheless a very important element in other types of art, particularly in tapa decoration and body tattooing. In Hawaii, Pacific tapa decoration reached its climax. Practically every known method of decoration was used, together with almost every variety of rectilinear and curvilinear design as well as a range of colors that included browns of several shades, reds, red-brown, rose, some blue, and white. Various blendings and gradations between these hues resulted in such delicate shades as mauve. The textural quality of Hawaiian tapa was also superior. It is certainly unfortunate that the skill of tapa-making and the art of its decoration have been lost forever in the Hawaiian Islands.

Featherwork of various types is of the utmost importance as an artistic and decorative medium, throughout the Pacific Island area. In Melanesia, feathers were largely used as headdress ornaments. While the same was true to an extent in many areas of Polynesia, there were some regions, such as Hawaii, in which they were used in a distinctive and different way. Elaborate and extravagant cloaks, capes, and helmets made of a plaited pandanus fiber base were covered on the outside with myriads of red, yellow, and some black feathers to produce bold designs of angular or circular nature (Fig. 100). Relatively few examples of this type of important chiefly apparel are still extant; but those which have

100 Polynesia, Hawaii, feather cloak.

survived evidence great accomplishment in the tieing-in of the feathers into a rich and colorful design. And these works become even more prodigious when it is taken into account that only the feathers of certain birds could be used, and that these birds and feathers were very small. Huge numbers of birds were thus required to produce one garment. Finally, it must be noted that the featherwork objects constitute, for Pacific island art, the epitome of aesthetic achievement in unusual materials and that they represent the most colorful of all Polynesian art expressions.

The nearest of the island groups to the area of eastern Polynesia are the Marquesas, which are located only seven hundred and forty miles northeast of Tahiti. An extensive and, in many instances, glamorous literature on these islands has given them an aura of romance and popular appeal almost as great as that of Tahiti.[51] But the physical or actual popularization of this group has been relatively minor, due to its geographical location: the Marquesas lie outside the limits of most of the Pacific navigation routes. Culturally, the Marquesans are closely allied to other Polynesian peoples; and, on the basis of recent archaeological work, the current opinion is that they were directly settled by migration from western Polynesia.[52] The rugged islands, broken up into innumerable valleys, were inhabited by many small tribes, most of which were hostile to one another but all sharing a uniform culture pattern. Rank was based largely on a graduated scale, working down from the chief through the priest and on to the heads of large families and to the tahuna, or specialist, whether he was a master sculptor or a house-builder. A singular feature of this culture in relation to the rest of Polynesia was the practice of polyandry. Unique to the Marquesas are various types of architecture and decorated head ornaments. Color is even more restricted than in most Polynesian areas; even the tapa cloth, which is of extremely fine textural quality, is usually found to have a delicate, monochromatic coloration in the natural gray-white, a yellowish tone, or a pink-to-almost-mauve tint. Sculpture, as is typical of this vast region, is also monochrome in treatment, being either a dark reddish-brown or black.

Marquesan houses were built on a high platform or base which was faced and surfaced with stone. The ground plan was rectangular, with a row of median ridge posts; but the elevation of the houses was unique since they had only three sides, the back of the structure being formed by an unbroken slope of the roof. The central ridge posts were usually planklike and were sometimes decorated with panels of geometric designs, while the front row of posts which supported the roof beams were often carved as half-length human figures. In characteristic Polynesian fashion, the house parts were lashed together with red, black, and white sennit arranged to form ornamental designs. Heavy reeds, set in vertical rows, served as the front wall; for the lower part of the side walls, the reeds were placed horizontally. The upper segments of the side walls, as well as the exotically sloped roof, were covered with thatch.

Like Hawaii, the Marquesas have their own distinctive art style, despite the presence of numerous shared features germaine to all of Polynesia. This appears in the stone figures from small to over life size, and in the various wood sculptures, including figures and heads used in diverse ways. Among the various figurative wood carvings, the "stilt-step" sculptures are particularly good examples (Fig. 101). Although small in size, these carvings illustrate the shapes and proportions characteristic of Marquesan-style figure sculpture in wood. The proportions are heavy, with the large head occupying a good one third of the total figure. Typical of all aspects of Marquesan art are the volumetric relationships of body parts. For the majority of these figure sculptures, regardless of material, the legs are handled as forms of massive scale, with the thighs arranged diagonally to create an area into which the heavy volume of the relatively short body is fitted. In fact, the thigh forms in this, as in many other examples, project in an upward diagonal to such an extent that the buttocks are structurally located halfway up the back. The figure is carved as a diagonal support set between the vertical and horizontal forms of the step, so that it can only be semi-round in form. Nevertheless, all of the features of fully round figures are evident in these relatively free, three-dimensional carvings. Marquesan stilt-steps were, so far as is known, of purely sociological significance; the fact that they were decorated indicates that they were, in all probability, created as personal prestige objects.

Of particular note for this style is the treatment of the enormously scaled facial features, carved in low relief on the rounded surface of the block head. Great wide

101   Polynesia, Marquesas Islands, stilt-step figure.

ovals, in some examples circles, represent the eyes and are defined by a surrounding or enclosing relief band; a slight ridge formed by the juncture of the concave facial plane below the eyes with the expanding lower edge of the forehead plane, traverses the face at ear level and bisects the orbital area, creating the appearance of tightly closed eyes. Between the eyes, this horizontal facial ridge curves down from each side and fuses to form a low nasal ridge which is terminated by two flanking solid and low-relief forms describing the wide nostrils. In characteristic manner, the mouth is represented by a very wide and slightly open oval, bound by a low-relief band. The ears are typically shaped as reverse spirals, curving toward the face above and below the median eye ridge. An unusual feature in the facial design is the bas-relief carving of two lizard forms, the heads of which are arranged so that they flank the mouth and the bodies approximately follow the curvature of the heavy jaws, with the tails ending just below the ears.[53]

Like this example, many of the footrest figures lack feet; the end of the heavy legs rests instead on small carved figures. In this particular work, a very small, full-length figure is carved at right angles to each leg and faces away from the main form; between the "feet" thus formed, a small head juts downward. On other stilt-steps, one or two small figures, half-forms, or even heads serve as supports under each leg. The variance of these terminal shapes is comparable to the wide array of geometric designs which frequently, as here, cover the entire surface of the major form. These designs consist of parallel grooves carved in different widths and arranged in various configurations such as vertical lines, chevron alignments, concentric circles, and expanding diamond patterns formed by the conjunction of chevron elements which are oriented in opposite directions. The frontal or outer surface of the foot protector which curves out and up from the top of the figure support is frequently, as here, given a comparable surface decoration. In this example, the deep, wide, parallel grooves follow the surface shape and contour in a horizontal direction. It is important to note that the arrangement of these horizontals is broken by a row of chevron elements. This same interruptive treatment also appears on the vertically grooved area of the face below, where one row breaks the regularity of the design as it extends downward from the forehead through the eye. This Marquesan decorative vocabulary is not extensive, but is employed with a great variance of elements. The segmentation of motives appears as a common practice, and results in what amounts to a distinctive patterning of surface design on each figure.

With only slight differences, which, as noted, give every Marquesan carved figure an individualistic flavor, these small footrest supports serve to illustrate the traditional style by which the human figure is rendered in this marginal Polynesian area. Sculptures ranging in size from six inches to about eight feet in height were carved in both stone and wood, functioning largely as votive or commemorative ancestor-deity figures, motivated by the dominating need-satisfying forces behind all Polynesian art traditions. That is, these objects were created to appease the need for continuity and stability, to symbolize the attainment of social status, and to give tangible evidence of individual prestige, or satisfy personal vanity. In meaning, they refer to ancestral-mythological beings who were culture heroes and progenitors.

All of the important variations in Marquesan figure representation can be observed in a canoe-prow carving from the British Museum (Fig. 102). Two of these differences are at once apparent: the greater freedom of pose in this intently alert, seated figure than in the stilt-step carving, and the globular rather than blocky shape of the head. This rounded shape appears with sufficient frequency to be considered a variant type of head definition within the art style. Facial features are handled in very much the same manner for both head types, although in this example a few changes can be noted which produce a somewhat more active expression. These alterations include such subtle elements as the sharp pointing of the corners of the mouth, the reduction in size of the nostrils, and, especially, the circular shaping of the eyes which echo the curvature of the head profile. This curvilinear accent is restated again in the single spiral design of the ears. Finally, the ridge that marks the

102 Polynesia, Marquesas Islands, canoe-prow board.

lower jaw is greatly recessed below the mouth and facial planes until it almost resembles a ring around the neck.

The body forms also are somewhat modified in this figure, which has a greater organic unity than is generally found in Marquesan sculpture. A slightly truncated, conical form gives the body an explosive thrust; the flattened arms terminate in an undifferentiated hand, with only the fingers summarily indicated. The hands are placed, as on most Polynesian figures, against the sides of the abdomen. The long concave line of the back develops as an unbroken continuation and reversal of the expanding curve formed by the back of the head; and this shape is somewhat repeated in the volumetric roundness of the buttocks. One should note the balance and relationship that exists between the three important and expressive volumes of the head, the abdomen, and the buttocks, the volume of the latter continuing forward into the heavy, rounded legs. Flat, slablike forms indicate the feet, each of which rest on a small, apparently squatting figure.

Another notable variation in this figure is that the surface is entirely without decorative designs. Instead, rough tool marks remain and give it a textural quality. This is not a unique feature, but appears in other Marquesan figure sculptures.

Of considerable importance in this canoe-prow carving is the long forward-projecting arm and its terminal form. The latter shape, with its high transverse ridge and sloping spadelike end is merely a rough blocking out of a particular type of fantastic head and/or face that appears mostly on various long, ovoid, Marquesan pouring bowls. Facial features, when present in this shape, are adaptations of the typical features, altered and arranged to focus on and emphasize the surrounding, flangelike form at the end as though it were an enormous, gaping mouth. The appearance of grotesque stylization in this art tradition conforms with the trend toward fantasy and distortion that has already been discussed, and which is found in all other marginal Polynesian arts.

A distinctive aspect of Marquesan art is the creation of various types of shell head-ornaments that function as insignia of rank and are worn on ceremonial occasions. These are not common to Polynesian traditions, but rather, as noted earlier, are an outstanding feature in the art of the Solomon Islands and in various other eastern Melanesian areas. An example which well illustrates this shellwork was collected by Cook on his last voyage to the Pacific, and was sent to the Museum in Göttingen, Germany, in 1781 (Fig. 103). It is composed of a large, circular disk of mother-of-pearl shell to which is attached, in a partially broken form, a cutout design of turtle shell. This is an agreement with the Melanesian "kapkap" tradition and technique. The pearl shell is attached to a headband made of heavy twisted and plaited sennit cord, with tapa cloth ties at either end; while a clump of feathers is tied into the headband, and attached to the shell directly over the center. These shell ornaments, known as "uhikana," were worn at the side of the head, that is, over the temple, mostly by warriors and male dancers. This is an unusually fine example of

103 Polynesia, Marquesas Islands, shell head-ornament.

delicate Marquesan shellwork. It should be observed that
the elegant pierced turtle shell is attached to the background by means of a smaller pearl-shell disk with an
attached, overlaid center of turtle shell which has a
punctuated decoration. The cutout designs are abstract,
but it is possible to detect certain shapes that suggest
ear or nose forms. The use of such isolated facial
features as decorative motives is a common style feature
in the vocabulary of Marquesan delineated art, especially
as it appears in the relief designs on the exterior surfaces of large bowls. Marquesan artists excelled in such

delicate, almost jewel-like work as found in these shell ornaments and in other fine objects, examples of which are the tiny, carved ear ornaments in bone (often human bone), and small hair tubes, many of which displayed carvings of full-length human figures in the same massive scale as noted in the larger ones of stone or wood.

Marquesan style is certainly one of the most individualistic of Polynesian art traditions. This is particularly true with regard to their tattooing, a practice carried on throughout Polynesia. The men's body decoration was the most complete in this entire Oceanic area, covering the entire person even to the crown of the head. The designs, in a blue-black color, were originally somewhat like those on the shell head-decoration just considered. But later, by the time of Herman Melville's stay there, the patterns had become modified into largely solid bands and panels.[54] By then, Marquesan art and life had undergone only slight modification.

One of the most dramatized of South Sea areas is the tiny land mass located eighteen hundred miles southeast of the Marquesas. It received its name, Easter Island, when it was discovered in 1722, because it was first sighted on Easter Sunday, and is the easternmost as well as the smallest of all Polynesian areas. On the basis of various archaeological and anthropological comparisons, colonization of Easter Island seems to have been accomplished by peoples moving southeast from the Marquesas Islands. The much publicized and dramatized "mystery" associated with this area is how the inhabitants of such a barren spot, only thirteen miles long by nine miles wide, could leave behind so many large volcanic-stone statues. Some of these were erected in architectural surroundings, while others were set up in isolation on uninhabited parts of the island. Aside from these remains, a number of incised and painted rock designs have been found in proximity to rustic stone habitations. Other art forms include: many small skeletalized and grotesque wooden figures; and a number of "tablets" or irregular slabs of wood incised with a zoned arrangement of semipictographs and semiglyphs which recorded, to the best of our present knowledge, the myths and legends of Easter Island. The recordings have been considered "script" and have been, as such, related to embryonic scripts from various parts of the East.[55] So far as is now known with any degree of reasonableness, however, this "writing" was likely a mnemonic device which aided the "takona," or specialist, to recall specific legends by means of inscribed references.

Among the more aesthetically satisfying of Easter Island art forms are the small wooden figures (Fig. 104). These are perhaps the most meticulously carved of all Polynesian sculptures, being rivaled only by the western Polynesian clubs. The majority of them depict skeletalized male figures in a fairly frontal pose, with small legs, an elongated torso, a long head, and with the arms cut free of the body but attached firmly by the hands to the end of the body form. In appearance these figures are a combination of anatomical and physical descriptive elements. For example, the rib cage is rendered in skeletal form; but the shallow abdomen, the arms, and the legs, as well as certain aspects of the head are physically rendered as living, fleshed forms, nonskeletal in character. Great care was taken in the definition of all physical and anatomical parts, although many of them are represented in a patterned or stylized manner. These statements of physical form include all points of articulation axcept the hip joints, which are rendered in a particular manner: the upper part of the thigh is flattened out and creates a saddlelike form into which the tenuous lower part of the body fits; the thighs continue around the form and develop into distinct and separate buttocks. All other parts of the body are organically described, and although somewhat conventionalized, they are anatomically descriptive, as for example the rib cage and the vertebrae.

The head is skeletalized and elongated, and certain structural elements are stressed in one way or another. The deep-set eyes, for example, are represented by a circle of gray-white fish bone, with an inlaid circle of shiny black obsidian acting as the pupil area. Other dis-

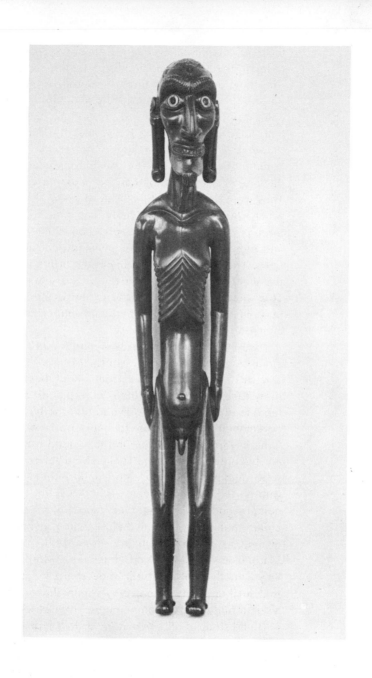

104 Polynesia, Easter Island, male figure.

tinctive facial elements include the bony representations of the zygomatic cheek structure; the thin, lipless mouth with its stressed teeth. In such figures, a long, pendent ear lobe hangs down toward the shoulders, and on the chin, a goatee is suggested in various ways. The thin, long head overhangs the body, and the skinny form of the neck is marked by exaggerated tendons and a projecting Adam's apple. The pre-European examples of these wooden figures had an extreme fineness of finish. They were carved in a blackish-red wood, the surface of which was given an extremely high polish, heightened through frequent use. The expression is one of complete and eternal rigidity, with an asymmetrical alignment of parts. The strict frontal rigidity of the figure is broken by the slight twist of the head to either one side or the other. This torsion, moreover, gives to these forms a degree of animation which is of particular importance in their aesthetic interpretation.

The best known of Easter Island art forms are the large stone carvings. These represent full-figures, half-figures, and busts ranging in size from about twelve to over thirty feet high. Many of them were placed on a wall at the end of a large, stone-paved area, the type of sacred ceremonial site common to many parts of Polynesia. Others were scattered around the island with no recognizable pattern or reason. These stone heads and figures were marked mostly by a horizontal beetling brow line, with no indication of eyes, and by a wide, tight-lipped, compressed mouth form. One aspect of these figures is clear: that they can, in their actual presence on the island, be equated with the stone work found in the Marquesas and the Austral Islands. Morphologically, however, the only features they share in common are that in their final shape, they retain the original four-sided structure of the stone matrix from which they were cut; and that, in all stone work of this type, the inordinately large head is by far the most important part of the sculpture. In all other respects, the carved, stone figures from these three areas display the distinct style characteristics of their own particular tradition.

105 Polynesia, Easter Island, fish club.

315

One of the most spectacular carvings from this area, now in the British Museum, is a fish club (Fig. 105). This is a unique design which has more of a Melanesian than a Polynesian quality of form interpretation. The basic forms of the composition seem to have been derived from a whale, whose enormous head and mouth are dramatized as the butt end of the club. The handle end tapers abruptly into a humanoid creation with legs like bird claws; and with a very simplified and conventionalized, relatively human body, hands, and head. On the back of the club, just below the humanoid form, a high-relief carving of a human head occurs. It appears that the forms were never colored, since the raw brown hardwood has a patina more consistent with constant rubbing and handling. As mentioned above, this is not a characteristic Polynesian design, but is far more Melanesian in flavor, suggesting in fact, the designs of the Sepik River of New Guinea. The appearance of fantastic or distorted grotesque forms is, however, in keeping with this trend throughout marginal Polynesia.

Breast pendants and ornaments are endemic art forms throughout the Pacific area. It is significant to note that in Easter Island, where wood was a scarce commodity, these were carved in this material. The characteristic shape is a crescent with confronting heads at either end (Fig. 106). Known as "rei-miro," they were apparently prestige objects; and on some of them, although not on this example, the so-called Easter Island script is lightly etched on the central section. It is interesting to observe that the heads at either end combine elements from the heads of both the large stone and the small wooden figures. The shapes of the mouth and the goatee are comparable to the big stone carvings; while the form of the head and the eye inlays agree with the smaller wooden sculptures. All of the varieties of art forms produced by Easter Island peoples agree essentially with the basic character of Polynesian art. The unique features are no more numerous or variant than in other marginal areas. But the features of this art can be related, in spite of other characteristics, to so many areas of

106   Polynesia, Easter Island, "rei-miro" pendant.

Polynesia, that the tradition clearly fits into the over-all
pattern of art in this vast area.

Far to the southwest of Easter Island, and over a
thousand miles southeast of western Polynesia, lie the
two big islands of New Zealand, the homeland of the
Polynesian Maori tribes. From where and at what time
these peoples came south from the tropics is purely
theoretical. It seems most likely that they came from
Tahiti and the Society group by way of Raratonga and
the Cooks, and possibly through the Austral Islands.
The Polynesian character of the Maori is not in doubt;
but the origin of the various components of their culture
is still to be reconstructed. Archaeological work has
suggested some facts, but much more remains to be
done before a reasonable and more than generalized
hypothesis about their beginnings can be presented.

When the tribes now known as the Maori migrated
from their original home, they brought with them several
variations of a common culture. They came in more than
one group, and at more than one time. When they arrived

317

in New Zealand, they further developed their cultural idiosyncracies in an individualistic fashion, since the tribes had apparently been hostile prior to their colonization of this new land, and the antagonisms were evidently redeveloped when they relocated. Of all the Polynesian peoples, the Maoris had to make the greatest adjustment to an alien environment. Their homeland staples, such as the coconut palm, the breadfruit tree, and the paper-mulberry, could not grow in this new climate, and the pig, an important protein source in Polynesia, does not seem to have survived the migration to the south. As a consequence, their basic food and clothing supplies were taken away from them. Thus, they had to be especially resourceful in finding substitutes for these vital essentials. That they made a superb adjustment to this new environment is now an established fact; but there must have been an interval when life was uncertain and uncomfortable in this colder country. It seems likely, in fact, that the early peoples may well have been nomadic, living on the great moa birds which were then plentiful on both the North and the South Islands.[56] As these birds became scarce, and as the Maoris began to learn more about their new land, completely distinct and unique forms began to emerge. For example, after a time these peoples discovered that the native, wild flax plant could be utilized in many ways to replace the coconut palm. As a result, flax cordage was devised as a substitute for sennit; and flax fibers were used to make the kind of clothing that was necessary in this colder climate. It was soon discovered, too, that the "air-conditioned" house type of the tropics was neither comfortable nor practical in New Zealand; thus, a new type of superior house was evolved, suitable to this subtropical-to-temperate region.

The so-called council house of the Maori was, without any doubt, the finest architectural structure built by any primitive peoples. In this colder region, it had to be more compactly built. As a result, the houses were constructed of tightly enclosing materials, and the roof and side walls were completely and heavily thatched in somewhat o an allusion to tropical Polynesian structures. To further insulate the houses, the interior of each edifice was slightly sunk below ground level, that is, a shallow excavation was made and served as a depressed floor level so that the lower part of the walls were built against solid earth. The superior or council houses were modeled on the less strongly built dwelling houses. A row of central supporting posts of wood, usually totara, held up a long central ridgepole. At the front of all the houses was a fairly deeply indented porch over which the ridgepole, in later structures supported by a frontal pole, projected. The center supports diminished in height from the front of the structure to the back, so that the ridgepole had a marked front-to-back slope. The walls—the two side walls, the end wall of the house proper, and the wall forming the back of the indented porch—were composed of wide, carved wooden planks alternating with specially plaited panels (Fig. 107). These are composed on a series of parallel, vertical reeds with horizontal cross-battens of thin laths. The vertical and horizontal elements were brought together and held with colored fiber lashings, which produced designs of a distinctive and bold character. The color of the horizontal laths was a red or a red-orange, and the ties were of black and white. The designs on the panels were always of a rectilinear nature by virtue of the technique involved in binding together the vertical and horizontal members. An important feature of these architectural forms is the way in which the structural members were tied to each other: a very large transverse flax rope was strung across the house, following the line of the crossbeams; these ties were wound round the ridgepole and then around poles parallel to the wall panels. When these ropes were pulled tight, the house was virtually locked into place. Maori houses were, therefore, lashed into place in a manner comparable to that employed in the construction of houses in other parts of Polynesia.

The interiors of the porches on these buildings were completely decorated. A continuation of the interior walls served as side walls, with the same alternation of decorative and carved panels. The back wall of the porch was also composed of like alternating panels, with a door to the left surrounded by carved jambs and a lintel. A sizable horizontal window was placed close to the door and on the right. This too was completely framed by carved jambs and lintels. The façade of the house was again elaborately decorated: wide, carved barge boards followed the slope of the roof; very wide vertical panels marked the end of the side walls; a carved frontal pole (probably a later feature) rose from the center of a high, carved sill which enclosed the porch. At the apex of the façade, a masklike face surmounted with a figure was generally placed to project above the roof line.

Although the carvings and decorations of these architectural forms cannot be considered polychromatic to the same extent as those, for example, of the Sepik River Tambaran houses, color is nevertheless important. The sculptures, with few minor exceptions, were given a monochrome red-ochre coloration, the depth of the red tones differing from area to area. The pigment was mixed with fish oil to give it a fair degree of permanence. All of the eye forms in the carvings were inlaid with South Pacific abalone shell, called "paua" by the Maori, which is more colorful and opalescent than its northern counterpart. The method of affixing these inlays differed from that of Hawaii. The area cut down to receive the shell had a central projection over which the carefully cut shell was fitted. This projection, rather than a separate peg, acted as the pupil of the eye. The lashed reed panels contributed a red-orange, black and white color series to the interior walls of the house and the porch. But perhaps the most important parts coloristically were the roof beams which were painted with decorative designs in deep red, black, and white. The range of patterns includes plantlike, curvilinear design combinations, and strictly geometric, rectilinear motifs, with all the intermediate design compositions utilized. Thus, with these painted beams set against the natural-color yellow reeds which formed the surface of the roof,

107 Polynesia, New Zealand, Maori, house panel, Gisborne style.

along with the wall panels of both types, the Maori superior or council house was extremely colorful.

It is scarcely possible to speak of Maori art as a single, unified style. Careful examination of the art objects reveals marked and important regional or tribal variations which have such distinct differences that it is difficult to extract the many common elements. For example, an interior panel taken from a carved house from the east coast area near Gisborne depicts a female form surrounded by complex design motifs. These together reveal many of the features that are usually considered common to Maori art (Fig. 107). Most prominent is the presence of a wide variety of curvilinear shapes and designs almost to the exclusion of rectilinear or straight-line elements. Large and active double spirals, other single and interlocking spirals, sweeping curved lines, and circular and ellipsoidal shapes and patterns give the grotesque female figure an extremely dynamic quality which carries the eye of the beholder with great rapidity from part to part, and from element to element. Even the vibrancy of the paua-shell inlaid eyes are not sufficient to hold the attention to the huge head for any length of time. It takes lengthy and intense visual concentration to discover the various forms involved in this intricate and elaborate composition.

The motivation behind these decorated houses and their carved architectural members was the desire to maintain tribal continuity and stability. For this purpose, the carvings functioned to express, through generic forms, the mythological tribal ancestors and the great culture heroes of the remote past; while in meaning, the large generic forms and their associated smaller forms extolled the great mythologico-historical background of the tribe. These sculptures, therefore, had a tribal prestige-vanity role that may be considered their second major significance. In the Gisborne house panel nine figures are represented or abstractly suggested. The dominant form is the large and dramatic figure of the female rendered as a grotesque form, which extends from top to bottom of the carving. She is depicted as

322

giving her breast to a small form, also grotesque, while another "child" figure is depicted below, in the area between her legs. To either side of the head, a profile, semiabstract figure can be seen; and under these, flanking the mouth area, is another, still more abstractly indicated pair of profile figures. The other two figures are just as abstractly formed, one on the left just below the elbow of the main form and the other on the right, immediately beneath the upraised arm. The abstract and distorted rendering of the six surrounding figures is a style feature interpreted by nearly all Maori groups in terms of local tribal design idioms. The basis for these abstractions is a dismemberment of the grotesque main form, and its reassemblage in such a way as to bring the abstractions into agreement with the existing space; and by doing this to present, in the recombination of shapes and parts, the basic descriptive elements of these forms. Their profile depiction adds, of course, to their abstract quality.

Structurally, this panel is carved in six or more planes of depth; and to understand the form and design relationships, these degrees of depth must be perceived. There is a rounding-out of the body of the large figure, with other relief depths recorded on it or in relationship to its surrounding background. Certain features should be pointed out: the use of the large double spirals to indicate the shoulder and knee joints and the use of other small spirals to suggest such additional points of articulation as the elbow and hand of the large figure. By following these joint indications, it becomes clear that the left arm of the main figure is raised up with the hand thrust into the big, looped form of the mouth. These grotesque heads, which are associated with mythological ancestor beings, have some analogy with the deity heads of the Hawaiian figures, particularly in the horizontal figure-eight mouth and the deep V-shape developing downward to the bridge of the nose. There is, however, a pronounced difference: Maori figures of this type have an intense movement and give a sense of overt participation with the spectator. Such qualities are not a part of the more aloof Hawaiian figures. In the Maori forms there is an almost hypnotic visual inclusion of the viewer in the dynamic activity and power of the expression.

In comparison with this panel, a lintel from the Taranaki region of the west-central coast area of the North Island (Fig. 108) reveals quite a different style character, although a number of elements agree with the Gisborne panel. The right-hand portion, which substantially balanced the extant left-hand forms, is missing. Originally, as was true of many of the over-door lintels, it had contained five figures: three frontally faced and two in profile at the ends. Clear distinctions between the Gisborne and the Taranaki styles are at once evident in any comparison of forms from these two carvings. Most conspicuous of these are the head shapes of the three frontal figures and the conformation of their bodies, arms, and legs. The head shapes are in particular diagnostic of this style, as revealed in the shaping of the cranium, the large looped forms of the eye area, the particular delineation of the nose, the low placement of the shell-inlaid eyes, the very wide, open oval of the mouth with the tongue projecting straight down from the roof of the mouth, and the special clusters of breaks appearing in the double-grooved forms that surround the eyes and mouth. The bodies are treated as fairly shapeless, unarticulated volumes; the hands and legs are completely inorganically developed in their relationship to the torso. They are instead simply attached to the surface, and not always at the anatomically correct spot. The small arms loop down and are terminated by undifferentiated hands, which clasp the legs. These in turn are drawn up and back, leaving the female genital area exposed. One final difference between the Gisborne and the Taranaki style is that the carvings of the latter are relatively static in appearance. The movement is controlled and rather stiff, and the representation is more formalized and nonorganic.

In these Taranaki designs, a very conspicuous style feature is the interlocking, looped design of the background, from which the rather pudgy figures project. As

324

108 Polynesia, New Zealand, Maori, house lintel, Taranaki style.

in all styles of Maori art, the surfaces are grooved, with interstices of clustered loops. At the terminals of such a lintel carving, a profile version of the active central figure type is dynamically presented. In this example—and only the left one is intact here—is a semiabstract presentation of the terminal figure. The sinuous statements made by the body forms should be noticed particularly for their aesthetic and functional expressivity. The significance of the forms on the lintel should also be considered. Over the door of the Maori carved houses, the female genital organs were usually prominently carved; this was done because the interior of these buildings contained and displayed such quantities of great mana that any individual who had been exposed to it was a menace unless some leveling influence could be brought to bear on his person. By placing over the doorway a powerful secular symbol the danger would be removed or at least alleviated.

The distinctive and characteristic features of varied Maori art appear perhaps best in the war-canoe stern boards (Fig. 109). These are tall, elaborately carved and pierced rectangular boards which were placed at a slight diagonal above the stern of the large war canoes. Their design is somewhat standardized so that it is difficult to place them on the basis of stylistic devices. The composition of each stern board consists of two long, flat, tusk-

109 Polynesia, New Zealand, Maori, canoe-stern board,
Bay of Plenty style.

like forms that develop upward from the base. On the left one, a clearly recognizable figure is carved in a crisp, sculptural style. The base of the tusklike form on the right terminates in a large profile of a grotesque head. The tops of the two long spurs end in an active, grotesque figure that embraces both of these solid, linear forms and then dissolves into the pierced background. Large linear double spirals, presented in their most extreme form in the available space, are used as the basic motives of the background composition. An important and esoteric characteristic of these carvings, and a difficult device to read, is the use of abstract segments of human form to fill in the areas between the double spirals and act as interstices. Throughout these carvings, as is stylistically typical of Maori art, there is an astonishingly strong control of design without any attendant loss of freedom and vigor. In other words, the motifs, while carefully and precisely arranged, show no evidence of stiff formalization.

An extremely comprehensive example of Maori art appears in the parrying blade of the "taiaha" (Fig. 110), a stafflike weapon ranging in size from just over three feet to something under six feet long. The parrying end is always carved as a spatulate form and defined as an elongated, projecting tongue. Considerable variations occur in the conformation of the head and facial features above the tongue. These taiaha forms are always Janus-shaped, that is, the same design appears on the back as on the front. On some examples, as on the one at the left, the shaft is given a carved decoration, although for the majority of these weapons no carving appears on the shaft above the head. Many of the basic form differences in the creation of these taiaha appear in these illustrations—for example, the varied proportions of facial forms in relation to the tongue and the method of handling the upper-jaw definition. In all these forms, there is a basic bilateral symmetry in the alignment of the decorative elements; this is not absolute, however, since slight variations are visible from one side of the design to the other.

110   Polynesia, New Zealand, Maori, "taiaha" carvings.

Not all Maori figure carving depicts the grotesque, mythological type of head. In many house carvings and other sculptures a more naturalistic form is represented. In most examples, this is also generic rather than individualized. The facial features are more nearly naturalistic, while the area of the face is characterized by a complete "moko," or facial tattooing. Maori moko was unique among Oceanic peoples. It consisted of a low-relief design carved into the skin, with a bluish-black pigment rubbed into the open cuts. This tattooing was not required as an indication of rank, but social pressure was such that a person of status or with aspirations toward social position would undergo the agony of a complete facial design, replete with full spirals and minor curvilinear elements. At death, in some instances, the heads of great persons were "cured" over a fire and then kept to be revered as tokens of the ancestors. Enemy heads were also preserved, but these were taunted as a means of belittling the enemy mana.

Of all the Polynesian art forms and traditions those of the Maori are the most individual and show the most variant developments within a broad, areal style. One highly singular artistic development that is found nowhere else in Oceania is the use of greenstone jade not only for weapons and tools, but also for delicately carved and highly aesthetic jewelry forms and pendants. The best known of these are the "hei-tiki," small pendants carved in the form of the grotesque type of figures. Even in these greenstone forms, endemic throughout New Zealand, it remains clear, however, that Maori art should not be considered as a single style entity but rather as a number of important, related styles. A careful analysis of local differences in Maori art would be most rewarding, not only for an understanding of the general style but also for establishing the connecting links in its relationships with other Oceanic traditions.

3

THE AMERICAN INDIAN

Unlike the migrants into Oceania, the Mongoloid Asiatic peoples who entered the Americas by way of its northwest corner developed, as is well known, both "high" cultures and "low" or primitive cultures. The migrations into the two American continents began, as indicated by deposits of shaped stone tools, many thousands of years before the beginning of the Christian era. Like the movements into the Pacific area, they were probably accomplished by prolonged migrations of small groups who must have come from various cultural backgrounds. At that time, the narrow area of the Bering Straits was probably a land bridge; but if not, crossing the narrow span of water would have provided little difficulty. The early pattern of life, during the adjustment of these peoples to their new homeland, was apparently a nomadic one, with constant movement for hunting, fishing, and food-gathering. The immigrants fanned out over the country from north to south, ultimately reaching the southernmost tip of available land. Many archaeological remains were left behind on these journeys. Finally, it is now believed that agriculture developed in the southwestern part of North America—that is, in the so-called Meso-American region of Central America and Mexico. It must have spread rapidly from tribe to tribe; and it may even have been known or simultaneously discovered at that early period in the southwestern part of the United States. However that may have been, the domestication of plants clearly led to a modification of the Indian culture pattern throughout the hemisphere. Agriculture was so important that these peoples became at least semisedentary. With a more reliable and stable economy came the leisure time necessary for the development of ceremonialism and attendant art forms. As a consequence, discernible centers of regional art styles evolved among the American Indians.

Indian art in North America should be considered in two distinct phases: the forms that existed prior to European contact (the knowledge of which has been largely derived from archaeological investigation), and the succeeding art and culture patterns that obtained in this hemisphere at the time of European contact (for which some historical documentation exists). The times of contact, however, differed considerably for the different parts of the country. In the southwest and the southeast, it dates from the sixteenth century, while in the northeast and the central eastern coast, contact occurred in the seventeenth century. Europeans did not enter the Great Lakes region until the end of the seventeenth century, and did not penetrate into the Great

Plains and the Northwest Coast, for the most part, before the early part of the nineteenth century. Archaeological knowledge of the Indians began to be accumulated in the early years of the nineteenth century and has been increasing constantly ever since as more and more field work has been done. Because of the clear demarcation of the two cultural phases, it is valid to consider the art of the American Indian first in its archaeological or pre-Columbian appearance, and then in its tribal or historical form.

a Pre-Columbian American Indian Art

An important area for the early development of a sedentary culture in the United States was in the northern part of the Southwest, in the area of the Little Colorado-San Juan Rivers. This is the "four corners" region, which takes in southwest Colorado, northwest New Mexico, southeast Utah, and northeast Arizona. The chronological limits for this area extend back as far as the early days of the Christian era and continue up through the early thirteenth century. Then drought, and probably various other factors, led to an abandonment of these sites. A second migratory or nomadic period followed, which eventually led to settlement in the area of the Rio Grande River to the south and southeast. Contemporary with this early period in the northern sector, the desert regions of south Arizona and New Mexico were also developing early cultures. In both these sections of the pre-Columbian Southwest, pottery was the most characteristic and typical art form, with various architectural developments a close second. Wall paintings were also common to both districts; and, particularly in the southern section, numerous small stone sculptures have been found which once served as votive offerings and mortuary gifts. This entire Southwestern region is exceedingly rich in archaeological remains, and continuing excavations are constantly adding to the present knowledge of the area, its inhabitants, and its culture.

The peoples who dwelt in the "four corners," or high northern region of the Southwest, were the much-publicized cliff-dwellers. They built their multistoried stone and adobe pueblo structures above the valley floor, within the recesses of high, overhanging cliffs. Many of their enormous community houses had as many as four or five stories, each one set back from the one below it. Access to each floor was by means of ladders that rested on the roof of the story below. Many of these houses were also built out in the open, the various ground plans being designed to afford a comparable protection to that furnished by the elevation of the cliffs. Each of the pueblos had one or more ceremonial structures, known as "kivas." These were generally circular in plan, and sometimes subterranean, with only the roof, through which the structure was entered, appearing above the ground. In other intances, they were only semisubterranean, with about half the side walls extending above ground. Like all southwest-style architecture, the roofs were flat and the buildings were undecorated.

Most important and widespread of the arts among the early, sedentary agriculturalists was the making and painting of pottery. Since prior to European contact the wheel was entirely unknown in the Americas, pottery was made by the coiling process. After the vessel was originally shaped in this manner, it was given its final form by scraping and by rubbing the surface with a special paddle. In the preferential use of shapes, painted decorative designs, and colors, the pottery of each pueblo was practically unique. There was an exceedingly wide range of shapes, both in kind and in size, embracing small cups, larger bowls, and still larger jars or pots. The colors included gray-white, tan, reddish-brown, black, and various shades of red. With the exception of a few pottery styles in the south, the painted designs were almost exclusively geometrical, rectilinear, and curvilinear. In the northern section of the area, there was a widespread preference for a dull-black, rectilinear design set off against a gray-white background (Fig. 111). The feeling for sculptural form that appears in the shap-

111   Southwest, Pre-Columbian, pottery.

ing of many of these pre-Columbia southwest vessels, and the sense of spacing applied to the painted design within the field and around the shape of this pottery, establishes many of these works as the collaborative result of two media: sculpture and two-dimensional painting. In many examples of this art, three distinct zones are delineated: the base or bottom section; the brim area at the top; and the large, middle segment, which receives the major decorative design. The base and the brim often are given only a solid-color treatment or a demarcating line, although in other examples both are given a design of their own, independent of the patterns in the major design area.

Of the pottery-producing sites, Chaco Canyon is one of the most important cliff-dwelling locations; and Pueblo Bonito is particularly significant among the large, free-standing pueblos of D-shape. These architectural forms are composed of a large, semicircular, stepped-back mass facing an open court, with the ends of the semicircle connected by a high enclosing wall. In the southern part of the ancient Southwest, the sites of the Hohokam peoples have yielded some fine pottery, many of them finely shaped bowls decorated with either bold curvilinear motives or sharp rectilinear forms in combination with curvilinear elements. The somewhat later Mimbres sites are conspicuous for their shallow mortuary plates, whose interiors are given either a purely geometric decoration around the rim or are painted with fantastic figures in the central field and concentric lines marking off the rim. The colors are generally gray-white and black.

Although many small stone carvings were produced in the Southwest, the most important and extensive center for that art in the early pre-Columbia times was in the Mississippi-Ohio River valleys and to the south and southeast. Since many built-up mounds have been found there, it is known as the Moundbuilder region. These mounds were of two kinds and served two purposes. In the north and in some parts of the central and southern areas, they were large, conical buried mounds, some of which reached a hundred feet high. In the south and especially in the southeast, many of the mounds are truncated, stepped pyramids which served largely as high bases for the so-called temples or palaces. The function of these buildings is as yet largely unknown. In both areas, it was the custom to bury with the dead a quantity of specially made mortuary offerings; knowledge of Moundbuilder art has been largely acquired through examination of these objects.

Excavations in the Ohio River valley have yielded numerous and varied examples of these mortuary objects. A single grave might have contained the following: numerous strands of fresh-water pearls; cutout mica decorations; a hammered breastplate of copper; a necklace of grizzly-bear teeth; salt-water shells; innumerable large and small chipped obsidian blades; and a number of carved pipes. All of these objects were made specifically as burial offerings, and they give a good indication of the contacts, whether direct or by trade, these people had with other groups throughout widespread parts of the country. Mica was brought from the Carolinas, copper from surface deposits in northern Michigan; grizzly-bear teeth and obsidian came from as far away as the Rocky Mountains, and salt-water shells from the Gulf of Mexico. The most important artistic objects to be dug from these mounds, with the exception of a few terra-cotta figurines, are the pipes, which are often carved.

These pipes were made from the so-called pipestone, which, when cut from its matrix, is easily carved and then hardens by exposure. They are called "platform pipes" because of their particular shape. The base, sometimes with a concave curvature, is four to six inches

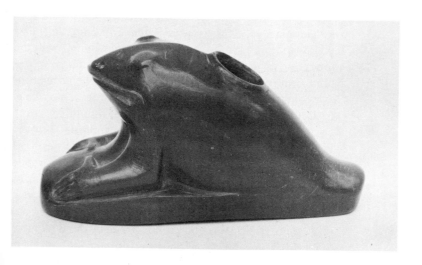

112   Moundbuilder, Pre-Columbian, carved stone frog pipe.

long; the bowl extends above it and is connected by a channel to one end of the pipe, which was used without benefit of a stem. The most frequently carved forms were animal, as in this example, which depicts a frog (Fig. 112). The pipes show a remarkable sensitivity to the natural shape of the animal, and a fine sense of the fusion between the form and its platform base. These small sculptures have a remarkable scale and are often extremely subtle renderings in terms of a simplified naturalism that conveys the reality of the animal with a succinct poignancy. This is excellently demonstrated in the frog pipe. Other examples have a more descriptive realism in their interpretation. Not all of the pipes are carved; the plain ones have a simple, tubular bowl placed at right angles to the platform base.

To the south, in the mid-Mississippi area of the Moundbuilder culture, the pipes are larger and heavier in construction and were made to be used with a reed stem (Fig. 113). Human figures in various tense poses are the dominant subjects of the pipe carvings in this region. These are made from a harder limestone and lack the platform base. They convey a more searching realism in form and detail. Probably from the Oklahoma-Arkansas area, this pipe is heavy in both scale and form and has a dynamic quality of expressivenes. The compact, difficult pose gives it a tenseness that is consistent with the rendering of all its parts. Distinctive style features in this pipe figure are the type of headdress, which agrees with other forms from this area; the large-scale facial features with the thick-lipped, half-open mouth, the teeth showing; and the decorations on the arms and on the legs. There is in this style a greater feeling for depth of form and a more pronounced differentiation of shapes and volumes than in the frog pipe. Such sculptures, as well as the smaller carved forms of the north, show a strong plastic tradition in which these examples are far from embryonic. Recent carbon-14 test datings have placed the beginnings of these art forms back to, or in some cases just before, the early years of the Christian era.

113 Moundbuilder, Pre-Columbian carved stone human pipe figure.

Aside from this type of Moundbuilder art, scattered examples of under-life-sized half-figure sculpture have been found and, in the southeastern part of the region, a number of remarkably carved stone bowls and very small limestone heads. Some wooden masks and carved boards from the latter part of this period have also been recovered in Florida. These sculptures convey the same strong sculptural tradition found in other parts of the eastern United States. Examination of this archaeological material makes it clear that a very strong plastic style of art developed quite early in this area. Future excavations and analysis of the recovered art objects will lead, in all probability, to an establishment of various style characterizations within this region.

Another important center for the early development of stone sculpture was the Northwest, in the area between and around the Fraser and Columbia Rivers in British Columbia and along the Washington and Oregon state borders. A considerable number of stone figures, bowls, mortars, and clubs, clearly identified as being from this region, serve to establish its significance and early date. In the southern district, that is, along the Columbia River, a more schematic-abstract style prevailed, in which renderings of humanoid figures, owls, turtles, and animal forms (possibly Rocky Mountain goats) were common. To the north, in the Fraser River region, the style had a bit more realistic and narrative character. Also, the sculptures from this district, consisting mostly of mortars, have more of an expressive relationship with the local ethnological material. Techniques of stone-working in both parts of the Northwest consisted largely of pecking and grinding the rock surface with harder stones and, particularly in the north, with sharp-edged cutting tools. Here, as in other parts of the Americas prior to European contact, the use of metal for tools was largely unknown. A few examples of Northwest stone sculpture still retain traces of color—a bit of red, black, or white.

In the Moundbuilder area, in the northern region and particularly in the Middle and Lower Mississippi Valley, mortuary pottery was also a common art form. These objects were decorated with incised and richly composed curvilinear designs. In the Arkansas area pottery effigy jars, a bit under life size, were created for the same purpose and evidence a sensitive modeling of facial structure and features. In the south and southeast sections of the region, a quantity of engraved shell disc-pendants have been found which suggest in decoration certain designs and motives of Meso-America. Some elbow-shaped pottery pipes and a few small shell maskettelike forms found in the area to the northeast of this major region give evidence of some extension of Moundbuilder influences and testify to the presence of a contemporary early culture. The same is true of objects from certain areas of the Plains west of the Mississippi.

The art of this pre-Columbian or archaeological period shows a wide spread of accomplished techniques and a development of artistic concepts in a variety of media. Although by the time of European contact the peoples responsible for this art had been replaced, except in the Southwest, by other Indian tribes, investigations have proved that these early inhabitants were also Indian peoples who may have been dispersed and absorbed by other tribes.

b Tribal or Historical American Indian Art

The tribal Indian art styles flourishing at the time of European contact differed in most areas from the earlier pre-Columbian traditions of those regions. This was particularly true in the Moundbuilder and the Northwest areas; but in the Southwest, although the locale had shifted, there was a marked continuity with the past. Several centuries prior to the first incursions into this area by the Spaniards, the Pueblo peoples had settled in the Rio Grande region of New Mexico, together with the older settlers to the west, the Hopi and Zuñi tribes. Architecturally, their structures were neither so large nor so imposing as their earlier homes to the north; but the character of the architecture remained essentially the same. Such features as the ceremonial kiva survived with only certain modifications of the older form. At the time the Spaniards arrived, pottery was still the major art expression of the Pueblo peoples, although woven textiles, which had flourished earlier, some wood-carving, and mask-making were also important. Only silverwork was missing from the artistic repertoire, since silver was first introduced by the Spaniards as silver coins. The nearby Navaho peoples also had their textiles; and they developed the art of sand-painting, acquired from the Pueblo peoples, into a major expressive medium. Later, they too were to become fine silversmiths; while the Apache, who were tinged with Plains influence, made as their important art forms fine, strong coiled baskets which they decorated with a few small, black, very stylized forms of animals and men set against the natural yellowish color of the background.

By the mid-nineteenth century, although the life patterns of the highly conservative Pueblo people had been very little modified by outside influence, some of the arts of the Southwest had been considerably altered, especially by commercial influences. This was particularly true of the pottery, silverwork, and Navaho textiles. For the past quarter of a century, however, under the influence and tutelage of the Government Indian Arts and Crafts Board, there has been something of a return to the older, more traditional forms.

As in pre-Columbian times, each of the Pueblos had its own particular pottery shapes and decorative patterns. Some designs, as on this Santa Ana jar (Fig. 114), are purely abstract, while others, such as on the large Zuñi water jars, have floral and geometric patterns with, on some, a stylized deer form set in oval zones. The design of the Santa Ana jar is divided into two related decorative zones: an enlarged lip or rim design and a wider major design area that extends above the shoulder of the vessel. The base is marked off with a light and dark zone, the latter related to the design of the central section. The main design is composed of four large abstract shapes, each of which contains similar small motifs such as large and small rectangles, small diamonds, sharp angles, rounded curves. A large, amorphous form appears as a central element. The rim design is formed by a repeated pattern, also large in scale, and gives a cohesive unity to the decoration as a whole. This is an excellent example of Pueblo pottery dating from just before the mid-nineteenth century.

Other well-known art forms of the historical period in the Southwest include the "kachina" masks and the small carved representations of the kachina spirits. The kachinas are beneficent gods or supernatural beings who figure prominently in Pueblo mythology and who bring fertility, long life, and other benefits to the Pueblo peoples. Their cult is one of the most important integrating forces in Pueblo culture, and is in the nature

114 Southwest, Santa Ana, pottery bowl.

of a secret society whose sanctum is the kiva. It is believed that the kachinas return to earth at certain regular intervals when, as masked and costumed members of the kachina cult, they emerge from the underworld by way of the kiva to participate in prescribed ceremonials. For the duration of the rite, the masked dancer actually "becomes" the supernatural being whom he is impersonating.

Representative kachina masks from among the Zuñi and Hopi Indians are often of composite construction, as illustrated by this example (Fig. 115): the face is an undifferentiated convex leather surface; small, rectangular openings mark the eyes and the mouth, the latter being framed lightly with wood strips; and the nose is

115 Southwest, Zuñi, mask.

often omitted. Wooden appendages are attached to
either side of the face to serve as ears, while a stuffed-
out cloth ruff surrounds the lower part of the face. An
animal pelt with the fur still attached covers the top and
back of the head; and a few feathers are affixed on the
top of the form. In masks from this area the morphological characteristics range from such simplified, elementary forms as found in this example to more naturalistic
interpretations of basic human features, and to fantastic
creations of fabulous shapes with a distorted scaling of

342

facial elements. Each of these mask forms, with their appropriate costume and iconographical details such as a staff or a bag of corn meal, represents a specific kachina spirit.

Before the kachinas appear, the men work in the kivas to carve small wooden figures from a soft wood (Fig. 116). These represent the kachina spirit and are correct in every detail, even to the precise costume and the accompanying iconographical details. During the ceremonies, these dolls are given to the children. In the past the carvings were taken home by each child and were hung in a spot where they would be constantly visible. This custom was motivated by the desire for continuity and stability, and the figures functioned didactically, instructing or acquainting the children with the history and mythology of the supernatural beings so faithfully represented. The mask forms, with their accompanying and inseparable costumes, were motivated by the need for security and survival as well as for continuity and stability. Their function was to bring the people of the community into the actual presence of these beings. The meaning of each form was related to and derived from beings who had lived in remote and mythological times

In the eastern United States the Iroquois peoples are the best known mask-producing group. Their activity in this field has been an outstanding cultural feature from the time of early contact to the present. Like the Pueblo groups, they have continuously maintained the practices of their culture and of this artistic element. Iroquois masks fall into two categories: the carved wooden forms discussed earlier in terms of their motivation, function, and meaning;[57] and those mask creations fabricated from cornhusks. Historical accounts show that both of these types antedate European contact.

When the early settlers arrived in what is now New York State, the Iroquois were known as the Five Nations. They constituted a strongly and democratically organized confederation of five tribes: the Seneca, Oneida, Onondaga, Cayuga, and Mohawk. In 1722 this confed-

116 Southwest, Zuñi, kachina doll.

eration was enlarged, becoming the Six Nations when their kinsmen, the Tuscarora, came north from the Carolinas to join them. The dating for the movement of the original five Iroquois tribes into the Northeast still remains conjectural, but it seems to have occurred in the sixteenth century, if not earlier. The precise area from which they came is also unknown: perhaps the most immediately previous location was the Ohio River valley, although they may at an earlier date have migrated to that region from the South. This seems likely, since many of their culture elements appear to be of southern origin. To take one example, their major form of habitation, the "longhouse," was a long rectangular structure with a barrel-vaulted roof and an entrance at one end. The exterior was covered with sheets of bark and the interior divided into sleeping sections. In general character this type of construction agrees with the mat-covered dwellings commonly used in the South at the time of European contact. Moreover, as was true in the South, the Iroquois houses were grouped in small villages surrounded by a protective palisade. The presence of masks, too, coincides with the use of masks in the South, particularly by the Cherokee and the Choctaw in the Carolinas, and by the Calusa Indians in Florida.

The Iroquois were a widely feared, warlike people, whose principal enemies were the northeastern Algonkin tribes. Their art, with the exception of the masks, consisted largely of decorating utilitarian objects to give them prestige value. Such works included carvings of human features on their ball-headed war clubs, which were sometimes inlaid with shell; modeled, globular cooking pots, whose long, angular necks were decorated with incised geometric designs and occasionally with small figures; elbow pipes, with carvings on the stems of small animal forms or, at times, human forms; and especially, the beaded decoration applied to women's leggings and dresses. Originally, the stitched-on designs of these garments were made with shell beads reminiscent of the beads used on their famous wampum peace belts. Later, however, European beads obtained in trade were substituted, leading to a considerable change in the artistic character of the decorations.

Masks, however, are the most important of the Iroquois art expressions, and have a distinctive style character. They are shallow-volumed in form, with a singular statement of facial elements: the wide-open round eyes are frequently outlined with tin; in some the nose is a large, distorted, and crooked form; and the huge, thick-lipped mouth is given a variety of grotesque shapes (Fig. 117). The surfaces of the facial planes are usually broken by numerous deep, parallel grooves—a powerful expressive device. Some of these masks are monochromatically painted with red or black; others are laterally divided and given a polychromatic treatment, half red and half black. Horsehair was attached to the head in simulation of hair.

Among the Algonkin tribes of New England and the Canadian Maritime provinces, the art tradition, except for the pre-Columbian shell burial masks, appears to have been predominantly symbolic, the floral motifs vying with abstract geometric elements. These dominant characteristics appear strongly in the art forms of the Penobscot peoples of Maine and the Naskapi Indians of Labrador. In both areas an important type of habitation was developed. This was the pyramidal, tentlike form known as the "teepee." All too often this word has been confused or equated with "wigwam," a term actually denoting the barrel-roofed structures of the Iroquois type. Among the Penobscot these conical teepees were covered with sheets of bark, while among the Naskapi to the north, the exterior was made from caribou hide. It appears that this type of architecture spread southwest from the Algonkin area into the region of the Great Lakes, and from there into the Plains, where it received its greatest development.

In the area extending northward from the New England states, the most important design motif was a pattern that has become known as the "double curve." Compositionally, this is a curvilinear, plantlike form that is repeated on either side of a solid center. According

117   Northeast, Seneca tribe, Iroquois mask.

to the beliefs of the tribal groups inhabiting this region, magical and supernatural power derived from plants, so that the design employed there had the same ceremonial status as the figures and masks ritually used in Africa and the South Pacific. This is well illustrated as an art form by the decoration of a tailored coat made by the

Naskapi of Labrador (Fig. 118), in which the lower border is decorated with one of the many variants of the double-curve motif. From a starting point along the leaflike center form, plantlike tendrils curve out to either side. Among the Penobscot and other peoples in the southern part of this region, motifs are frequently stitched onto the surface with small shell beads; while among the Naskapi they are lightly etched into the hide and then picked out with red ochre to contrast with the natural yellowish background of the material. The border along the front, across the yoke, and on the shoulders and the sleeves, is decorated in the same manner. Farther south, along the reaches of the St. Lawrence River, this same motif appears on the birch-bark containers. The outer surface of the bark used for these objects is scraped to produce a lighter interior surface. Thus, a contrast of light and dark occurs, reminiscent of a photo-negative effect, with the double-curve clearly dominant in the decorative pattern. Some animal forms appear in later examples of this St. Lawrence River art, but they are still involved with the double-curve motif.

Certain cultural and artistic concepts from the Northeast traveled up the St. Lawrence River to the Great Lakes area and a mingling of influences took place there, since both the wigwam and the teepee forms of architecture were prevalent. There is also evidence of techniques more commonly associated with Indian peoples to the east and north. Mention should be made of two of these techniques in particular: a method of using moose hair in embroidery and plain outline stitching; and the employment of dyed porcupine quills for various purposes. Both of these techniques were found in the Great Lakes area, as were other local or regional developments that referred to the traditions of the Great Plains region to the west. The use of eastern decorative devices was applied mainly to small animal pelts, such as beaver and mink, on which significant designs were elaborated by means of quillwork in the early examples and by combining the techniques of beadwork and quillwork in the later ones. Among the artistic forms of the

118 Northeast, Naskapi, hide coat.

Great Lakes Indian tribes, the plaiting of basswood and reeds was a unique development generally used in the creation of long, rectangular carrying bags (Fig. 119). Against a background formed by the natural brownish color of the material are set black-dyed designs consisting of rows of thunderbirds, and various stylized or conventionalized representations of them, creating a dark-light surface-covering pattern. Later, when the area came under the influence of the French entrepreneurs and fur-trappers, the motifs on these carrying bags were

119 Great Lakes, Menomini, carrying bag.

remarkably influenced by seventeenth-century French
tapestry designs. The effect of acculturation is quite
marked in these objects and provides an excellent illustration of what could develop in regard to the modification of a traditional art style as a result of early contacts
between Indian and European.

It is evident that there was a close relationship
between the Great Lakes area and that of the Great
Plains to the west. This midwestern territory, which was
entirely a product of acculturations, developed relatively
late as the consequence of one historical factor: the
acquisition of the horse brought by the sixteenth-century
foray of the Spaniards into the Southwest. Prior to that
time, the Plains Indians were sedentary agriculturalists
living along the margins of the plains, who at certain
seasons went on tribal hunts after buffalo. This provided
a supplemental factor to their usual diet of deer and

vegetables. With the arrival of the horse, from wild herds in the Southwest, the Plains Indians for the most part became seminomadic. They followed the great buffalo herds, relying on them primarily as their staple food, and agriculture was reduced to a meager, secondary supplement. The horse brought mobility to these peoples, and with this freedom of movement there was a surplus of food. Such a chain of events led inevitably to an increased amount of leisure time in which social relationships, ceremonials, and significant tribal art forms could be developed.

The majority of Plains Indian art forms has a decorative and personal significance. Early investigators believed that all of these forms had a meaning comprehensible to anyone in the tribe. In the latter part of the nineteenth and the early part of the present century, however, three men explored this concept in detail.[58] Through their efforts it was discovered that the designs used to decorate one object might be identical to those used on another of the same function, but these motifs meant different things depending on their creator. In other words, personal or individual meanings were given in each instance to designs that were ostensibly the same. Thus no such thing as a mutually comprehensible design vocabulary existed in this area. Rather, each motif and design combination was used in such a way as to give it a new and esoteric meaning; the forms used to decorate a group of Plains moccasins (Fig. 120), with their variegated patterns in porcupine and quillwork and beads, could only be deciphered by the women who made them. No one else was capable of determining the content, or subject matter, of her designs.

The personal-prestige character of Plains art appears in more than just the decorated moccasins. It is also discernible on the deerskin shirts worn by the warriors, where strips of porcupine quillwork and/or beading were often combined with scalp fringes in a prominent design (Fig. 121). The type of design and colors used tended, as on the moccasins, to show certain tribal preferences. The Siouan-speaking Dakota tribes, for example, used

351

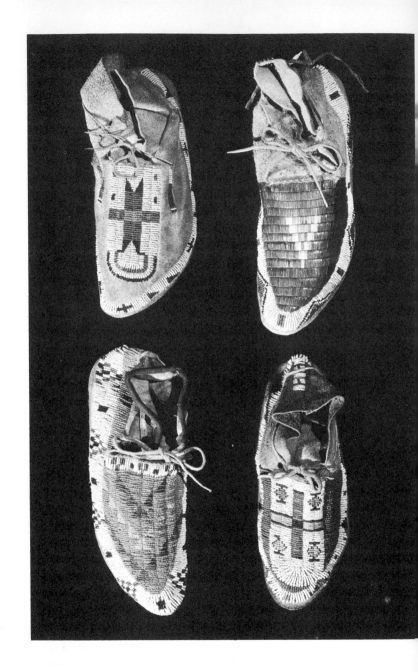

120 Plains region, Sioux and Crow, moccasins.

light colors, especially white and light blue; while the Blackfeet tribes used darker and heavier colors such as deep red and dark blue. Colors were tonally soft and limited in range so long as the decorations were done in quillwork alone. This was also true when the comparatively large and opaque "pony beads" were brought in by trade prior to the days of strong and continued European influence. But later, when the smaller, translucent European beads arrived in the Plains, a wide range of colors and shades was made available which modified tribal decorative styles to a considerable degree. In many objects, as illustrated by the moccasin at the upper right-hand side of Fig. 120, beads are combined with quillwork.

Painting on a flat surface was more developed among the Plains Indian peoples than among any other "low" or primitive culture group in the Americas. This type of art appeared predominantly on three categories of objects: the "parfleche"; the teepee cover; and the buffalo robe. It was also utilized for surface designs on the comparatively small war shields and on a few shirts or jerkins. The parfleche was a rawhide container that was shaped, cut, and lashed together to form a rectangular trunk or carrying case. The technique used in the creation of these objects should be related and integrated with that employed by the eastern Algonkin Indians for shaping and cutting sheets of bark, which were then lashed together to form carrying bags of various shapes and sizes. The parfleches were decorated in somewhat the same way, by incising a design on the hide and then peeling off the darker, outer surface. On some examples the design was pressed into the surface, and the area was then filled with color. The earth pigment used for this was mixed with animal fat and then sized with a type of glue to make it relatively permanent. Designs on these rawhide carrying cases were always abstract and rectilinear in character, with patterns frequently composed of small rectangles, squares, and hourglass shapes.

In this area, men with great power (largely acquired through dreams) often had teepee covers painted with

121 Plains region, Dakota, hide shirt.

basically naturalistic designs, the forms deriving from
locally known and admired or symbolic animals. Such
painted animal forms as the beaver and the buffalo
flanked the doorway, while at the top and the bottom
symbolic designs and colors denoted the morning and
the evening sky. On the smoke flap at the top, the
delineation of a Maltese cross motif signified that the
power represented by the animals was acquired in a
dream. The cross was symbolic of the butterfly which,
according to beliefs in this region, brought these dreams
to men. On other less important teepees, strips of quillwork or beadwork were attached that were largely

354

emblematic of rank. In all forms of Plains Indian decorative art the geometric designs were done by the women and all of those depicting naturalistic forms were created by the men. The men also had the job of gathering the necessary poles for and erecting the framework of the dwellings. The teepee covers were, however, made and fitted over the framework by the women. Originally, tough buffalo rawhide was used for the covers, making these structures waterproof and to a large extent protective against all types of weather.

One of the most important art forms of the Plains Indians was the painted buffalo robe.[59] While the teepee designs had a religious significance, the decorated robes, like the shirts, moccasins, and horse trappings, were created essentially for their prestige value. The paintings on many of the robes have been called biographical, since they recount, in pictorial terms, the exploits of the artist. As in this example (Fig. 122), they tended to describe a series of roughly concentric circles on the broad field made by the smooth underside of the buffalo hide. The scenes on this robe suggest the summer encampment where all the tribal bands gathered for the ceremonial Sun Dance. Since they contained naturalistically rendered subject matter, which was taboo for the women to handle, buffalo robes were decorated by the men. Here, the time, as mentioned above, is indicated by the placement of the sun in the upper left-hand corner. The designs were made principally by pressing the outline of the forms into the surface of the hide with a buffalo bone. Color was then applied either by filling the incision with reddish pigment or by painting all or part of the outlined form. The full range of these devices has been exploited in the painting of this robe. There is, however, practically no aesthetic demonstration of a sense of rhythm or balance, and only a rudimentary suggestion of depth or perspective is evident. In spite of these deficiencies, many of the robe paintings have a naïve and appealing quality derived from the indications of fluidity and action. Although it has never been done, these works could be integrated with the great number

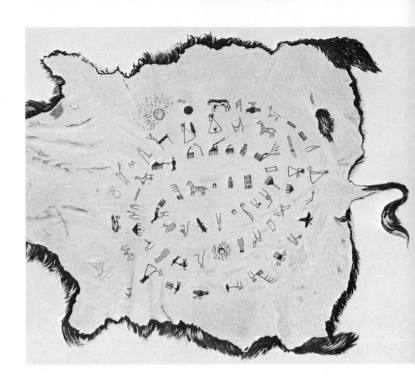

122 Plains region, Dakota, painted buffalo robe.

of pictographs found on rock surfaces in many parts of the United States. These cuttings, whether on exposed or sheltered rocks, were made by the Indians for some particular purpose, and at some particular time, as yet generally unknown.

In plastic quality, Plains Indian art is particularly deficient: only a few stone-headed war clubs and some ceremonial pipes had any plasticity in their artistic character. On the other hand, these artists excelled in two-dimensional decoration, whether in painted forms or in beadwork and/or quillwork. The great spirits revered by these people were usually aerial and ambient. Sometimes they were symbolized by design forms, but more usually they were represented, in their "medicine bundles," by certain natural, unshaped objects with magical significance. The art style of the many Plains Indian tribes was substantially of a decorative type, with designs composed mainly of abstract, geometric, sometimes symbolic elements arranged in accordance with the principles of design symmetry. With certain impoverishments, this art tradition persisted across the Rocky Mountains and on into that high region, known as the Plateau Area, which stretches westward to the Coast Range.

West of this coastal range of mountains, along the Pacific shores of the United States and Canada and extending up into the southeastern part of Alaska, several art areas can be singled out: the California region in the south; the Salishan style center extending from its northern border, the Fraser River, down to the Columbia River valley, and including the Puget Sound district in Washington state; and the territory of the Northwest Coast proper, reaching north of the Fraser River and taking in southeastern Alaska. The California region was missionized very early in the historical period, and had at that time only a comparatively meager art tradition. The most accomplished medium was that of basketry.[60] Among the Salishan peoples, as noted in the discussion of the Duwamish spirit canoe ceremony,[61] a rudimentary type of sculptural art was created, the exception being a single type of more elaborated mask. The third area, that of the Northwest Coast, deserves special consideration as a center for the creation of greatly developed art forms.

The Northwest Coast was one of the richest art-producing territories of the primitive world. Although very different in style, the art forms of this region and its peoples are comparable, both quantitatively and qualitatively, to those of the Sepik River area in New Guinea. Ecologically the Northwest Coast provided an environment rich in an easily obtainable, though seasonal, food supply, the salmon, and with abundant forests filled with the readily available, easily carved cedar wood. Since the food could be stored, the long winter season was a time of leisure given over to ceremonials and to the making of ritual and other art objects. Although wood was the most commonly used material, work in bone, argelite, copper, and shell, as well as distinctive textiles, was also characteristic of this region. The wide range of art forms included masks and single figures; superposed figures on the monumental, so-called totem poles; storage boxes, rattles, and clubs; blankets and headdresses. That the art was the work of professionals is at once apparent, but unfortunately, little information has been recorded about the artists.

Like the Sepik River area, the Northwest Coast is a homogeneous art center in which a considerable number of elements were common to all of the tribal styles. These commonly shared elements must first be extracted before the residue, the distinctive characteristics of tribal style, can be determined. At present, this has only been done in brief[62] and to attempt such an isolation and identification of tribal style features in a general work goes beyond the limits of available space. As in the consideration of the Sepik River area, the aim will be to examine representative art forms to determine the stylistic characteristics endemic to the entire region.

The major tribal groups on the coast were, from south to north: the Kwakiutl on Vancouver Island and southern British Columbia; the Haida, in the Queen Charlotte Islands; the Bella Coola, along the river by that name in northern British Columbia; their nearby neighbors, the Tsimshian; and in southeastern Alaska, on the offshore islands, the Tlingit. While there were cultural and linguistic distinctions between the groups, the general life pattern of these peoples was, like their art, basically homogeneous. It is evident from the art that there was not only a fluidity of art motifs throughout the region but also an interchange or trading of the actual objects.

The mask and the totem pole are among the most developed art forms of the Northwest Coast. An astonishing variety in both kind and design characterizes their masks, together with a prominent use of polychromy. The majority of these forms are among the most plastic of all mask expressions; but to produce the desired aesthetic and dramatic effects required the combination of sculpture and polychromy. Human features and animal forms, often in combination, provide the subject matter, which is usually given a dynamic expression. Although some sensitive naturalistic representations do occur, particularly among the Tsimshian, the forms and facial features are most often large and bold in scale, created as forceful, sculptural statements that are by no means an imitation of reality. Many of these strong qualities are illustrated in a Bella Coola mask (Fig. 123). The power and breadth of rendering of the heavy sculptural shapes should particularly be noted in the use of broad, sweeping planes and of varied projecting and deeply receding shapes and zones. The vigor of the sculptural statements in this mask cannot be surpassed by forms from any other primitive area. Moreover, the forms and their interrelationships are strongly stressed by color. The dark areas on the photograph are painted a rich brick red; in juxtaposition to them are zones colored in light, bright blue and in a thin whitewash. The total effect is spectacular —a visual experience retained by the observer long after the original viewing. Cedar bark, a material used extensively throughout the entire area, was shredded and attached to the mask as a fringe.

The dramatic impact of the Bella Coola mask derives from the manner in which the vibrant colors emphasize the large-scale features and create an interlocking unity of shape relationships. The great sweep of the low-relief flat eyebrows, defined by the characteristic, angular curve common to so many sculptures from this area, is painted a bright red. This color is continued down the form of the heavy nose, under the deep eye area, and in winglike designs flanking the nostrils and mouth. White is used to stress the depressed eye area and the pierced, projecting, tubular eye forms. This color is also employed to define the heavy nostrils, the great projecting mouth, and the narrow surrounding area. White integrates the relationships between the shapes of the mouth, nostrils, and eye area as they exist within the brick-red zone of

123 Northwest Coast, Bella Coola, mask.

the eyebrows, nose, and flanking facial surface. Such treatment yields a close-knit unity of shapes and expression. Extraneous designs, such as the two featherlike elements painted on the sides of the face just below the eye area, probably had a symbolic meaning that helped to create the total significance of the form. The aesthetic vigor and artistic drama of this integrated, polychrome composition is typical of many of the art forms created by the peoples of the Northwest Coast.

A variety of mask forms with movable parts was developed which is unique to the area. A common form was that in which the lower jaw was carved separately and hinged to the back of the upper jaw so that the wearer could, at appropriate moments in the ceremony, open and close the mouth by means of a hidden string device. Another kind of movable composite mask form was the double- or even triple-faced type. These consisted of two (or three) carved forms: the outer one, slightly larger than the other, was carved in two halves and the exterior and interior surfaces were both carved and painted. This outer mask was hinged and fitted over the smaller one so that when the two halves of the outer form were closed the smaller mask was hidden from view. At a certain dramatic moment in the rites, the outer mask was opened by means of manipulated strings attached to the hinges, and a new character was revealed by the appearance of the "hidden mask." These are among the most dramatic and complex masks evolved by primitive peoples.

The social dynamics of the Northwest Coast cultures were largely focused on the demonstrations of social position or rank, both of which were hereditary; but either could be increased by marriage, by warfare, or by various other methods. Prerogatives of rank included the rights to wear certain masks which had crest or heraldic meaning at ceremonials of secular or religious significance, and to participate in the dramatizations of various religious experiences. These dramatic, or often melodramatic, events were re-enactments of the specific moments when the right to wear each specific power mask had been acquired through encounters with the supernatural beings. The great spirits were generally represented either with animal features, as fabulous monsters, or as conventionalized human forms. In the southern district, among the Kwakiutl, religious dances were the most common form of dramatic presentation. These were graded and so restrictive that the performers were considered members of secret societies. This restrictive aspect occurred mostly because the specific dances were inherited, and the performances were given either for the purpose of initiation or as theatrical exhibitions. In both cases, the mask was a vitally important part of the ceremony. To the north, masks were largely worn at secular occasions as a means of displaying the crests and insignia that served as emblems of rank.

The best-known forms of Northwest Coast art are the totem poles. This term, however, is actually a misnomer, for the forms do not represent totems. Rather, they portray specific family crests and their associated myths. The poles were erected as burial, memorial, or commemorative objects. Several examples of these carvings are illustrated on an old photograph of Haida poles (Fig. 124). Each of the three examples with a board across the top is a burial pole and has at the back a box in which the body of the deceased was placed; the tall pole at the extreme right exemplifies the commemorative type of carving. Some contain a single crest figure, while others have several forms arranged in a complex and interlocking vertical composition. Animals, often conventionalized, human forms, and hybrid creatures are represented in the relief carvings which are cut into the surface from the front and side planes to produce massively scaled, often fabulous shapes and creations. These forms follow the curvature of the original surface of the pole and in many examples, as here, utilize about three quarters of the surface. The back of many of these poles are left uncarved.

Two other approaches to the arrangement of formal elements were employed in the carvings of these superposed figures. A stylistic device of the Tsimshian, for

124 Northwest Coast, Haida, burial or "totem" poles.

example, was arranging the figures in horizontal zones. Vertical unity was obtained by the repetition of related or similar shapes. The Tlingit, in southeastern Alaska, carved poles of lesser diameter than the southern type and also depicted clearly separated figures set in horizontal bands. The forms, however, were less sculpturally related to each other than visually accented by the use of color. There was, nevertheless, some overlapping of these three stylistic devices.

In the southern part of the Northwest Coast area, another variant of these pole carvings developed among the Kwakiutl, which was eclectic and flamboyant in style. In fact, the general character of the art forms created by this tribe was the most visually spectacular of the entire region, just as other cultural features received the great-

125 Northwest Coast, Kwakiutl, whistle as human figure.

est development among these peoples. A good example of this is the extent to which they developed the "potlatch" ceremony. The potlatch was fundamentally a ritualistic feast and gift-giving which was held upon such important occasions as the emplacement of a memorial pole or the celebration of the winter dances. It was so highly evolved among the Kwakiutl, however, that a local chief would impoverish his entire family by giving away or destroying all of his property in order to gain the prestige of rank or position over a rival chief. Nothing could dispel the considerable cloud under which the recipient of these potlatch gifts was placed until he could stage a more elaborate feast, disposing of more property than he had obtained. The emphasis on bigger, better, and more elaborate ceremonies, although engendered by different purposes and with very different art forms, is somewhat reminiscent of the attitude of New Ireland peoples toward the Malagan ceremonies. Among the Kwakiutl, there was a good deal of this vying for power through the staging of potlatches. Ultimately, the practice became so ruinous that the Canadian government was forced to place the potlatch ceremony under severe restrictions.

The eclectic and dramatic nature of Kwakiutl art is discernible not only in their totem poles but also in their masks and many other art forms. This approach is well illustrated by a small dance whistle (Fig. 125). The obverse of this object is carved as an exceedingly tense human figure with a fantastic head. The mouth serves as the sounding aperture of the whistle and is shaped as an enormous, squared opening, pulled down into this form by the two hands that grip the lower lip. Appropriately enough, the visual impression created by this form is of a figure in the act of screaming or shrieking loudly. This is implemented by the renderings of the eyes, nose, and facial folds. It is an incredibly dynamic small figure which seems to have been made all the more intense by the organic, integrated quality of the body forms. Many examples of Kwakiutl art parallel this whistle in their vigorous, outspoken forms and their intensity of expression.

Another characteristic art style which seems to have evolved in the northern parts of the territory, although found in the south as well, was a highly abstract, symbolic type appearing on a variety of objects. This is noticeable primarily in the designs on the lightly carved wooden boxes; in the relatively late and thoroughly acculturated forms of their silver jewelry; and especially in the decorative motifs used on blankets woven by the Chilkat, a subtribe of the Tlingit. Woven of mountain sheep wool and shredded cedar bark, these blankets, according to tradition, came to the Chilkat as a result of intermarriage with the Tsimshian, and were then given their characteristic development by the Chilkat (Fig. 126). Their distribution spread far and wide along the coast, ultimately reaching Vancouver Island. In color, these blankets are a dull black, a blue-green, and a yellow-brown. They have a unique shape and are surrounded on the sides and bottom by a long fringe of shredded bark.

The blankets were designed so that the back would hang down straight; the two sides were intended to be gathered up and brought around to the front, thus creating somewhat of a trapezoidal ground for decoration. A woven margin, the inner limits of which are defined by fine, black lines, surrounds the entire work. Within this, the design area is bordered by a zone consisting of a wide band of black and another in the natural, brown-yellow color of the fabric. The decorative field proper is divided into three parts: the wide, central section; and two, smaller, flanking ones. The central portion is decorated with a single, frontally posed, animal form, that is, a crest insignia, while in the flanking areas are symmetrically arranged, profile animal forms. Throughout the design, the forms are handled as symbolic abstractions of natural form. For example, the dominant eye motif seldom represents an actual eye. This applies to the ear and wing motifs, as well. Interpretations of the subject matter contained in these abstractions apparently depended, to a very large extent, on the intentions of the woman who wove them. This supposition is upheld by

126 Northwest Coast, Chilkat, blanket.

several instances, as for example, when such veteran Northwest Coast investigators as Boas and Swanton each interpreted the same design differently. This occurred mainly because the basis of their knowledge of the design in question was derived from two different informants, each of whom believed that he knew the significance of the motifs. Aesthetically, these blankets, regardless of meaning, have an endlessly interesting and absorbing arrangement of variously related, naturalistic and abstract design elements.

Other interesting art-producing regions did exist within the limits of the North and South American continents. However, as was true of Oceania, it has been necessary to select representative examples of work from those style centers that best exemplify the characteristics of American Indian art on the primitive level.

Two rich areas that fall into this category of art forms and traditions not sufficiently representative to be discussed in such a general work as this are those of the South American Indian tribes, and the Eskimo groups of the northern littoral.[63] Neither of these areas has been as thoroughly investigated or evaluated artistically as it deserves; but to do so here would go beyond the purpose and scope of this work.

PART **III**

CONCLUSION: Some General Considerations

In the light of historical evidence, it must be recognized that the first forms of primitive art which attracted any widespread attention as objects of artistic quality and aesthetic value were the sculptures of Negro Africa. This was not merely fortuitous; rather, it came about because, of all the multitudinous styles and forms created and developed in the world of primitive people, those of Africa are the only ones so largely restricted to a single medium—sculpture. The understanding of morphological or exterior relationships and qualities in African art could therefore be more readily approached from this consideration alone. They could be aesthetically viewed and enjoyed, independently of their inner qualities of motivation, function, and meaning more easily than art works from other primitive areas. It is no wonder, then, that young artists during the early years of this century both delighted in, and felt supported by, what they had discovered in African art forms.[64]

What were the aspects of this art that held, for the more creative of the twentieth-century artists, such deep fascination? The most significant element which appealed to these modern artists was the nonrepresentational quality of African sculpture. They found in these works an interpretative approach or creative attitude toward the rendering of natural forms that was independent of any degree of verisimilitude in the attainment of sculptural integrity and artistic force. In the African forms they saw an art of pure shape that depicted in various ways the functions and interrelationships of natural form, whether animal or human. It was, however, the erroneous belief of these young enthusiasts that African sculptures were free, spontaneous creations unhindered by the academic restraints imposed on artists of Europe. They did not know, when they extolled the freedom of these primitive forms, that this too was an art of traditions and that these traditions exerted a direct control over the development and persistence of African art styles. Nor were they aware that the forms grew from and agreed with the cultural concepts of each group of people.

During the half century that has passed since the days when these young artists exuberantly described its quality and its magic, a sounder knowledge of primitive art, its forms and styles, has been amassed. Along with this has come an increased awareness of the cultural contexts in which these works developed, making it possible to appraise the creations of primitive peoples in a valid way. Prior to their disappearance or modification as a consequence of European influence and acculturation, all primitive works of art were created in terms of their own particular and traditional styles so that each object should be characterized in the light of that style. Furthermore, for a complete understanding of the art forms, the motivations, functions, and meanings of each work must, in so far as possible, be considered within its cultural frame of reference.

Another point in relation to primitive art as a whole is that the methods by which analysis is made of the aesthetic properties and qualities in these forms is derived from the same set of artistic principles that are applied to any other forms, whatever the time or place of their origin. However, the use of universal principles of aesthetic and artistic analysis, although certainly applicable to all of these objects as art forms, neither implies nor invites comparative evaluations of kind or style between these works and art forms of unrelated areas, whether spatial, temporal, or cultural. Comparative analyses made between objects of primitive and nonprimitive origin yield no meaningful information since the forms neither grew out of comparable backgrounds, nor were they created in terms of any common artistic idiom. On the other hand, it is often valid to compare and relate the nature of aesthetic expression characteristic of certain primitive art forms with those from another region in the primitive world. In fact, the most valuable aspect of comparative analysis is that it can be used for the distillation of essential characteristics of style and aesthetic expression as they exist in objects of similar cultural background. These fundamental qualities can then be related or contrasted, allowing characterizations of the larger, more comprehensive regions to be made.

With this in mind, it is possible to summarize the essential features of the major areas discussed in Part II, and to bring each area into focus in relation to the other regions of the primitive world.

The art of Negro Africa can be stylistically divided into two areas, West and Central Africa. Within each of these basic style centers, a considerable number of local variations and substyles may be discerned. There was, however, throughout a long period of time, extensive contact and diffusion of both cultural and artistic elements between contiguous regions. As a result a marked homogeneity is recognizable within the great number of tribal variations, a homogeneity not found in other art-producing regions of the primitive world. Of what, then, does this homogeneous quality consist, and in what ways is it apparent?

African art is distinctly a sculptor's art.[65] Although the styles range from naturalistic through conventionalized and schematic approaches to form with, in some instances, a formalistic almost abstract expression, it is

371

all clearly derived from and based on the understanding and interpretation of natural forms. The subject matter, therefore, was experienced physically by the artist in his participation in the daily routine of life and, especially, in the socio-religious ceremonials when physical and emotional tensions were at their most expressive peak. From these experiences, the perceptive artist would select the expressive moments and bring these observations to bear on his interpretation of traditional designs. There are no academic ties, in the European sense of the term, to realistic or scientific aspects of reality. Instead, the component shapes of the body may be repressed, eliminated, stressed, or enormously exaggerated in such a manner that a creative synthesis results. This often appears as a new and revealing interpretation of life forms which functions as an aesthetic statement of reality. When this is created by a great artist, it becomes a new reality with vigor of its own. In the sculpture of Negro Africa, therefore, the predominant aesthetic quality resides in the creation and interrelationship of forms derived from nature but arranged in compositions of nonrepresentational type that have the energy and poignantly vital expression of life forms.

From the stylized Sudan and the formalized Bakota, to the vibrant Baoule and emotionally expressive Central Congo, the artistic character of natural forms and of human emotions are expressed aesthetically by sculptural and tangible forms. These pervading qualities of interpretative and expressive integrity, as stated in the dynamic forms, endows the art of this part of the primitive world with its strong aesthetic character and homogeneity.

Considered in this light, it is apparent that, in basic character as well as in fundamental culture patterns, the art traditions of western Oceania differ considerably from those of Africa. While African creations are based largely on interpretations of natural form, the morphological concepts in western South Pacific art derive mainly from imaginative variations of natural objects, whether obtained in dreams or through various other unreal mental experiences. There is a very marked distinction between African forms based on natural experiences and observations of natural phenomena, and those of the South Pacific, which were based on images from the subconscious or from psychotic states. In consequence, the art of Melanesia was charged with a vital, often fantastic content, while that of Africa was closely related to aspects of natural reality. The contrast in the content or subject matter between the art forms of these two areas underscores the difference in approach. This approach to content is what serves to mark one art area off so clearly and considerably from another in the Pacific world.

Although Melanesian cultures are conspicuous for the presence and the colorfulness of their heterogenous art styles, it is possible to isolate certain salient aesthetic features. Form interpretations displaying any close morphological relationship to nature are rare, although they can all eventually be traced back to naturalistic sources. It would seem, therefore, that even those Melanesian forms based on subconscious or hallucinatory experiences with a supernatural being had their basis in natural events or phenomena. This agrees with the nature of form characteristic of twentieth-century surrealistic art, in which abnormal and weird forms originate in the vagaries of human, extra-normal perceptions. The quality of fantasy thus dominates the character of these artistic and aesthetic expressions. In this regard, Melanesian art is at considerable variance from that of Africa where, for the most part, forms lack this abnormal or specialized development of naturalistic character. Melanesian art forms also combine a variety of materials in their final expressive character; and they frequently utilize vivid colors and surface designs to achieve the desired final effect. The often fantastic expressions apparent in so many of these forms evolve from the relationships of the designs and/or patterns to the interaction of formal elements.

Polynesian art, in relation to that of Melanesia, is less varied in materials and in techniques, depending more on a sculptural mode of expression than on color. In almost all Polynesian areas, two types of figure representation prevail: 1) a more naturalistic form with important characterizing features derived from reality; and 2) a more stylized, grotesque tradition. The second type, discussed with regard to the motivation, function, and meaning of the Hawaiian temple figures,[66] was derived from the concept of aggression, power, and vigor as ideal qualities with which the mythological-ancestral beings and culture-heroes were endowed. These figures were created as forms mirroring the qualities which the people strove to acquire for themselves. This was an intellectualizing process and differed in kind and intent from the grotesque, fantastic forms of Melanesian art which, as noted above, were emotionally developed through experiences in states of unreality. Hence the emotionally charged, dramatic, or at times even melodramatic aura associated with the majority of Melanesian works is conspicuously missing in Polynesian art. The southeastern Pacific forms had, instead, a didactic character that would appeal to the mind, and only in a narcissistic way to the emotions. Another important difference should be noted between the grotesque or distorted forms of these two areas: in Melanesia, they were often used together with many other prescribed objects in prolonged rituals; while in Polynesian traditions, the works, although frequently grouped together, do not function in direct relationship to each other. Unlike the vast regions of Melanesia and Africa, Polynesia was almost without masks, though it abounded in large stone works, both architectural and sculptural in type. Stone work has been found in parts of Melanesia, however, and future archaeological work may prove that it was extensive there, too, providing further fields for comparison, stylistically and aesthetically, between the two Oceanic territories.

Although numerous points of stylistic analogy can be noted among certain of the art styles in Melanesia, the forms are substantially so much at variance with each other that the large region must be considered as one of heterogeneous art traditions. In contrast, the art styles of Polynesia, while each area had its distinct style characteristics, shared so many elements in common, that they may be considered parts of a more homogeneous artistic unit. As was true of Africa, there were numerous underlying aspects of culture, as well as stylistic devices used in the art forms, that appeared consistently throughout Polynesia and gave a certain unity to the area as an art-producing region. But, whether homogeneous or heterogeneous in character, all three areas shared one common feature: the importance of art as a dominant aspect or feature of culture.

This was true, also, of the North American Indian whose art traditions are varied and, in many instances, highly distinctive. A number of the forms, media, and techniques are unique to this part of the world as, for example, moose-hair embroidery, porcupine quillwork, and fresh-water shell headwork. Other singular techniques are the birch-bark etchings of the Northeast, and the method of incising used to decorate the buffalo robes of the Plains, which to some extent was a modification of the treatment given to the birch-bark containers. In turn, the construction of these Northeastern containers was related to the extraordinary technique found in the Northwest Coast by which slabs of cedar were grooved, moistened, and then bent so as to form a boxlike container. Other special forms of art found only in North America were the particular developments of pottery and the singular types of stone work.

The essential character of the art forms created by the original inhabitants of this continent was decorative and largely two-dimensional. By comparison with the arts of Africa and the South Pacific, there are relatively few high points. Among these are included such forms as the pre-Columbian stone work and the Northwest Coast historical sculptures, which are comparable, in terms of aesthetic achievement, to the finest creations from any other part of the primitive world. Homogeneity in North American Indian art is restricted, for the most part, to regional stylistic zones, although influences frequently traveled with great strength from one part of the continent to another. There is still much to learn about the backgrounds of this art since the forms are diverse and the meanings of the compositions so varied that almost every design has its own significance. Certain generalizations are valid, however. In this sense, it can be said that Northwest Coast masks were of great importance in the dramatic presentation of social position or rank, as well as in the enactments of religious phenomena. In either case, these masks and other sculptures demonstrated visually the expressive purposes for which they were worn in the histrionic revelations of supernatural experiences. Consequently, this art was generally extremely expressive and purposeful.

As in Melanesia, many of the forms were obtained from experiences in states of unreality, such as dreams or hallucinations. But here the similarity ends. None of the surrealistic fantasy so characteristic of form expression in Melanesia is discernible in the Indian arts of North America. Even in the dramatic abstractions of the Northwest Coast, there is none of the spontaneous, emotionally charged aura found in western Oceanic art forms. Precise designs, real or visual symmetry of parts, esoteric symbolism, and abstractions of natural form are all apparent in the primitive art forms of North America. There exists, in this part of the primitive world, a clear relationship between design, shape, and function. That is, the designs on a given object were adapted very carefully to the contours of the shapes and forms, while the object itself was frequently shaped in such a way as to reveal its purpose. In addition, there was as great an emphasis on the decoration of wearing apparel and common utilitarian objects—e.g., the carrying bags—as can be found in any other part of the primitive world.

While there are no special principles unique to either the creation or the analysis of these art forms, there are nevertheless certain features common to the arts of all primitive areas. These have been considered in detail in the Introduction, but it seems worthwhile to recapitulate to some extent here in the conclusion. Of paramount importance is the complete integration of the art within its cultural context. Other significant, shared features include: the lack of personal creation with its attendant stress on individual interpretation within the bounds of local or area style traditions; the anonymity of the artist in most, but by no means all, cases; and the vast number of relatively small areas of local style that prevail. There is no single art style in the primitive world that is common to, and extends over, a very large area, the one exception being the relatively large territory of the Great Plains in North America.

Another aspect of the artistic creations of primitive man that is commonly shared is the immediacy and directness with which the visual impact of the artistic power is felt by the viewer. For those of the nonprimitive world, this is somewhat due to the uncommon appearance of these forms. It also results from the fact that these primitive forms exist and are combined in a manner outside the familiar frame of reference, so that there is no background against which to interpret or evaluate them. But this is more than just the consequence of a strangeness or unfamiliarity with the art forms. Rather, it is a result of the primary use of all media by primitive man to express creatively and interpret artistically the underlying concepts of his subject matter, whether human, animal, or plant forms. The primitive artist makes no attempt to render the external aspects and details of form with pictorial exactness; it is the essence or inner meaning that must be translated into imagery. The primitive artist seeks to give tangible substance to the subjective concepts involved in each particular creation. From this fact, all persons interested in art have much to learn.

Chronologically, primitive art, with few exceptions, can largely be dated from the eighteenth and, especially, the nineteenth and early twentieth centuries. After contact between primitive peoples and peoples of the Western world, acculturation set in through mission work, trade, and, finally, through colonial control, which imposed restrictive laws and altered greatly the original culture patterns. With the modification of religious beliefs and practices, and with the changes in social and economic customs, primitive cultures no longer required their traditional art forms. The very motivations, functions, and meanings of the forms were no longer valid. Only in a very few areas are any traditional, primitive art forms being produced today; and even these seem, by comparison with the older forms, spiritless and of modest technical quality.

In many of the once primitive areas, a new art is in the process of emergence. This exists in several of the new African states, among the American Indians, in New Guinea, and elsewhere. Also in existence in these areas is the tourist art, which is somewhat based on very degraded versions of traditional forms, and the commercial mission school art. The new art is an attempt to express, in such media as watercolor, oils, and sculpture, the concepts and thoughts of the artists which sometimes relate to the old, traditional myths. In some instances, particularly in African sculptures, attempts have been made to develop a style that has something in common with the idiom of the traditional art. This is an important and active development; but only the future will tell to what extent a new and original art will be produced. It seems unlikely that any of the old styles will exert much of an influence, since they are now meaningless. Nor does it seem likely that the traditional arts can ever be revived, for the thoughts, hopes, and aspirations that gave them such momentum, power, and expression are now gone. The old arts, however, will forever remain as one of mankind's great artistic achievements and as a steady testimonial to how firm and vital a role art can play in the life of man.

NOTES

1 "*Rites de passage*" was coined as a term for ceremonies accompanying changes in status; cf. A. van Gennep, *Les Rites de Passage*, Paris, 1909.

2 For further information on Papuan Gulf ceremonials, cf. F. E. Williams, *Drama of Orokolo*, Oxford, 1940.

3 For further discussion of New Hebrides grade societies and culture, cf. John Layard, "Degree-Taking Rites in Southwest Bay, Malekula," *Journal of the Royal Anthropological Institute*, 58, 1928, pp. 139-223.

4 For further discussion of Duwamish ceremonials and culture, cf. Paul S. Wingert, *American Indian Sculpture, A Study of the Northwest Coast*, New York, 1949.

5 A good discussion of the recent studies on dating in the Sudan can be found in: G. P. Murdock, *Africa: Its Peoples and Their Cultural History*, New York, 1959.

6 For further information on the knowledge of early dates for Benin culture, see: P. J. C. Dark, Introduction and Notes to Plates, *Benin Art*, compiled by Werner and Bedrich Forman, London, 1960.

7 The treatment of the eyelids in this example, as in other Yoruban works, is very close to a peculiarity of the Sudanese Baga style: the completion of the eyelids is treated as though it were hidden by the fleshy bridge of the nose.

8 Among the Bakota, and in the area extending southwestward along the Ogowe River, a well-known and often-illustrated type of naturalistic white-faced mask was used. This is often cited as among the more realistic of African Negro art creations; indeed, many of the examples are just that. To the northeast of this region, another center of more dramatic, expressive mask forms existed. These are too little published and deserve to be better known.

9   For a discussion of motivation, function, and meaning of ancestor figures, cf. pp. 20-2, 66.

10 The Kwango is a large river that flows north and empties into the Kasai River near its confluence with the Congo.

11 The aesthetic qualities of fetish figures are also discussed earlier, cf. p. 24.

12 The Bayaka used three types of masks: 1) the large, semihelmet type which resembles closely the forms of their neighbors, the Basuku; 2) a very large face mask; and 3) a unique form consisting of a small, highly stylized, enframed face dominated by the typical Bayaka nose and carved on a small handle. These latter-type masks are fabricated of wood, fiber, and clay, with a bulbous mass of raffia fringe depending from the base. The composite form is held before the face of the wearer by the carved handle.

13 For a discussion of initiation-type art forms, cf. pp. 39-41.

14 Although composed of entirely different stylistic elements, the head of this figure should be compared with the Benin bronze royal ancestor heads for a comparable expression of kingship and power, cf. Fig. 14.

15 The most important of the other court styles are those of Benin and Ife in Nigeria; a lesser center should be noted in Dahomey.

16 For a further discussion of raffia in Congo art, cf. E. Torday & J. R. Joyce, *Les Bushongo*, Brussels, 1910.

17 It is important to note that neither type nor class of cup is restricted to the Bushongo. Effigy cups have been clearly identified as of Bapende and Basonge styles; while geometric cups of distinctive shapes have been found among the Bayaka and various neighboring tribes to the Bushongo area.

18 Tukula, used largely as a cosmetic or for painting the body and face on ceremonial and special occasions, was made from the powdered dust of camwood. This powder, red in color, was then mixed with water and oil so as to form a solid block or cake which, when moistened, produced a chalklike, transient pigment. This medium was used extensively in Central Africa, not only as a cosmetic, but as a substance with sufficient magical power to activate, when rubbed on the surface, the spirit content of a figure or mask.

19 Records of the meaning and function of Kifwebe masks, as obtained in early days of contact, may be found in J. Maes, *Aniota-Kifwebe*, Antwerp, 1924.

20 For other references to exaggeration and amplification of scarification patterns, see the discussion of Baoule forms, pp. 84-5.

21 For a further discussion of Buli style, cf. F. M. Olbrechts, *Plastiek van Congo*, Brussels, 1946; published in French as *La Sculpture de la Congo*, Brussels, 1960.

22 The Stuttgart example has details of the hair, nipples, and body scarification picked out in black. It appears likely that this was done later.

23 Reference to the historical movements of the Badjokwe peoples to and from the Kasai-Sankuru region can be found in E. Torday, *Notes Ethnographiques sur des Populations les Bassins du Kasai et du Kwango Oriental*, Brussels, 1923.

24 The transliteration of this tribal name has now been altered by the Tervueren Museum, to Balega; in the current literature, it has recently appeared under this new designation.

25 Among the other peoples of the Northern Congo who likewise produced art forms are the Ababua, Basengele, Bwaka, Bakwese, Togbo, and Bobati. Compared to the developed styles of other parts of the Congo, however, the styles were simple in form and meager in the success of their aesthetic expression (cf. Olbrechts, op. cit.) In East Africa, near the Lake Tanganyika region, several strong figure and mask styles occurred which, in a general discussion of this type, cannot be included; otherwise the art of the Makonde would certainly have had careful consideration.

26 For a discussion of the importance of physical contact with the korovar figures, see S. Chauvet, *Les Arts Indigènes en Nouvelle Guinée*, Paris, 1930.

27 A number of Maprik houses are still extant in their pristine condition, although the incentive toward their construction and maintenance is dying, due to the consequences of acculturation. This change or loss of motivations has already taken place in the Middle Sepik area where the houses have already lost, or are fast losing, their significance. Cf. R. Gardi, *Tambaran*, London, 1960.

28 Gardi, ibid., p. 14.

29 Ibid.

30 For a discussion of the motivations, functions, and meanings of Sulka masks, cf. pp. 39-41, 65.

31 It should be stressed that the idea was current over a wide area of Melanesia that by contact with the "presence" of spirit-ancestor power sources, represented in the art forms, some of this power could be absorbed. The contact with these power sources in the Maprik Tambaran houses is a good illustration of this important aspect of Melanesian art.

32 For a discussion of Papuan Gulf art forms, their motivation, function, and meaning, cf. pp. 33-6, 64.

33 The best known of these archipelagoes are the Trobriands, the d'Entre-Casteaux, and the Louisades.

34 The spatulas are used in many areas of Melanesia where the betel-nut-chewing habit prevailed. This habit, widespread in Southeast Asia as well as in western Oceania, entailed first putting a pepper leaf on the tongue; on top of this was placed a cracked nut from the Areca (betel-nut) palm; and then finally, slaked lime, obtained from shells, was chewed, producing a copious flow of brilliant red saliva and eventually staining the teeth black. A mild stimulation resulted from the betel nut.

35 A discussion of the importance of the "kula ring" in the development of a barter system can be found in B. Malinowski, *Argonauts of the Western Pacific*, London, 1922.

36 For a discussion of the importance of magic in the Massim area, see B. Malinowski, *Coral Gardens and Their Magic*, London, 1935.

37 For a discussion of the motivations, functions, and meaning of Malagan art, cf. pp. 46-8, 66-7.

38 Illustrations of shell inlay in canoe-prow carvings can be seen in Paul S. Wingert, *Outline Guide to the Art of the South Pacific*, New York, 1946.

39 For a discussion of New Hebrides grade societies, cf. pp. 48-53.

40 For more detailed accounts of the Fiji-Tonga relationships, see W. Mariner (John Martin, compiler), *An Account of the Natives of the Tongan Islands in the South Pacific Ocean*, 2 vols., Edinburgh, 1817.

41 Sennit cord was made of twisted fibers from the coconut husk and was used throughout Polynesia as a sewing and/or lashing material.

42 For the meaning and function of Fijian temple tapa, cf. p. 262.

43 Suspension hooks, carved with the human figure, are most common in the Sepik River area of New Guinea, and are rare in eastern Melanesia and throughout Polynesia. Cf. Karl Erik Larsson, "Fijian Studies," *Etnologiska Studiar*, 250, Goteborg, 1960, p. 75.

44 Present research on Samoa and Tonga as centers for the expansion into Polynesia, and on the role of the Societies, is discussed in H. L. Shapiro & R. C. Suggs, "New Dates for Polynesian Prehistory," *Man*, January, 1959.

45 The Raratongan fisherman's god is illustrated in Paul S. Wingert, *Art of the South Seas*, Museum of Modern Art, p. 27.

46 The Raratongan district gods are illustrated in Wingert, op. cit., p. 28.

47 The best known of Austral Island decorative art objects are the paddles. Like the Mangaian adzes, these ceremonial objects were modified somewhat in shape and, in certain instances, in proportions as well.

48 The motivation and function of Hawaiian temple figures are discussed further on pp. 59-61.

49 This figure was collected by Midshipman Knowles of the H.M.S. *Blonde*, which in 1824 took back to Hawaii the body of King Liholiho, who had died on a recent trip to London. The documentation in the British Museum register states that it is "possibly the goddess Kihu." Cf. *Man*, 1932-3.

50 For a discussion of the motivation and function of Hawaiian figures, cf. pp. 59-61.

51 This literature on the Marquesas includes such works as: K. von den Steinen, *Die Marquesaner und ihre Kunst*, Berlin, vols. 1 & 2, 1925, vol. 3, 1928; and Willowdean Handy, *L'Art des Iles Marquesas*, Paris, 1938.

52 For a more extensive discussion of the settlement of the Marquesas, cf. R. C. Suggs, *The Island Civilizations of Polynesia*, New York, 1960.

53 The appearance of these lizard forms is provocative: were they symbols of death, evil, or a wizard as they were in some areas of Polynesia? Or were they merely decorative forms with no symbolic meaning? If they had some special significance, then were the stilts used merely for diversion or were they used on some occasion with ceremonial significance?

54 A classical although somewhat romantic story of Marquesan life is that recorded by Herman Melville in his *Typee*, London, 1846.

55 A discussion of Easter Island "script" and its supposed relationship to embryonic Eastern forms is to be found in A. Metraux, *Easter Island*, New York, Oxford, 1957.

56 Moa birds, once plentiful throughout New Zealand, were extinct, with the exception of a small species, well before the arrival of Europeans.

57 For a discussion of the motivation, function, and meaning of Iroquois masks, cf. pp. 36-8, 64-5.

58 These men were Clark Wissler, Alfred Kroeber, and Robert Lowie.

59 The motivation of these robes in prestige-vanity needs can be integrated with the discussion of this aspect, pp. 30-1.

60 At the time the Spaniards arrived, steatite sculpture of fantastic fish forms was being carved in the Los Angeles area and the nearby offshore islands. These objects were known as "cloud-blowers," and were used ceremonially. Recently, many faked copies of these objects have appeared.

61 For a discussion of the Duwamish ceremonies and art, cf. pp. 56-9.

62 The characterizations of individual tribal styles in this area can be found in V. Garfield, P. S. Wingert, & M. Barbeau, *The Tsimshian, Their Arts and Music*, New York, 1951, part 2.

63 Throughout the important art-producing regions of South America, aside from the various "high"-culture areas, various distinctive representational traditions are evident. Particularized and highly singular art forms developed in several areas, especially the numerous mask

and masklike forms of which the costume mask is the most significant example. These include the samples of disguises, such as the conical hide masks of the Ona in Tierra del Fugo and their neighbors, which were used as impersonations of spirits at boys' initiation rites. More elaborate forms were created in the Upper Xingu River area to the south of the Amazon region in east-central Brazil. These masks were usually conical forms that fitted over the head, with the facial features painted in various conformations on the bark-cloth surface. The designs and/or features were rendered in tans and browns on the natural-colored fabric. Mask forms of this area also include head-dresses of carved wood with attachments of woven straw and painted calabashes, which are fantastic in appearance and visually exciting. In the Amazon region of Brazil, the conical bark-cloth costume masks were used. In color and design, these were somewhat reminiscent of certain Melanesian forms. This does not mean, however, that these forms grew out of the Pacific designs. The geometric motives of the two areas are common decorative elements found in widely spaced areas totally disparate in culture and physical stock throughout the world. Their ''origin,'' if such must be found; undoubtedly lies in independent development. The costume masks on which these designs are found are composed of grasses, leaves, basketry, bark, and feathers. They were used by many tribes to evoke various spirits and mythological beings. These South American masks are dynamic in expression and varied, if not elemental, in technique.

In the northern littoral of the North American continent, the Eskimo developed particular ceremonials and entertainments in which mask forms were employed. These were often of composite character and included attachments of wood, bone, feathers, and shell. Many of them were asymmetrical in composition, and they often referred to evil spirits or spirits of specifically therapeutic character. The majority of these Eskimo masks was used either to propitiate or to humor malevolent spirits, such as those of winter and disease. The differentiation of types and styles is considerable, and representations include various combinations of grotesque or distorted human, animal, and imaginative forms; and it is not unusual to find masks in which one side of the face is completely unlike the other, thus producing a flagrant asymmetry. Some other examples of these masks have pendent forms which give them the character of mobiles, with bits of bone, feather, hides, or other materials attached in a state of suspension. These create an obvious emphasis on movement when the mask

385

is used. These forms, with the extraneous materials attached, were used in combination with specific costumes in dramatic performances.

64 For a discussion of the relationships of primitive and modern art, cf. R. Goldwater, *Primitivism in Modern Painting,* New York, 1938.

65 Roger Fry, *Vision and Design,* London, 1924.

66 See the discussion of Hawaiian temple figures, pp. 294-7.

BIBLIOGRAPHY: Selected Works

General

Adam, L., *Primitive Art,* Penguin Books, London, 1949.
Basler, A., *L'Art chez les Peuples Primitifs,* Paris, 1929.
Boas, Franz, *Primitive Art,* Oslo, 1927.
British Museum, *Handbook to the Ethnographical Collections,* 2nd ed., London, 1925.
Brooklyn Museum, *Masterpieces of African Art,* New York, 1954.
Gennep, A. van, *Les Rites de Passage,* Paris, 1909.
Goldwater, R. J., *Primitivism in Modern Painting,* New York, 1938.
Heydrich, M., & Frölich, W., *Plastik der Primitiven,* Stuttgart, 1954.
Hoebel, E. A., *Man in the Primitive World,* 2nd ed., New York, 1958.
Muensterberger, Werner, *The Art of Primitive Man,* London & Amsterdam, 1955.
Sydow, E. von, *Die Kunst der Naturvölker und der Vorzeit,* Berlin, 1923.
Webster, H., *Primitive Secret Societies: A Study in Early Politics and Religion,* New York, 1908.

Africa

Baumann, H., & Westerman, D., *Les Peuples et les Civilisations de l'Afrique Noir,* Paris, 1948.
Dark, P. J. C., Introduction and Notes to Plates, *Benin Art,* compiled by Werner and Bedrich Forman, London, 1960.
Dieterlen, G., *La Religion Bambara,* Paris, 1951.
Donner, E., *Kunst und Handwerk in Nord-Ost Liberia,* Berlin, 1940.
Egharevba, H. U., *A Short History of Benin,* Lagos, 1936.
Fagg, W. B. (with photographs by Eliot Elisofon), *The Sculpture of Africa,* London, 1958.
———, *The Webster Plass Collection of African Art,* British Museum, London, 1953.

Fry, Roger, *Vision and Design*, London, 1924.

Gerbrands, A. A., *Art as an Element of Culture, Especially in Negro Africa*, Leiden, 1957.

Gluck, J. F., *Afrikanische Masken*, Baden-Baden, 1956.

———, *Die Kunst Negre-Afrikas*, Stuttgart, 1956.

Goldwater, R. J., *Antelopes and Queens* (Bambara Sculpture), Museum of Primitive Art, New York, 1960.

Griaule, M., *Folk Art of Black Africa*, New York, 1950.

———, *Masques Dogon*, Paris, 1938.

Harley, G. W., "Masks as Agents of Social Control," *Papers of the Peabody Museum*, Cambridge, Mass., 1950.

———, "Notes on the Poro in Liberia," *Papers of the Peabody Museum*, Cambridge, Mass., 1941.

Herskovits, M. J., *Backgrounds of African Art*, Denver Art Museum, 1945.

———, *Dahomey*, 2 vols., New York, 1938.

Himmelheber, H., *Negerkunst und Negerkünstler*, Braunschweig, 1960.

——— & U., *Die Dan*, Stuttgart, 1958.

Holas, B., *Cultures Materielles de la Cote d'Ivoire*, Paris, 1960.

Kjersmeier, C., *African Negro Sculpture*, New York, 1948.

———, *Centres de Style de la Sculpture Negre Africaine*, 4 vols., Paris, 1935-8.

"L'Art Negre," *Presence Africaine*, vols. 10-11, Paris, 1951.

Lavachery, H., *Statuaire de l'Afrique Noire*, Neuchâtel, 1954.

Lem, F .H., *Sculpture Soudanaise*, Paris, 1948.

Leuzinger, Elsy, *Africa: The Art and Culture*, New York, 1960.

Luschan, F. von, *Die Altertümer von Benin*, 3 vols., Berlin, 1919.

Maes, J., *Aniota-Kifwebe: Les Masques des Populations du Congo Belge*, Antwerp, 1924.

Murdock, George P., *Africa: Its Peoples and Their Cultural History*, New York, 1959.

Olbrechts, F. M., *Plastiek van Congo*, Antwerp, 1946; translated as *La Sculpture de la Congo*, Antwerp, 1960.

Paulme, Denise, *Les Sculptures d'Afrique Noire*, Paris, 1956.

Radin, P., & Sweeney, J. J., *African Folktales and Sculpture*, New York, 1952.

Rattray, R. S., *Religion and Art in Ashanti*, Oxford, 1927.

Sadler, M. E., *Arts of West Africa*, Oxford, 1935.

Schmalenbach, W., *Die Kunst Afrikas*, Basel, 1953; translated as *African Art*, New York, 1957.

Sweeney, J. J., *African Negro Art*, Museum of Modern Art, New York, 1935.

Sydow, E. von, *Africanische Plastik*, Berlin, 1954.

Talbot, A. P., *Peoples of Southern Nigeria*, 3 vols., Oxford, 1926.

Tessman, G., *Die Pangwe*, 2 vols., Berlin, 1913.

Torday, E., *Notes Ethnographiques sur des Populations les Bassins du Kasai et du Kwango Oriental*, Brussels, 1923.

———, & Joyce, J. R., *Les Bushongo*, Brussels, 1910.

Underwood, L., *Bronzes of West Africa*, London, 1949.

———, *Figures in Wood of West Africa*, London, 1947.

———, *Masks of West Africa*, London, 1948.

Vatter, E., *Religiöse Plastik der Naturvolker*, Frankfurt am Main, 1926.

Wingert, Paul S., *Sculpture of Negro Africa*, New York, 1950.

Oceania

Beaglehole, J. C., *The Exploration of the Pacific*, London, 1934.

Bodrogi, T., *Oceanian Art*, Budapest, 1959.

Edge-Partington, J., *An Album of the Weapons, Tools, Ornaments, Articles of Dress of the Natives of the Pacific Islands*, 3 vols., Manchester, 1890-8.

Leenhardt, M., *Folk Arts of Oceania*, New York, 1950.

Linton, R., & Wingert, P. S., with R. d'Harnoncourt, *Arts of the South Seas*, Museum of Modern Art, New York, 1946.

Nevermann, Hans, *Sudseekunst*, Berlin, 1933.

Oliver, Douglas, *The Pacific Islands*, Cambridge, Mass., 1952.

Robson, R. W., *The Pacific Islands Handbook*, New York, 1944.

Rousseau, M., "L'Art Océanien," *Le Musée Vivant*, no. 39, Paris, 1951.

Tischner, H., *Oceanic Art*, London, 1954.

Wingert, Paul S., *Arts of the South Pacific Islands*, New York & London, 1953.

———, *Outline Guide to South Pacific Art*, New York, 1946.

a Melanesia

Bateson, G., *Naven*, Cambridge, 1936.

Chauvet, S., *Les Arts Indigènes en Nouvelle Guinée*, Paris, 1930.

Codrington, R. H., *The Melanesians, Oxford, 1891*; Yale, New Haven, 1957.

Cranstone, B. A. L., *Melanesia, a Short Ethnography*, British Museum, London, 1961.

Deacon, A. B., *Malekula*, London, 1934.

Firth, Raymond, *Art and Life in New Guinea*, London & New York, 1936.

Haddon, A. C., *The Decorative Art of British New Guinea*, London, 1894.

———, & Hormell, James, *Canoes of Oceania*, 3 vols., Bernice P. Bishop Museum, Honolulu, 1936-8.

Harrison, T., *Savage Civilization*, New York, 1937.

Ivens, W. G., *Melanesians of the Southeast Solomon Islands*, London, 1927.

Kooijman, S., *The Art of Lake Sentani*, Museum of Primitive Art, New York, 1959.

Krämer, A., *Die Malanggane in Tombara*, Munich, 1925.

Larsson, Karl Eric, *Fijian Studies*, Etnologiska Studier, 25, Göteborg, 1960.

Layard, J., "Degree-Taking Rites in Southwest Bay, Malekula," *Journal of the Royal Anthropological Institute*, no. 58, 1928.

Lewis, A. B., *Carved and Painted Designs for New Guinea*, Chicago Natural History Museum, Series 5, Anthropological Design, 1931.

———, *Decorative Art of New Guinea: Incised Design*, Chicago Natural History Museum, Series 4, Anthropological Design, 1925.

Luquet, G. H., *L'Art Neo-Caledonien*, Inst. D'Ethnol., Paris, 1926.

Malinowski, B., *Argonauts of the Western Pacific*, London, 1922.

———, *Coral Gardens and Their Magic*, London, 1935.

McCarthy, Frederick D., *Australia's Aborigines, Their Life and Culture*, Melbourne, 1957.

Mason, Leonard, "Art of Micronesia," *Encyclopedia of World Art*, New York, 1962.

Mead, Margaret, *Sex and Temperament in Three Primitive Societies* (Sepik), New York, 1935.

Meyer, A. B., & Parkinson, R., *Schnitzerein und Masken vom Bismark Archipelago und Neu Guinea*, Königliches Ethnographiches Museum in Dresden, Pub. 10, Dresden, 1895.

Nevermann, H., *Masken und Gehiembinder in Melanesien*, Berlin, 1933.

Parkinson, R., *Dreissig Jahre in der Südsee*, Stuttgart, 1907.

Powdermaker, H., *Life in Lesu* (New Ireland), New York, 1933.

Reche, O., *Der Kaiserin-Augusta-Fluss*, Hamburg, 1913.

Reichard, G., *Melanesian Design*, 2 vols., New York, 1933.

Rensalear, H. C. van, *Asmat Art from Southwest Dutch New Guinea*, Amsterdam, 1956.

Roth, A. K., *Fijian Way of Life*, London, 1953.

Seligmann, C. G., *The Melanesians of British New Guinea*, Cambridge, 1910.

Speiser, Felix, *Ethnographische Materialien ins den Neuen Hebrides und den Banks Inselm*, Berlin, 1923.

———, *Ten Years with the Natives in the Western Pacific,* London, 1913.

Williams, F. E., *Drama of Orokolo,* Oxford, 1940.

Williams, J. R., *Missionary Enterprises in the Pacific,* London, 1870.

Williams, Thomas, *Fiji and the Fijians,* vol. 1, London, 1860.

Wirz, Paul, *Die Marind-anim von Holländisch-Süd-Neu-Guinea,* 2 vols., 4 parts, Hamburg, 1922-4.

Woodford, C. M., "The Canoes of the British Solomon Islands," *Journal of The Royal Anthropological Society,* 39, 1909.

b   Polynesia

Archey, G., "Maori Carving Patterns," *Journal, Polynesian Society,* 45, 1936.

———, *Maori Design.*

Best, Elsdon, *The Maori,* 2 vols., Wellington, 1924.

———, "Maori Storehouses and Kindred Structures," *Bulletin, Dominion Museum,* 4, Wellington, 1926.

Brigham, W. T., "Old Hawaiian Carving," *Memoirs, Bernice P. Bishop Museum,* 2, 1906.

Buck, Peter H. (Te Rangi Hiroa), "Arts and Crafts of the Cook Islands," *Bulletin, Bernice P. Bishop Museum,* 179, Honolulu, 1944.

———, *Arts and Crafts of Hawaii,* Bernice P. Bishop Museum, Honolulu, 1957.

———, *Coming of the Maori,* Wellington, 1951.

———, "Material Representation of Tongan and Samoan Gods," *Journal, Polynesian Society,* 3 parts, 47, 1935.

———, *Vikings of the Sunrise,* New York, 1938; retitled: *Vikings of the Pacific,* Univ. of Chicago Press, 1960.

Chauvet, S., *L'Ile de Pâques et ses Mystères,* Paris, 1935.

Dodge, E. S., *The Hawaiian Portion of the Polynesian Collection of the Peabody Museum of Salem,* Salem, Mass., 1937.

———, *The New Zealand Maori Collection in the Peabody Museum of Salem,* Salem, Mass., 1941.

Duff, Roger, *The Moa-Hunter Period of Maori Culture,* Wellington, 1950.

Ellis, W., *Polynesian Researches,* 4 vols., London, 1831-2.

Emory, K. P., "Hawaii: Notes on Wooden Images," *Ethnologia Cranmorensis,* III, 1938.

Firth, R., *Economics of the New Zealand Maori,* 2nd ed., Wellington, 1959. (First edition, published in London, entitled *Primitive Economics of the Maori of New Zealand.*)

Hamilton, A., *The Art Workmanship of the Maori Race of New Zealand,* Wellington, 1896-1901.

Handy, E. S. C., "History and Culture in the Society Islands," *Bulletin, Bernice P. Bishop Museum*, 74, Honolulu, 1930.

———, "The Native Culture in the Marquesas," *Bulletin, Bernice P. Bishop Museum*, 9, Honolulu, 1938.

Handy, W. C., *L'Art des Iles Marquises*, Paris, 1938.

Krämer, A., *Die Samoa Inselm*, 2 vols., Stuttgart, 1903.

Linton, Ralph, "The Material Culture of the Marquesas Islands," *Memoirs, Bernice P. Bishop Museum*, 8, Honolulu, 1923.

Luquiens, H. M., *Hawaiian Art*, Honolulu, 1931.

Malo, D., *Hawaiian Antiquities*, Honolulu, 1903.

Mariner, W. (John Martin, compiler), *An Account of the Natives of the Tongan Islands in the Pacific Ocean*, 2 vols., Edinburgh, 1817.

Melville, H., *Typee*, London, 1946 edition.

Metraux, A., *Easter Island*, New York, 1959.

———, "Ethnology of Easter Island," *Bulletin, Bernice P. Bishop Museum*, 160, Honolulu, 1940.

Routledge, Mrs. S., *The Mystery of Easter Island*, London, 1919.

Shapiro, H. L., & Suggs, R. C., "New Dates for Polynesian Prehistory," *Man*, January, 1959.

Skinner, H. D., "Evolution in Maori Art," *Journal of the Royal Anthropological Institute*, 46, London, 1916.

Stienen, K. von den, *Die Marquesaner und ihre Kunst*, Berlin, 3 vols., 1925-8.

Suggs, Robert C., *The Island Civilizations of Polynesia*, New York, 1960.

Turner, G., *Samoa a Hundred Years Ago and Long Before*, London, 1844.

North America

Boas, Franz, "The Social Organization and Secret Societies of the Kwakiutl Indians," *Annual Report, United States National Museum, Smithsonian Institution*, Washington, D.C., 1897.

Bunzell, Ruth, "The Pueblo Potter," *Columbia University Contributions to Anthropology*, 8, New York, 1929.

Coulton, H. S., *Hopi Kachina Dolls*, University of New Mexico Press, Albuquerque, 1959.

Davis, R. T., *Native Arts of the Pacific Northwest*, Palo Alto, Calif., 1949.

Dockstader, F. J., *Indian Art in America; the Arts and Crafts of the North American Indian*, New York, 1961.

Douglas, F., & d'Harnoncourt, Rene, *Indian Art of the United States*, Museum of Modern Art, New York, 1941.

Driver, Harold E., *Indians of North America,* Univ. of Chicago Press, 1961.

Ewers, J. C., *Plains Indian Painting,* Stanford University, Palo Alto, Calif., 1939.

Fenton, W. N., *Masked Medicine Societies of the Iroquois,* Smithsonian Institution Report no. 1940, Washington, D.C., 1941.

Garfield, V., Wingert, P. S., & Barbeau, M., *The Tsimshian, Their Arts and Music,* Part 2, New York, 1951.

Griffen, James (ed. James Griffen), *Archeology of Eastern United States,* Univ. of Chicago Press, 1952.

Himmelheber, H., *Eskimo Künstler,* Stuttgart, 1938.

Inverarity, R. B., *Art of the Northwest Coast Indians,* Univ. of California Press, Berkeley, 1950.

Jenness, Diamond, *The Indians of Canada,* 5th ed., Ottawa, 1960.

Kroeber, A., "The Arapaho," *Bulletin, American Museum of Natural History,* vol. 18, parts 1, 2, 4, New York, 1907.

———, "Decorative Symbolism of the Arapaho," *American Anthropologist,* vol. 3, 1901.

Lowie, Robert H., "Crow Indian Art," *Anthropological Papers, American Museum of Natural History,* 21, part 4, 1922.

Martin, P. S., Quimby, G. R., & Collier, D., *Indians Before Columbus,* Univ. of Chicago Press, 1947.

Morris, E. H., *Archeological Studies in the La Plata District, Southern Colorado, and Northwestern New Mexico,* Carnegie Institute, Washington, D.C., 1936.

Orchard, W. C., "The Technique of Porcupine Quill Decoration among the North American Indians," *Indian Notes & Monographs, Museum of the American Indian,* Heye Foundation, 1916.

Quimby, George I., *Indian Life in the Upper Great Lakes,* Univ. of Chicago Press, 1961.

Radin, P., "The Winnebago Tribe," *Bureau of American Ethnology Annual Report,* 37, 1923.

Shetrone, H. C., *The Moundbuilders,* New York, 1930.

Speck, F. G., "The Double-Curve Motive in Northeastern Algonkian Art," *Memoirs, Anthropological Series, Canadian Dep't. of Mines, Geology Survey,* vol. 42, no. 1, Ottawa, 1914.

———, *The Iroquois,* Cranbrook Institute, Mich., 1955.

———, "Material Culture of the Menomini," *Indian Notes & Monographs, Museum of the American Indian,* Heye Foundation, 1921.

———, *Naskapi, Savage Hunters of the Labrador Peninsula,* Univ. of Oklahoma Press, 1935.

393

Valliant, G. C., *Indian Arts of North America*, New York, 1939.

Wingert, Paul S., *American Indian Art, a Study of the Northwest Coast*, New York, 1949.

Wissler, Clarke, *The American Indian*, 3rd ed., New York, 1938.

———, "The Decorative Art of the Sioux," *Bulletin, American Museum of Natural History*, 18, 1904.

———, *North American Indians of the Plains*, Handbook 1, American Museum of Natural History, New York, 1934.

Wormington, H. M., *Prehistoric Indians of the Southwest*, Denver Natural History Museum, 1947.

body-painting, 14, 31, 263, 380
bone, 13, 157, 197, 212, 311, 355, 358, 385
bonito, 247-9
boomerangs, 263, 264
Borneo (Indonesia), 190
Bougainville (Solomon Islands), 78
bow and arrow, 227
bow-rest shaft, 170
bowls, 31, 62; Austral Islands, 292; Baluba, 167-70; Baoule, 87; Cameroon, 129; cliff-dweller, 332; Hohokam, 334; Ibo, 118-20; Lake Sentani, 195; Marquesas, 310; Micronesia, 265, 267; Moundbuilder, 337; pre-Columbian Northwest, 338; Solomon Islands, 247-9; Tami-Huon, 210, 214-15; Yoruba, 114, 115, 117
boxes: Bakota skull and skeleton preservation, 55, 140; Bushongo, 45, 158; Northwest Coast, 358, 366; see also containers
bracelets, 65
brass, 13; Bakota, 55, 140, 141; Cameroon, 128; Dahomey, 109-10
Brazil, 385
breastplate, 335
British Columbia (North America), 338, 358
British Museum, 150, 247, 249, 307, 316, 383
bronze, 13, 98; Ashanti, 69-70, 107-8; Benin, 21, 78, 110-12, 380; Ife, 21, 78, 110, 112
buffalo, 350; Plains teepee, 354, 355; see also water buffalo
buffalo robes, Plains Indians, 70, 353, 355-6, 375
Buka-Bougainville (Melanesia), 239-40, 241
Buli: see Baluba
bull-roarers, 227, 264
Bundu Society (Africa), masks, 98-100
burial trees, 265
Bushongo (Bakuba) (Africa), 44-6, 66, 152-8, 159, 164, 167; commemorative royal portrait figures, 44-5, 46, 65, 152-5, 157; cups, 68-9, 152, 155-7, 158, 380
butterfly, 354
Bwaka (Africa), 381

C

calabashes, 109, 385
California (North America), 357
Calusa Indians, 345
Cameroon, 127-34, 135, 138, 256; carved stools, 128, 129-30; ceremonial and prestige objects, 130; masks, 129, 130-4; sculptured objects, 129
camwood, 380
Canada, 357

cane, 39, 201, 222, 225, 230

cannibal forks, 257, 258, 260

cannibalism, 191

canoe-prow carvings, 382; Marquesas, 307-9; Massim, 231, 232-4; Ponape, 267-8; Raratonga, 286-8; Sepik River, 197

canoe-shaped dishes, 217

canoe stern boards, 325-7

canoes: in Duwamish ceremony, 57; Maori, 325; in Oceania, 232; Papuan Gulf, 227; Polynesia, 271, 286; Solomon Islands, 244

capes, 301

carbon-14 tests, 336

caribou hide, 346

Carolinas (North America), 335, 345

Caroline Islands (Micronesia), 266

carrying bags, American Indians, 62, 376

carving, 13, 14, 20-5, 31, 32, 42; Oceania, 187, 189-90

cassowary bird, 197

casting, 13; see also brass; bronze

cat's-eyes: see sea snail

Cayuga Indians, 343

cedar, 366, 375

celt, 65

Central Africa, 79, 135-41, 147-8, 164, 371, 380

Central America, 6, 8, 330

Central Congo, 44, 71, 158, 148-66, 167, 175, 176, 372; see also Bapende; Basonge; Bena Lulua; Bushongo

ceramics, 13, 14

ceremonial objects, 16, 18, 32-3, 42, 70

ceremonies, 27-30; Africa, 82, 372; ancestor worship, 20-1, 23; Bambara, 88; Baoule, 42; Basonge, 160; childbirth, 29; communal, 49, 50, 58, 59, 120; comparison of, 25-6; deity worship, 23; divination, 25; Dogon, 94; Duwamish, 56-9, 379; grade societies, 49-53; Ibibio Ekpo Society, 38; Ibo, 118; initiation, 29-30; Iroquois False Face Society, 36-7; Korubla, Senufo, 93; magical, 24, 25-6; Malagan, 46-8, 234-9; marriage, 29-30; Melanesia, 191; mortuary, 21, 29; Nigeria, 120; Northwest Coast, 361-2; Papuan Gulf, 33-6, 379; Pueblo kachina cult, 341; Solomon Islands, 249; spirit worship, 22, 23; Sulka, 40, 41; Tami-Huon, 212; Yoruba Gelede Society, 117

Chaco Canyon (North America), 334

chant, 26, 60, 160

charcoal, 243

charms, 62, 105; see also amulets

Cherokee Indians, 345

chiefs: Africa, 83; as art patrons, 18, 19; in Dahomey brass castings, 109; and

Society, 39; Ibibio, 120; Iroquois False Face Society, 37; Malagan, 47; Maori, 322; Marquesas, 307; New Hebrides grade societies, 50, 53; Papuan Gulf, 35; Pueblo, 343; Solomon Islands, 245, 247; South Dutch New Guinea, 218; Sulka, 40, 41

Cook, James, 294, 309

Cook Islands (Polynesia), 285, 286-91, 317

copper, 55, 140, 141, 335, 358

cornhusks, 343

costumes: Bapende, 148; Eskimo, 386; Malagan, 237; and Mundugumor masks, 204; New Caledonia, 254; Pueblo kachina cult, 341, 343; South America masks, 385; and spirit worship, 22

court styles, 154, 380

cowrie shell, 65, 130, 204

creativity, 9, 15-17, 18, 31-2, 45, 63, 69, 70-1, 77, 370, 377

crests, 361, 362, 366

crocodile, 109, 197

crowns, 62, 65

cultural factors, 8-9, 11, 16-19, 62-3, 65, 71-2, 75-6, 78-9, 370, 371, 377; Africa, 82-3; American Indian, 330-1; Australia, 263, 265; Bambara, 88-9; Basonge, 160; Cameroon, 127; Dahomey, 108-10; and decorative art, 70; and function of art forms, 33; Hawaii, 60; Ibibio, Ekpo Society, 38; Iroquois, 37, 343, 345-6; Melanesia, 191; Malagan, 47, 48; Maori, 317; Marquesas, 303; New Hebrides grade societies, 50, 51, 52-3, 68; Northwest Coast, 357-8, 361; Oceania, 186-8; Papuan Gulf, 35; Plains, 350-1, 353-5; Polynesia, 269-72, 292-3; Poro Society, 101; Pueblo, 340-1; Solomon Islands, 247; South, 345; South Dutch New Guinea, 218

cups, 31; Bayaka, 147, 380; Bushongo, 45, 68-9, 152, 155-7, 158, 380; cliff-dweller, 332; Tami-Huon, 210

D

Dahomey (Africa), 108-10, 134, 380; brass castings, 109-10

Dakota Indians, 351, 353, 354

Dan (Africa), masks, 101, 102

dances: Bambara Tji Wara Society, 89; Ibibio, 120; Ibo, 120; Kwakiutl, 362, 365; Malagan, 237; Marquesas, 309; New Hebrides grade societies, 51, 52; Papuan Gulf ceremonies, 35; Plains Indian Sun Dance, 355; Pueblo kachina cult, 341; Senufo Korubla ceremonies, 93; Sepik River, 206-7; Tambaran, 210; Yoruba Gelede Society, 117

decorative art, 14, 61-2, 68-71; American Indian, 375, 376; Austral Islands, 383; Bushongo, 45; and ceremonial art, 70; Great Lakes, 348; Iroquois, 345; Mangbettu, 179; Melanesia kapkaps, 241; Oceania shells, 62; Plains, 351, 353, 355, 357; Solomon Islands, 242-5; Tahiti, 286

deer, 340, 351, 354

deerskin shirts, 351, 354
deity worship, 23, 25-6; Africa, 83; Baoule, 42, 87; Fiji, 263; Hawaii, 59-61, 68, 294, 297; Ibibio-Ibo "plays," 28; Marquesas, 307; Polynesia, 270, 286, 293; Tahiti, 282, 285; Tonga, 280; Yoruba, 114
d'Entre-Casteaux (Melanesia), 382
"destroyers," Ekpo Society spirits, 38
diffusion, 10-11; Africa, 371; Cameroon, 127; Melanesia, 194; New Ireland and Solomon Islands, 239; Sepik River, 198
diffusionists, 188, 256
dishes, 217, 257, 258, 260
"district gods," 288, 383
divination, 23, 24-6, 87
Dogon (Africa), 88, 93-5, 97; ancestor figures, 97; mask of Andumboulou, 94-5, 97; "Tellem" figures, 97
double-curve motif, 346-8
Dravidians (India), 186
drums, 62, 68-9; Basonge, 160; Bushongo, 158; Cameroon, 130; Solomon Islands, 240-1; South Dutch New Guinea, 217, 220, 221
Dutch, 193
Dutch New Guinea: see New Guinea; South Dutch New Guinea
Duwamish Indians, 56-9, 66, 357, 379

E

earth paints, 104
earth pigments, 197, 198
East Africa, 180, 182-3, 381
Easter Island, 272, 292, 311-17; figures, 312-14; fish clubs, 315-16; pendants and ornaments, 316-17; "script," 312, 316, 384; stone statues, 311, 314
Eastern civilization, 30, 69, 72
Eastern Congo, 76, 166-73
economic factors, 17, 18, 26, 30, 71, 378; Africa, 82, 83; American Indian, 330; Ashanti, 108; Bambara, 88-9; Baoule, 43; Dahomey, 110; Duwamish, 58; Iroquois False Face Society, 37; Massim kula ring, 232; Melanesia, 190-1; New Hebrides grade societies, 51-2, 53; Northwest Coast, 357; Papuan Gulf ceremonies, 35; Plains, 350-1; Sulka, 40
effigy art, 152, 155-7, 179, 380
Ekpo Secret Society: see Ibibio
embroidery, 155, 348, 375
Enggano Island (Indonesia), 188-9
engraving, 13
equilibrium, as motivation, 29-30; Duwamish, 56, 58; Malagan, 47; Sulka, 40, 41; Yoruba Gelede Society, 117
Eskimo, 8, 368, 385-6
ethnic groups: American Indian, 329; Oceania, 186; Polynesia, 269

European: figure of, 64; in Yoruba Gelede Society mask, 116, 117
European contact, 53, 370; Africa, 82; American Indian, 330-1; Badjokwe, 175; Bakongo, 144; Baoule, 42, 84, 87; Basonge, 160; Benin, 110; cliff-dweller, 332; Fiji, 262; Great Lakes, 350; Hawaii, 294; Ibibio Ekpo Society, 38; Ife, 110; Indonesia, 194; Iroquois, 343; Malagan, 47; Mangbettu, 179; New Hebrides grade societies, 49; New Ireland, 239; Northwest, 338; Oceania, 186, 199; Plains, 353; Polynesia, 292; Samoa, 275; South, 345; Sudan, 88; Sulka, 40, 41; Tonga, 282; see also acculturation; Dutch; French; Portuguese; Spanish; Western civilization

F

face-painting, 31
False Face Society: see Iroquois
family, 23, 82-3, 97, 118
fan handles, 285
Fang (Pahouin, Pangwe) (Africa), 145, 154, 180; guardian or mortuary figures, 54-5, 66, 135-8; musical instruments, 179; skull containers, 54-5
feathers: Australia, 263; Brazil costume masks, 385; Eskimo masks, 385; Hawaii, 301-2; Marquesas head ornaments, 309; Oceania, 301; Pueblo kachina masks, 342; Sepik River, 197, 201
fertility, 88, 94, 97, 154, 340
fetish figures, 24, 145, 161-4
fiber, 14, 319, 380
fig tree, 273
figures, 13, 18, 20, 22-4, 31, 32, 42, 338; Africa, 98, 381; Bakongo, 142-4; Benin, 111; Bougainville, 78; Cameroon, 129, 130; Dahomey, 109; Duwamish, 57-9; of European trader, 64; Iroquois, 345; Kwango River, 145; Lake Sentani, 196; Malagan, 47, 48, 235; Mangbettu, 179; Mound-builder, 337; New Hebrides grade societies, 49, 52; Northwest Coast, 358; Polynesia, 374; Sepik River, 197; Sudan, 97; see also specific peoples and areas
Fiji Islands (Melanesia), 190, 257-63; cannibal forks, 257, 258; 260; decorated bark cloth, 273; decorated clubs, 257, 258, 261; hook figures, 257, 259, 260-1; houses, 257, 262-3; priests' bowls, 257, 258, 260; and Samoa-Tonga art, 272-3, 277, 279, 280, 282, 285, 383; tapa cloth, 257, 261-2
Fire-spitters: see Senufo
fish clubs, 315-16
fish forms, 384; Malagan, 48, 236, 237; Sepik River dance object, 207; Solomon Islands, 245-7, 248, 249; Tami-Huon bowls, 214
Florence Museum, 167, 182
Florida (North America), 337, 345
Florida (Solomon Islands), 244
flutes, 203
Fly River (Melanesia), 222

404

Hamburg Museum, 164, 198

Hawaii (Polynesia), 138, 269, 272, 293-302, 304, 320, 383; deity figures, 297-301, 323-4; end of figure carving, 294; featherwork, 301-2, and Polynesian culture, 292, 374; tapa decoration, 301; temple figures, 59-61, 68, 294-7, 374

hawk, 50

head deformation, 179

headdresses, 358, 385

head-hunting, 191, 218, 244

headmen, 29, 83

heads: to decorate musical instruments, 179-80, 181; preservation of, Maori, 329; see also Benin; Ife; Warega

heheve masks, Orokolo, 222-3, 225

hei-teki, Maori pendants, 329

heiau, Hawaii temples, 294, 296

helmet masks: Bundu Society, 98; Cameroon, 130; Sulka, 39; see also semihelmet masks

helmets, feather, 301

hide, 13, 14; Eskimo masks, 385; Naskapi coat, 348, 349; Naskapi teepee, 346; Ona masks, 385; Plains shirts, 351, 354; Plains teepee, 355; see also rawhide

high culture: Americas, 6, 329, 384; vs. primitive culture, 4-6, 7, 9-11, 16, 63, 69

historical phase, American Indian art, 339-67

Hohokam Indians, 334

Hollandia (New Guinea), 183

hook figures: Fiji, 257, 259, 260-1, 280; Sepik River, 383, Tonga, 280

Hopi Indians, 339; kachina masks, 341

horns, 13

horse: acquisition of, Plains, 350; in Barotse neckrests, 182; in Senufo equestrian figure, 92-3

horse trappings, 62, 355

horsehair, 346

houses, 14; for Baoule figures, 42; Batak, 190; building materials, 14; cliff-dwellers, 332, 334; Fiji, 257, 262-3; Gisborne, 321-4; Indonesia, 188-9, 190, 194; Iroquois longhouses, 345; Maori, 318-25; Maprik, 201, 203, 381, 382; Marquesas, 303-4; murals on, Micronesia, 265; New Guinea, 194; Papuan Gulf, 33, 34; Polynesia, 271; Samoa, 275-6; South, 345; Tambaran, 382; Tonga, 275-6; see also architecture; men's houses

human form, 9, 10, 18, 21, 22, 23, 42, 70, 77-8, 97, 377; see also anthropomorphism

Huon Gulf: see Tami-Huon

Louisades (Melanesia), 382
Lower Congo (Africa), 141-2, 145, 152, 154, 180; Bakongo figures, 142-4; fetish figures, 145
Lower Sepik: see Sepik River
low-relief carving, 13
Lualaba-Lomami region (Africa), 158
"lum," Tami-Huon men's house, 212

M

magic, 17, 23-4, 25-6, 70, 72; Basonge fetish figures, 163; Bayaka, 145; Indonesia, 190; Massim, 232, 382; Melanesia, 191; Northeast, 347; Plains Indians, 357
Maine (North America), 346
Makere: see Mangbettu
Makonde (Africa), 180, 381
Malagan, 46-8, 234-9; as communal ceremony, 59; masks, 47, 48, 235, 236-7, 238; and New Hebrides grade societies, 53, 68, 249-50; pole sculpture, 235-6; sakabul, 237, 239; sculptures, 66-7, 68
Malekula (Melanesia), 48-52, 59, 66, 67-8
mallets (pig-killers), 52, 250-2, 253
Maltese cross motif, 354
mana, 60-1, 269-71, 325, 329
Mangaia (Polynesia), 286; ceremonial adzes, 288-91, 292, 383
Mangbettu (Makere) (Africa), 179
Maori (New Zealand), 272, 317-29; canoe stern boards, 325-7; culture, 317-18; Gisborne house panel, 321-4; greenstone jade, 329; houses, 318-25; moko tattooing, 328-9; and Polynesian culture, 292; taiaha carvings, 327-8; Taranaki houses, 324-5
Maprik (Melanesia): Abelam, 208, 210-11; figures, 203; houses, 201, 203, 381, 382
Maprik (Prince Alexander) Mountains (Melanesia), 198
marionettes, Ibibio figures as, 123
Maritime Provinces (Canada), 346
Marquesas Islands (Polynesia), 11, 272, 285, 303-11, 314, 383, 384; canoe-prow carving, 307-9; clubs and crowns, 62; culture, 303; figures, 307-9, 311; houses, 303-4; and Polynesian culture, 292; shell head-ornaments, 309-11; stilt-step figures, 304-7; tattooing, 311
marriage ceremonies, 29, 30
mask-making: Iroquois False Face Society, 37; Papuan Gulf, 33; Pueblo, 339
maskettes: Bapende, 61, 150, 151; pre-Columbian Indians, 338
masks, 18, 21-4, 30, 31, 32, 42, 62; Africa, 98, 374, 379, 381; Bakota 379; Baluba, 167; Baoule, 42, 83, 87; Bushongo, 152; Calusa, 345; Central Congo, 158; Cherokee, 345; Choctaw, 345; Kwakiutl, 365; Kwango River, 145; lacking in Ashanti forms, 105; lacking in Polynesia, 374;

modeling, 13

modern art: see contemporary art

Mohawk Indians, 343

moko, Maori facial tattooing, 328-9

Monkey God: see Baoule

moose-hair embroidery, 348, 375

morphological aspect of art, 75-6

mortar, 170, 338

mortuary ceremonies, 21, 29; Malagan, 46-8, 234-9; New Britain, 254

mortuary objects: Moundbuilder, 334-7, 338; pre-Columbian Southwest, 331

Moslem influence, 92, 93

motivation: see aesthetic factors; balance; continuity; creativity; equilibrium; prestige; security; stability; survival; vanity

Moundbuilder Indians, 334-7; 338; influences on other areas, 338; mortuary objects, 334-7, 338; pipes, 335-7, 338; pre-Columbian vs. historical phase, 339

Mundugumor (Melanesia), masks, 202-4, 206

Murua Islands (Melanesia), 232

Musée du Congo Belge, 172

Muserongo (Africa), 180

musical instruments: 179-81, 220; see also drums; flutes

mythology, 22-3

N

narrative forms, 14, 69-70; American Indian buffalo robes, 70; Angola stools, 70; Ashanti bronze castings, 69-70; Congo, 70; pre-Columbian Northwest, 338

Naskapi Indians, 346; decorated hide coat, 348, 349; teepee, 346

nation, Africa, 82, 83

naturalism, 21, 78; Africa, 134-5, 371-2, 373, 379

Navaho Indians, 339

neck rings, 100

necklaces, 335

neckrests, 31, 62, 69; Baluba, 167; Barotse, 180, 182-3; Bayaka, 147; Bushongo, 45; Central Congo, 71; Massim, 234; Tami-Huon, 210, 213

New Britain (Melanesia), 138, 190, 212, 214, 215-17, 222, 230, 234, 241, 262

New Caledonia (Melanesia), 190; ancestor figures, 256; masks, 254-7

New England (North America), 346-8

New Georgia (Solomon Islands), 244

New Guinea (Melanesia), 33, 75, 76, 138, 186, 190, 191-215, 217-34, 262, 268, 378; Abelam, 208, 210; ancestor figures, 191; Geelvinck Bay korovar ancestor figures, 192-4, 381; Lake Sentani, 195-6; Maprik, 208, 210; Massim, 231-4; North Dutch New Guinea, 192, 195; Papuan Gulf,

56, 217, 222-30; Sepik River, 196-209, 211, 316, 357, 383; South Dutch New Guinea, 217-20, 221; Tami-Huon, 210, 212-15

New Hebrides (Melanesia), 68, 186, 190, 249-52, 253, 256, 257; grade societies, 48-53, 59, 66, 67-8, 249-50, 254, 379; pig-killer mallets, 250-2, 253; rambaramp mortuary figures, 254; skull preservation, 254; slit-gongs, 250, 252

New Ireland (Melanesia), 190, 239-40, 241, 249-50, 297; Malagan, 46, 53, 59, 234-9

New Mexico (North America), 331, 339; Pueblos, 339

New South Wales (Micronesia), 265

New York State (North America), 36, 343

New Zealand (Polynesia), 231, 269, 272, 384; Maori, 271, 317-29; and Polynesian culture, 292-3

Ngere (Africa), 103

Nias (Indonesia), 188

Niger-Benue (Africa), 110, 127

Niger River (Africa), 118, 120

Nigeria (Africa), 11, 38, 78, 108, 110-27, 134, 135, 380; see also Benin; Ibibio; Ibo; Ife; Yoruba

North Island (New Zealand), 318, 324

Northeast Indians, 343, 345-8, 349; birch-bark etchings, 375; cedar containers, 375; double-curve motif, 346-8; influence on Great Lakes area, 348; Iroquois, 343, 345-6, 347; Maritime Provinces, 346; New England, 346-8; St. Lawrence River, 348

Northern Rhodesia (Africa), 180

Northwest (North America), pre-Columbian Indians, 338, 339

Northwest Coast Indians, 331, 357-67; Bella Coola masks, 359-61; birch-bark containers, 375; Chilkat blankets, 366, 367; culture and economy, 357-8, 361; Duwamish, 56; Kwakiutl, 364, 365; masks, 358-62, 376; sculptures, 375; totem poles, 362-3; see also Haida Indians; Tlinglit Indians; Tsimshian Indians

nose-sticks, 30, 212

Nukuoro (Micronesia), 265-7

Nyimi, Bushongo kings, 152-5

O

objective aspect of art, 75-6

obsidian, 312, 335

Oceania, 187-90, 367, 372-5, 376, 382; betel-nut chewing, 382; culture, 186; influences, 188; shell ornaments, 62; tools for sculpture, 199

Ogowe River (Africa), 379

Ohio River valley (North America), 334, 345

Oklahoma (North America), 336

Ona (South America), 385

Shamba Bolongongo, Bushongo figure of, 152-5
shark, 207
sharkskin, as abrasive, 199
shell, 13; Algonkin, masks, 346; American Indians, 375; Australia, 263, 264,
    265; canoe-prow carving, 382; Eskimo masks, 385; Fiji pendants, 263;
    Hawaii deity figures, 297; Iroquois clubs, 345; kapkaps, 62, 68-9; Maori
    houses, 320, 322, 324; Marquesas head ornaments, 309-11; Melanesia
    head ornaments, 309; Moundbuilder, 335, 338; Northwest Coast, 358;
    Oceania ornaments, 62, 187, 232; pre-Columbian maskettes, 338; Sepik
    River, 197, 201, 208; Solomon Islands, 242-5, 249, 309; tools, 199, 208, 250
shell beads, 345, 348
shields: Australia, 263, 264-5; Borneo, 190; Papuan Gulf, 225-7; Plains, 353;
    South Dutch New Guinea, 218-20
shirts, 351, 353, 354, 355
shrines, 118, 119, 120, 263
Siassi Islands (Melanesia), 214
Sierra Leone (Africa), 98, 99
silver, 13, 339, 340, 364
skeleton preservation, 53-6
skins, 14, 24
skull preservation, 53-6, 193, 252, 254
slit-gongs, 52, 240-1, 250, 252
snake, 48
social factors, 17, 18, 26, 30, 71, 378; Africa, 82-3; Basonge, 160; Cameroon,
    130; Dogon, 94; Duwamish, 58; Hawaii, 59-61, 294; Ibibio, 38, 39, 120;
    Ibo, 120; Maori, 328; Marquesas, 307; Massim, 232; Melanesia, 191;
    New Hebrides, 49, 52-3; Northwest Coast, 361, 376; Polynesia, 269-71,
    293; Sulka, 40; Yoruba, 114, 117
Society Islands (Polynesia), 272, 282-6, 317
solar disc, 50
Solomon Islands (Melanesia), 183, 190, 239-49; Baka-Bougainville, 239-40,
    241; Bougainville figures, 78; ceremonial bowls, 247-9; ceremonial
    paddles, 239-40, 241; fish-form figures, 245-7; kapkap, 241-2; lime
    containers, 245; pendants, 242-5; shell head-ornaments, 309; shellwork,
    242-5, 249; slit-gongs, 240-1
songs, 34, 57, 160
South (North America), 345
South America, 368, 384-5
South Dutch New Guinea (Melanesia), 33, 217-19, 220, 222, 225, 241;
    carved shields, 218-20; drums, 217, 220, 221
South Island (New Zealand), 318
Southeast Asia, 8, 186, 188, 382
Southwest (North America), 339-43; introduction of horse, 350-1; kachina
    cult masks and dolls, 340-3, 344; pre-Columbian vs. historical phase,

sculpture, 199; Sepik River, 208; pre-Columbian Northwest, 338; stone-working, 338

Torres Straits (Melanesia), 222

totara, Maori houses, 319

totem poles, 358, 362-3

totems: Australia, 264, 265; Cameroon, 130-1; Lake Sentani, 196; Malagan, 237; Massim, 232, 234; Northwest Coast, 362; Sepik River, 208; Solomon Islands, 249

tradition, in primitive culture, 7, 9, 23, 28, 30, 63, 77-8, 378

tribal phase, Indian art: see historical phase

tribe, 7, 16; Africa, 82, 83

tridachna: see clam shell

Trobriands (Melanesia), 382

Tsimshian Indians, 358, 384, 366; totem poles, 362-3

tukula, 158, 166, 380

turtle, 338

turtle shell, 36, 62, 241, 309, 310

Tuscarora Indians, 345

tusks, of boar, 49

U

uhikana, Marquesas shell head-ornaments, 309

Utah (North America), 331

utilitarian objects, 13, 14, 31; American Indians, 376; Austral Islands, 291; Baluba, 167, 170; Baoule, 87; Barotse, 180; Bayaka, 147; Bushongo, 155; Iroquois, 345; Kwango River, 145; Lower Congo, 142; Micronesia, 267; Plains, 62

V

Vancouver Island (North America), 358, 366

vanity, as motivation, 30-1, 62; Bushongo cups, 44, 45-6, 155; Hawaii temple figures, 61; Malagan, 47; Maori, 322; Marquesas figures, 307; Massim spatulas, 231; New Hebrides mallets, 250; Tahiti fly-whisk handles, 285

vegetable pigments, 14, 197, 198

village, 16, 23, 34, 82, 83, 191, 345

viscera, 24

votive offerings, 97, 307, 331

W

wall paintings, 331

wampum peace belts, 345

War Memorial Museum, 231

Warega (Balega) (Africa), 176, 178-9; figures, 176, 178-9; heads, 176; ivory mask miniatures, 61-2; masks, 61-2, 176